ID0906728

The News People

John W. C. Johnstone
Edward J. Slawski
William W. Bowman

The News People

A Sociological Portrait
of American Journalists
and Their Work

UNIVERSITY OF ILLINOIS PRESS
Urbana Chicago London

The research reported in this volume was made possible by a grant
from the John and Mary R. Markle Foundation, New York.

Library of Congress Cataloging in Publication Data

Johnstone, John Wallace Claire, 1931–
    The news people.

    Bibliography: p.
    Includes index.
    1. Journalists--United States. I. Slawski,
Edward J., 1941– joint author. II. Bowman,
William W., 1947– joint author. III. Title.
PN4871.J6   070.4'0973   76-14890
ISBN 0-252-00310-1

Contents

Preface

This book deals with an occupational group currently very much in the public eye: news-media journalists. The study on which it is based was conducted during the fall, 1971, at the height of the struggle between the press and the Nixon administration—the period just after the publication of the Pentagon papers but prior to the Watergate break-in and events which followed. Although these circumstances have little bearing on the purposes of the study, and relate only indirectly to the issues it addresses, the time of the research clearly increases both the delicacy of the subject matter and the care with which the results must be presented.

In view of this, we feel it is essential at the outset to clarify our goals in this undertaking. What we attempt here is neither a defense nor an attack on the news media. We seek neither to congratulate newsmen for their vigilance in the role of public watchdog, nor to damn them for their reportorial excesses or shortcomings. Our goal is sociological inquiry, not social criticism.

Experienced news people will recognize at once that we are claiming to present an objective sociological analysis of journalists. Most of these same persons will also be quick to point out how tenuous and guarded any such claim must be. Some will say it is not possible at all. Although we do present "hard data" about journalists, and report them in a facts and figures style, we are also aware that our own judgments have dictated which facts to report, how much attention to accord them, and how they have been interpreted. Social data are never neutral. About the most we can claim, then, is that we are aware of no conscious (or unconscious) feelings about journalists which have colored our perspectives, and we know of no conflict of interest between our goals in this undertaking and our professional or individual interests. Each of us is a sociologist employed by a university; none of us belongs to any professional journalism society, nor teaches students preparing to do media work; and none of us is dependent for his livelihood in whole or in part from work prepared for (or against) the news media. Moreover, the style of presentation we have adopted here is deliberately sober and academic—though, we hope, not dull or obtuse.

Several other points about the nature of this book should also be clarified here. First, journalists and journalism are discussed outside the context of current issues surrounding the press. Thus, we do not deal with the pros or cons of shield laws for newsmen; we do not promote, assess, or critique current philosophies or ideologies of the press; we do not argue that newsmen should or should not engage in advocacy reporting; and we do not try to evaluate media performance. Second, while we do focus on newsmen and their work settings, we do not deal with the final product of their labors—the news. This, of course, is a shortcoming of the study, for perhaps the main reason for being interested in the characteristics of newsmen and how they go about their work is that these may tell us something important about the nature of news. And while we believe this to be true, it must remain an unexplored assumption: we do not attempt here to link characteristics of news people or news organizations with the specific nature of the messages they produce.

Finally, in this volume we are dealing with the entire population of journalists in the American news system—not just national newsmen, the Washington press corps, the more visible television anchormen or commentators, or the star columnists or personalities in the industry. In fact, ours is the first attempt we know of which deals systematically with the social characteristics of newsmen at large—those behind the scenes of the cameras as well as in front of them; those buried in the newsrooms of metropolitan dailies as well as those by-lined on the front page; those who prepare anonymous dispatches for the wire services or anonymous editorials for their papers; and those whose identities are known only in very limited geographical environs. In this respect, the volume departs sharply from most current writing on the American press, which focuses disproportionately on news celebrities, landmark institutions, major news stories, or the more colorful or powerful figures in press history. Although influential journalists do certainly fall within our purview, our concerns here are much more with the news system as a whole, and by necessity, therefore, with rank-and-file news people and with the more mundane day-to-day routines of newswork. Our main concern here, in short, is to present a representative overview of the nature of newsmen and newswork in contemporary America.

Any social science project of the scale undertaken here requires inputs and contributions from large numbers of people, and it is simply not possible for us to identify by name all of the persons whose efforts went into this study. Our main debt, for example, must be to the nearly 1,400 members of the working press in the United States who shared with our interviewers intimacies of their lives and work. It is to this group more than to any other that the present volume is dedicated: without their cooperation and support, the study could not have been conducted. We are also indebted enormously to Lloyd N. Morrisett and to the John and Mary R. Markle Foundation of New York, without whose moral and financial support the study would not have been possible.

Many other persons shared their ideas and insights with us at one point or another in the project, and we wish specifically to thank the following: Edward Barrett, James Boylan, Warren Breed, James A. Davis, Herbert Gans, Paul Gapp, Leonard Iaquinta, Richard McKinley, James Norr, Theodore Peterson, Peter H. Rossi, Paul Sheatsley, Roger Skolnik, Harry Skornia, and James Wiley. Ron Dorfman, David McQueen, and Marshall Rosenthal also provided us valuable ideas and leads in studying journalists in the alternative media. Special thanks must go to Eve Weinberg: whatever field successes were achieved in this study can be credited directly to her insights and efforts. We are also indebted to Benjamin King and Carol Richards, who designed a complex sampling plan and then made it work. We also thank Toshi Takahashi, who typed all of the survey instruments and manuscripts emanating from the study, and caught many of our errors and oversights in so doing. Finally, we wish to acknowledge the computing assistance provided by the National Opinion Research Center and by the Computer Center of the University of Illinois at Chicago Circle. It should go without saying that none of these persons or groups is responsible for any of the shortcomings of the study, or for any statements or interpretations made in this volume.

1
Background and Design of the Study

Sociological studies of the mass media usually focus on one of three related problems: on the processes by which mediated messages are generated; on message content itself; or on the diffusion of information through a population, and its impact on individuals, groups, or the society as a whole.

During the past few decades considerably more attention has been paid to the second and third of these concerns than to the first. With regard to message content, for example, investigators have analyzed the characteristics of news, propaganda, popular culture, and other media fare, and have done so for varied purposes—to make inferences about the motives of communicators, to assess audience taste, or to speculate about the changing American culture. A sizable number of content studies have also dealt with more focused topics, such as the portrayal of minority groups, of occupations, or of violence in the media. Equally prominent are studies of media effects: there has been no dearth of investigation into how information diffuses through social networks, of the impact of the media on politics, of the effects of television on children, or of the uses people make and the gratifications they derive from exposure to the media.

Systematic studies of how the news media come to shape the particular images of social reality that they do have been much less frequent, however, and it is possibly this gap which led a number of social scientists in recent years (Berelson, 1959; Ennis, 1961; Gans, 1972) to declare the field of mass communication research to be dead. Especially lacking in this regard have been inquiries which treat the news media as complex organizations and their functionaries as representatives of an occupational group. It is primarily in response to this latter deficit that the present volume is addressed.

Previous Studies of Journalists

Despite a voluminous literature on the development of American journalism, and numerous biographical accounts and case histories of central figures and institutions in the field, there are comparatively few studies which deal systematically with the characteristics of individual journalists. Indeed, there has been no previous inquiry which has had as its universe the entire population of working newsmen. At the same time, however, several important studies of more specialized groups of journalists should be noted.

A pioneering work on one such subgroup was Rosten's (1937) study of Washington correspondents. Rosten presented detailed information on the social composition of the Washington press corps, their news sources, and their attitudes on important issues in contemporary politics and journalism. He found that in the 1930s, Washington correspondents were likely to have come from relatively substantial economic beginnings; were disproportionately from the Midwest, particularly Illinois and Indiana; had done well in college; and were liberal in their attitudes. In all, Rosten prepared an in-depth analysis of 127 members of the Washington press corps.

Twenty-five years later, Rivers (1962) updated Rosten's study. Rivers discovered a greater sense of freedom among the correspondents than Rosten had found during the late thirties, noting that reporters felt under considerably less pressure from their home offices to prepare stories in particular ways. Correspondents in the sixties were also much better educated than might have been anticipated from the general trend of increasing education in the population. In addition, they were not so likely to be from the Midwest as had been the case earlier: New York and Pennsylvania were now the dominant states producing correspondents, and the Northeast was the leading region. Reporters in Washington were as well paid when Rivers did his research as they had been when Rosten studied them. Both of these authors have provided valuable accounts of an extremely important subgroup in American journalism.

Newsmen in the nation's capital are attractive research subjects not only because of the importance of the events they cover but also because of the prominence of their sources of information. Yet the very prominence of these sources creates pressures for newsmen—pressures which result in a continuous conflict between the press and the government. Rivers (1960, 1965, 1971, 1973) has extensively explored the adversary relationship between representatives of the government and representatives of the press, and argues that only such developments as objective reporting afford the reporters some protection from the relentless pressure exerted by sources.

Three other studies of relationships between reporters and officials should be noted here. Cohen (1963) attempted to explain news-gathering activity in Washington in terms of antagonism between the desire of policy officials for privacy in the conduct of diplomacy and the desire of reporters to publicize these governmental activities. According to Cohen, the press may play one of three roles with respect to the conduct of foreign policy: observer, participant, or catalyst. Cohen did not deal with any of the background or career characteristics of his sixty-two respondents. In another study, Nimmo (1964) classified reporter and source roles in order to clarify the relationships which develop between reporters and public information officers. He identified three types of relationships: cooperative, competitive, and compatible. Nimmo also traced the impact of a variety of external influences on political communicators—influences such as organizational factors, audience responses, personal friendships, and personal feelings of confidence and skill in source-channel negotiations. The latest entry of studies of Washington reporters is provided by Chittick (1970). Chittick's analysis is somewhat broader than those of his predecessors in that he examines more relationships—relationships between leaders of pressure groups, policy makers, information officers, and members of the press. He found that the background characteristics of these persons had no significant bearing on their relationships to one another in the policy-making process. Chittick concluded that antagonism is inherent in the democratic management of foreign affairs, and that the press shares in this antagonism with others who are influential in the development of foreign policy.

All of the authors cited above have dealt with very limited though important subgroups of journalists. A concern with elite newsmen also appears in Kruglak's (1955) and Maxwell's (1956) studies of foreign correspondents working abroad, and in Lambert's (1956) study of correspondents from abroad working in this country. Newsman-source relationships have also been studied among somewhat less elite subgroups of journalists, as in Valleau's (1952) study of state capital reporters in Oregon, Gieber and Johnson's (1961) research on the city hall "beat" reporter, and Dunn's (1969) study of state legislative reporting in Wisconsin. Reporter-source problems also surface in the coverage of specialized content areas such as medical news (Krieghbaum, 1957), science news (Krieghbaum, 1967), and education news (Gross, 1965; Gerbner, 1967).

Studies of the training and careers of journalists are rare, though Breed's (1950, 1955) analysis of how journalists learn newsroom norms and organizational policy stands out as a classic treatise on the socialization of news personnel. The management and control of newswork has received attention in several more recent works, in particular, those of Tuchman (1969, 1972, 1973), Sigelman (1973), and Epstein (1973).

Empirical studies of journalists in other countries have also begun to appear in the literature in recent years, the most notable of these being Tunstall's (1970, 1971) studies of Westminster Lobby correspondents and specialist reporters in Great Britain. Tunstall's analysis of specialist correspondents in the British national news media comes closest in overall scope to that of the present study, though that inquiry, too, is restricted to an elite group of newsmen—one which according to the author (Tunstall, 1971, p. 5) represents only about 2 percent of all British news personnel.

To date, then, the social science literature on journalists has been restricted to studies of relatively small subgroups of newsmen, most typically political reporters, and has tended to deal with limited aspects of their lives and work—most typically their relationship with news sources. As yet, no inquiry has examined the full range of journalistic manpower in the American news media, and no study has focused simultaneously on backgrounds, careers, attitudes, and work.

The Realm of Journalism

In this volume, we present the results of a large-scale national study of practicing journalists in the United States. The principal goal of the undertaking is to present a comprehensive sociological portrait of the occupational group most directly responsible for the day-to-day informational needs of our society, and to provide accurate information on the nature of journalistic manpower in contemporary America. The volume describes the social origins of newsmen, assesses patterns of training and recruitment to the field, traces career histories and job aspirations, maps the division of labor within news-media journalism, examines professional behavior and values, and assesses working conditions, financial rewards, and sources of job satisfaction and dissatisfaction.

Given the scope of the inquiry, our frame of reference is necessarily broad, and bridges several fields of sociological inquiry. First and foremost, the focus is demographic since the study seeks to delimit the social parameters of a specific segment of the labor force. Our concerns also branch into social psychology, however, since we deal with the socialization of individuals into an occupation, with their occupational goals and aspirations, and with the impact of a chain of background and career experiences on their professional orientations. Finally, we try not to lose sight of the fact that news-media journalists are members of organizations, and that the final product of newswork results from collective rather than individual effort. The analysis is also social structural, then, in that it deals with how the settings within which journalists work shape both their day-to-day routines and their perspectives on newswork. Analysis of the status hierarchy which pervades the American news industry also necessitates a social structural perspective.

The population under study here may be defined initially as the full-time editorial manpower responsible for the informational content of English-language mass communications in the United States. Several criteria must be spelled out in order to more clearly delimit this population.

First, we are concerned here only with personnel who prepare content for *public* communications media, which is to say, channels of mass communications targeted at the public at large rather than at private audiences, special interest groups, or groups which constitute audiences by virtue of their common affiliations. Although we would not exclude as public those media which define their target audiences in terms of characteristics such as sex, educational level, or race, we do mean to exclude those aimed at members of specific occupational groups, secondary organizations or associations, or narrowly defined interest groups. To be more specific, the study does not deal with editorial personnel who write or edit company newsletters or magazines, those who prepare content for trade or professional publications, or those who gather and circulate information to government officials, corporate managers, or the rank-and-file membership of organizations and associations.

Second, our focus here is restricted to persons who produce "reality" rather than "symbolic" media content—news, information, and opinion as opposed to fiction, drama, art, or other categories of symbolic fare so prominent in our media.

Three types of communication personnel fall within this definitional framework: editorial personnel employed within the news media proper; those employed elsewhere who prepare information for dissemination to the news media; and freelance journalists and writers. Although data on all three groupings were collected as part of this project, attention in this volume is restricted to the first category—those working full-time within news organizations. The universe for the study may be formally defined as all salaried full-time editorial personnel employed in daily and weekly newspapers, magazines, and periodicals concerned with news and public affairs, the wire services, and the news departments of broadcast media.

At this point additional discussion is necessary to clarify which media fall within the realm of journalism, and which among these can be classified as informational. Though it is extremely difficult to establish and defend firm boundaries between journalism and other communicative realms, some attempt to do so was necessary in order to proceed with this study. The approach which was adopted was based on two premises, one concerning the principal function of journalism in a society, and the other the principal source of journalistic content. We here characterize journalism as the institutionalized running-record of a society, the day-to-day representation of ongoing social process as filtered through the apparatus of the news industry. Journalistic content focuses essentially on the present, and is designed for immediate consumption rather than for the permanent record of the society. As such, its principal societal function is to sustain ongoing social process. Journalistic content also deals with occurrences which originate in the real world, though as Boorstin (1962) and Molotch and Lester (1974) have elaborated, much of what passes as news today could be termed "pseudo events" or "promoted events"— occurrences designed, staged, and promoted for the purpose of being defined by the media as real. It is with this important qualification in mind, then, that we delimit as journalism that realm of public communication which derives its subject matter from surveillance of the environment, and which diffuses information, interpretation, and opinion about events in close temporal contiguity with their occurrence.

With the latter consideration in mind, we decided to limit the study to news media which transmit information with a periodicity more frequent than once a month. With respect to periodicals, the study is confined to news magazines published either weekly or bi-weekly.

Journalistic manpower is here defined as all news-media personnel who have editorial responsibility for the preparation or transmission of news stories or other basic information units. This definition embraces those whose principal responsibilities lie in news gathering, news processing and editing, or the supervision or management of news operations. Persons who write about occurrences they observe firsthand have editorial responsibility since they select the information which enters the news system; those who interpret or comment on events also do because they suggest the significance which should be attached to information; and those who edit, manage, or supervise the work of other editorial employees have obvious "gate-keeping" power over the transmission of information.

Even with these guideline definitions, a number of arbitrary decisions were necessary in order to operationally define the universe to be studied. For example, we decided arbitrarily that video cameramen and audio specialists would not be considered as journalistic manpower for purposes of this study. This decision was based on the fact that in many if not most broadcast organizations, responsibility for structuring how events in the field will be reported lies with the reporter or newsman in charge of the news team rather than with the video or audio specialists. This is obviously untrue in some cases, but we could think of no simple way in which to make the necessary distinctions. Full-time newspaper photographers also fall into this category, and to be consistent we excluded them from the inquiry as well. On the other hand, we reasoned that editorial cartoonists do have direct editorial responsibility for the information they communicate, and these personnel were therefore included in the sampling universe. One might argue that these persons produce "symbolic" rather than "reality" content, but they do typically draw their inspiration from the social and political events of the day. On the assumption that most comic-strip cartoonists would not even purport to depict current events, however, we decided they did not qualify as journalistic manpower.

Method of Study

The information reported in this volume was obtained from interviews conducted with a national probability sample of practicing journalists. Due to the lack of pre-existing data on journalistic manpower as defined here, it was necessary in the early stages of the study to invest considerable time, effort, and expense in assembling the materials necessary to sample the relevant universe. No precise estimates were available even regarding the size of the manpower pool in question. Although the 1960 census enumerated 102,555 persons in the occupational category "editors and reporters" (U.S. Bureau of the Census, 1963a, p. 1),[1] this figure would include personnel employed in all sectors of the communications industry rather than just the news media. Moreover, no lists could be obtained which adequately represented the universe: there is no single organization to which even a substantial minority of practicing journalists belong, and one does not have to be licensed to practice journalism in the United States.

The sampling strategy which was developed was a three-stage plan in which procedures in the second and third stages were dependent on the results obtained in the preceding stage. The first task was to compile lists of daily and weekly newspapers, news magazines, news services, and radio and television stations and networks. To begin, names were listed of all qualifying organizations with head offices located within the seventy-two primary sampling units of the National Opinion Research Center's national area probability sample. Three sources were utilized for this purpose: the 1970 *Ayer's Directory of Newspapers and Periodicals*, the 1971 *Broadcasting Yearbook*, and the 1970 *Editor and Publisher Yearbook*. Since the number of eligible radio stations and weekly newspapers proved to be large, only a systematic random fourth was listed.

From these sources a list was compiled which included 372 daily newspapers, 239 weekly newspapers, 24 periodicals, 34 news services, 140 radio (only) stations or networks, and 252 television (or television-and-affiliated radio) stations or networks. These organizations were then contacted by telephone for information on the number of full-time editorial staff members they employed. In order to clearly delimit editorial manpower, representatives of the organizations were first asked for the total number of full-time staff they employed—including editorial, advertising, production, distribution, and managerial personnel, as well as any staff assigned to bureaus or branch offices. They were then asked how many of these persons were *editorial* personnel, which were defined as all "full-time reporters, writers, correspondents, columnists, newsmen, and editors." In broadcast organizations, only editorial staff in news and public affairs departments were enumerated, and where approriate, the informants were asked to subtract photographers, librarians, cameramen, or audio technicians from the totals.

This information was successfully obtained from 94 percent of the 1,061 organizations contacted, and for the remaining 6 percent was estimated from known correlates of staff size—circulation and size of market. This preliminary survey completed the first phase of sampling, and provided us with basic data on the national distribution of journalistic manpower. We could now estimate the number of journalists working in various regions of the country as well as in various sectors of the news industry. In the country at large, we estimated a total manpower pool of 69,500 full-time personnel working within the news media. Thus, fewer than half (45.7 percent) of the 153,000 persons who reported themselves as "editors or reporters" in the 1970 census were in fact employed on a full-time basis in the American news media.

In the second stage of sampling, 308 news organizations, stratified by organization type and geographic location, were sampled from the longer list with probabilities proportionate to size. These 308 organizations were then recontacted by telephone and asked for the names and job titles of their editorial personnel. In the case of smaller organizations, this information was usually provided directly over the telephone, while most of the larger organizations agreed to mail us printed rosters. Field workers also made visits to several extremely large news organizations to provide clerical assistance in assembling or sampling the lists, since in some cases it was more feasible to obtain only systematic samples of the employee rosters. Although this phase of the work was extremely time-consuming, total or partial listings were successfully obtained from 282 of the 308 organizations in the sample. Twenty-six organizations declined outright to participate any further in the study, but rather than accept these refusals as sample losses, efforts were made to obtain partial listings from other sources—such as from names appearing in mastheads, by-lines, or feature stories, or by listing news personnel identified by name on news broadcasts. The rosters compiled in this phase of the work provided the frame from which individual respondents were then selected.

In the final stage, a probability sample designed to yield 1,340 completed interviews was drawn. This sample was stratified by job title, so that persons in more influential positions within news organizations had a higher probability of selection than did "rank-and-file" journalists. The "elite" stratum was defined operationally as all personnel holding job titles of editor, manager, news director, assistant editor, bureau chief, producer, columnist, critic, commentator, Washington correspondent, or combinations of these titles. Persons in these positions constituted 24.9 percent of the total manpower pool. The sample was drawn in clusters of two or three persons, with larger organizations yielding more than one cluster. The probability of selection in the "elite" stratum was .06454, while in the non-elite stratum it was .02559. This sampling plan thus resulted in a 6.45 percent representation of media "influentials" and a 2.56 percent sampling of "rank-and-file" journalists. Since selection probabilities were known, the two strata could also be combined into a single sample by introducing appropriate weights.

Field work for this survey was conducted during September and October, 1971. An interview schedule combining open-ended and closed questions was developed and pretested twice, first on a small group of newsmen in the Chicago area, and then on forty journalists scattered throughout the country. In the survey proper, all interviews were conducted by telephone by regular National Opinion Research Center (NORC) field workers located in eleven major urban centers. A large number of the interviews were therefore completed by long distance. Respondents were first sent advance letters informing them about the study and of their selection into the sample, and following this were contacted by a field worker for an appointment to be interviewed. Although all persons were asked if they would prefer to be called back at home, 54 percent chose to be interviewed at the office, 45 percent at home, and 1 percent at other locations. The median length of the interviews was 49.2 minutes.

Interviews were completed with 1,313 of 1,550 eligible respondents, an overall completion rate of 84.7 percent. Within the "elite" and "rank-and-file" strata, the completion rates were 84.1 and 85.2 percent, respectively. Of the interviews which were not completed, 7.0 percent resulted from refusals, 8.2 percent from failure to locate or make contact with respondents, and .1 percent (two cases) from interviews being broken off after they had begun. In overview, then, the field strategy can be considered highly successful: in 74 percent of the cases the interviewers felt their respondents had been "very interested" in the interview, and only 2 percent rated their respondents as "uninterested." Our belief that the telephone would be a natural medium in which to interview journalists thus proved, happily, to be justified. Although enormous telephone bills were generated, the costs of conducting these interviews in person would have been even greater.

In addition, thirty-six interviews were completed with a supplementary sample of Washington correspondents drawn from members of the press corps listed in the 1971 *Congressional Directory*. All persons selected into this special sample were employed by news organizations which during the previous three years had been cited for their journalistic excellence by national professional organizations of newsmen. This supplementary sample was selected in order to bolster representation in the study of persons working for unambiguously "elite" news organizations. Because these persons were not selected as part of the probability sampling procedures, however, their responses are not included in the analysis except where specifically indicated.

Finally, a special case study was undertaken of editorial personnel working in the so-called "underground" press. Field work for this project was conducted exclusively by the junior author. Personal interviews were completed with thirty alternative news people, and field notes were collected on the operations of ten alternative news organizations. This study was restricted to organizations located in New York, Detroit, Chicago, and San Francisco.

A Note on Terminology

One difficulty which became evident in the pretest interviews was finding a common vocabulary for interviewing personnel from both the print and broadcast sectors of the media. In addition to the obvious differences in technical terminology between the two sectors—a problem which itself necessitated several drafts and redrafts of questions—there was the more immediate problem of how interviewers should address their respondents. Because of its historical roots, the term "journalist" conveys pronounced print-media connotations, and we were concerned that use of the term might alienate news people in broadcast journalism. Indeed, the term does not even have universal currency among newspaper people today: in the pretests, some respondents rejected the term as being too pretentious or felt it denoted a higher level of professional standing than they wished to claim for themselves—as with one young reporter who remarked that she had not been in the field long enough to be called a "journalist."

In order to find out just how much currency the term does have today—as well as to establish an acceptable vocabulary for carrying out the interviews—the following question was asked at the beginning of all interviews: "Do you think of yourself as a 'journalist,' or as something else?" Persons who preferred to be known by other titles were referred to by those terms in subsequent questions concerning their occupational field. In the sample as a whole, however, almost two-thirds (65.8 percent) accepted the term "journalist" as a proper designation of their occupation, while about a third rejected it in preference to some other term. Interestingly, the term was acceptable almost as often to broadcast newsmen as to those in other media sectors: among radio and television personnel, 62.6 percent thought of themselves as "journalists," compared with 66.5 percent in the print media, and 67.2 percent in the wire services. It would appear, then, that the label does have fairly widespread usage in the field today. The most commonly mentioned alternative designations were "newspaperman" (by 8.6 percent), "reporter" (by 7.1 percent), "writer" (by 2.7 percent), "editor" (by 1.7 percent), or one of several terms denoting broadcasting affiliations ("broadcaster," "broadcast journalist," or "electronic journalist") by 3.1 percent. In total some 22.8 percent in the print media preferred to think of themselves simply as "newspapermen," "reporters," or "writers," while 15.8 percent in the electronic media used the term "broadcaster" or a related term. Yet if one had to select a single occupational title to designate editorial personnel in the American news media, "journalist" would still be the best term to use. Our own usage of this label throughout this volume, then, is consistent with the self-designations of at least a majority of our respondents.

Organization of the Book

As will be appreciated, an enormous volume of factual and attitudinal data was generated by these field procedures, and our overriding concern in this volume is to present and interpret these data as thoroughly and coherently as possible. The results from the main survey are reported in Chapters 2 through 8, which are organized within a temporal framework. Chapters 2, 3, and 4 focus on newsmen's backgrounds and prior career experiences; Chapters 5 up to the middle of Chapter 8 deal with current situations and dispositions; and the last half of Chapter 8 assesses goals and aspirations for the future.

To begin, Chapter 2 reviews several broad demographic features of journalistic manpower. After locating journalists in terms of areal distribution, city size, industry sector, and personal characteristics such as age and sex, the discussion shifts to an analysis of racial, ethnic, and socioeconomic origins. Our main goal here is to identify the social strata in our society from which news personnel most typically emerge. Geographic origins are not considered here, however, but are discussed as part of the analysis of migratory behavior in Chapter 4.

Education and training are the exclusive concerns of Chapter 3. Here we describe the very substantial differences in educational background which are found among contemporary American journalists, and assess trends in formal schooling over the past few decades. To deal with this latter topic, of course, it is necessary to interpret cross-sectional data from a cohort perspective: we do not report any information on persons previously employed in the news media who are currently retired, deceased, or employed elsewhere. Strictly speaking, then, our data are representative only of the survivors of cohorts, and the reader should be reminded that over time even carefully selected samples of survivors become less and less representative of their original cohorts. Chapter 3 also reviews newsmen's opinions on the types of training they feel are most valuable for persons entering the field today, and we note here how these perspectives vary across different sectors of the news industry. The chapter then concludes with a discussion of the mid-career educative behavior of journalists.

Labor turnover and manpower flow within the news media are the central themes of Chapter 4, and the bulk of this chapter is devoted to an analysis of newsmen's employment histories. Three aspects of labor turnover are discussed here: job mobility—the extent to which journalists change their employers; inter-organizational labor turnover—patterns of manpower flow within and between various types of news organizations; and geographic mobility—migratory shifts between critical points in the life cycle: birth, college, first employment, and current employment. The first section of the chapter discusses entry paths into news-media journalism, and in this section we evaluate the influence of socioeconomic origins and formal schooling on the types of entry routes taken. Following this, we return to a temporal perspective, and link rates of job changing with career stage—looking separately at persons in the print and broadcast media. The origins and destinations of all previous job moves reported to us by our respondents are then aggregated, and from these data we are able to identify the parameters of manpower exchange between different news organizations as well as the patterns of geographic flow of journalistic manpower. From this description, it should be clear that the main thrust of the analysis in this chapter is at the level of aggregates rather than individuals. We do not deal here with newsmen's motives or reasons for changing employment, and defer consideration of that topic for the discussion of job satisfaction in Chapter 8. The analytic perspective of Chapter 4, in short, is demographic rather than social-psychological.

Chapter 5 deals with status differentiation within the news industry. This topic is approached in two ways: first, by examining the control of newswork within organizations; and second, by discussing the organizational prestige hierarchy within the news industry at large. The first half of the chapter focuses on what newsmen do: it examines the division of labor between news gathering, editing, processing, and the management of news operations, and charts how participation in these functions changes over the course of individual careers. By assessing the clusters of job functions newsmen perform at various ages, we also try to identify the main career paths which are followed in news-media journalism. Other aspects of newswork, such as specialization of function and editorial autonomy, are also discussed here, and are interpreted in relation to the structural characteristics of news organizations. The second half of Chapter 5 focuses away from intra-organizational status differentiation, and considers the fact that news organizations themselves vary markedly in influence and prestige. Here, we identify the news organizations which journalists nominate as fairest and most reliable, and the ones they depend on most often in their own work. These ratings are next transferred to the case records of individual newsmen, and we are then in a position to describe journalists employed by organizations of greater or lesser prominence—as judged by other journalists. Chapter 5 concludes by comparing the characteristics of newsmen classified simultaneously by their status position within a news organization, and by the prominence of their organization within the journalistic community.

Over the years, a good deal of discussion has appeared in the professional journalism literature regarding the status of journalism as an occupation, and in particular, regarding its quest for recognition as a profession. Chapter 6 ties in with this body of literature by reviewing the criteria by which occupations are judged as professions, and then indicating the ways in which journalism meets or does not meet them. We then indicate the extent to which newsmen are attached to professional organizations and associations in their field, and by use of multiple regression analysis, identify the factors which relate most strongly to these attachments. Informal social contacts among journalists are then analyzed in a similar fashion. Since professions are also said to be distinguishable by the peculiar work-orientations of their practitioners, the final section of the chapter deals with the factors which journalists consider to be most important about their work.

Professional orientations are considered again in Chapter 7, where newsmen's beliefs regarding the proper functions of the American news media and their own obligations and responsibilities as professional journalists are analyzed at length. This chapter, which is an expansion of an earlier paper published by the authors (Johnstone, Slawski, and Bowman, 1973), factor analyzes attitudinal responses made by newsmen, and from these data locates professional orientations along a continuum which fits closely with what Cohen (1963) identified as "neutral" and "participant" value orientations. We then employ regression analysis to try to trace the etiology of these values.

Chapter 8 returns to more mundane matters, and examines the nature of rewards—both tangible and intangible—in news-media journalism. The first half of this chapter deals exclusively with income levels in the news media in 1970, compares levels of remuneration in different sectors of the media and among different categories of individuals, and then utilizes regression analysis to trace sources of variation in earnings. Following this, we turn to the elusive question of job satisfaction, and again employ multiple regression analysis to identify the main sources of variation. This section of the chapter also assesses newsmen's commitments to remain in the field, and after zeroing in on the twenty-five to thirty-four age group, compares the characteristics of persons differentially committed to long-term careers in news-media journalism.

Chapter 9, the final data chapter, presents a descriptive overview of journalists working in the alternative media, and touches on most of the themes introduced in preceding chapters. The chapter begins with a discussion of the scope of alternative journalism in the United States during the early seventies, and we attempt here to estimate the size of the editorial manpower pool employed in these media. Following this, the discussion deals successively with the nature of newswork in the alternative media, the characteristics of "underground" news organizations, the backgrounds and general characteristics of alternative news personnel, and finally with how these people view both mainstream and alternative journalism.

Chapter 10 concludes with a brief overview of the main features of American journalists circa 1971, and with comments on the types of changes which might be expected in the field in the future. This chapter does not systematically review the main findings of the study, as these are presented separately in the chapter summaries. The reader who so chooses can thus gain a quick review of the main findings of the study by reading the summaries to Chapters 2 through 9.

Although numerous tables and charts are presented in this volume, many more might well have been included: the volume of data generated in the study permits tabular breakdowns of an almost limitless variety. We include here only those tables and charts which we feel are essential as a base of evidence to support the occupational profile we are attempting to construct.

Although the text and statistical materials are closely inter-woven, we have also attempted to prepare the text so that it can be read independently, and for this reason, the tables and charts are grouped separately at the end, each table and chart being identified first by chapter number followed by its particular number. Finally, we should acknowledge that our approach to the data analysis is exploratory, and that we have attempted to highlight results which we feel have practical significance rather than merely statistical significance. At the same time, however, we comment in the text only on those results which satisfy the usual conventions of sampling reliability.

Notes

1. Tabulations from the 1970 census had not been released when this study was begun. In the 1970 census, 152,984 editors and reporters were enumerated. Source: U.S. Bureau of the Census, Census of Population, 1970. Subject Reports, Final Report PC(2)-7a, *Occupational Characteristics*. U.S. Government Printing Office, Washington, D.C., 1973. (Hereafter cited as U.S. Bureau of the Census, 1973a.)

2

Basic Characteristics
of Journalistic Manpower

This chapter reviews several demographic characteristics of journalistic manpower. First, estimates are presented of
the size of the national manpower pool in the news media, and
of its dispersion through different sectors of the news industry
and different regions of the country. Following this, data are
presented on the age and sex composition of journalistic manpower, with particular emphasis on the representation of
women in the news media. The chapter then concludes with a
discussion of the cultural and socioeconomic origins of contemporary journalists.

Size of the Manpower Pool in the News Media

From information obtained in the preliminary survey of news
organizations, the total full-time editorial manpower in English-
language news media in the United States can be estimated at
69,500. Table 2.1 reveals that three-quarters of this manpower
is located in the print sector of the media, another 20 percent in
the broadcast media, and about 5 percent in the wire services.
Over half are employed by daily newspapers alone.

These estimates are for salaried editorial staff employed full
time by news organizations, and do not include the part-time
correspondents, freelancers, and "stringers" retained on an
occasional or assignment basis by most newspapers and wire
services. Precisely how many additional persons there are who
work for the news media on a part-time basis is not known, but

what evidence there is suggests that the number may be considerable. One indicator of this is the volume of news stories
and articles written by freelancers which are edited by news-
media personnel. Some 34.2 percent of the journalists interviewed in the study reported that their job responsibilities
included editing or processing news stories or articles prepared
by freelancers. From the numbers of such stories they said they
had worked on during the previous month, the total flow of
such materials into news organizations might run as high as
100,000 pieces per week. Moreover, this does not include news
releases prepared by persons employed full time in government,
business, public relations firms, or other organizations. Based on
similar data, the total circulation to the news media of materials
of this latter type would be estimated at between 1,300,000
and 1,400,000 a week.

Altogether, then, the total number of persons who make
editorial contributions to the news media is considerably larger
than the number employed full time by the media. Some
160,000 persons reported their occupations as editors,
reporters, authors, publicity writers, or public relations specialists in the 1960 census,[1] and if we were to add in those in other
occupations who make occasional contributions, the combined
full-time and part-time manpower pool in American journalism
might well be double or triple the 69,500 full-time personnel
estimated in Table 2.1. Many full-time employees in news
organizations double as part-time or freelance contributors to
other media. Some 18.6 percent of those interviewed said they
had done freelance work on the side during the previous year,
and as many as 31.9 percent said they had done so at one time
or another during their professional careers.

Nonetheless, the full-time editorial pool in public communications is a relatively small one, and it is revealing that it is still
as concentrated as it is within the print media. Recent research
evidence indicates that the public now relies more on television
than on newspapers as a source of information about what is
going on in the world,[2] and that television has the reputation
as the most credible information source among the major
media.[3] What is evident, then, is that the public's primary
information source is staffed by a relatively small cadre of news
and public affairs personnel—some 7,000 at most.

Geographic Distribution

Both economic rationality and historical impetus can cause industries to become concentrated within specific geographic regions. From its beginnings, the American news industry has been concentrated in the Northeast, originally because that region was the center of population and of trade and commerce, and over time as a result of the growth stimulated by its initial presence there. Today the news industry is centered in the New York metropolitan area, in part perhaps because New York is the financial capital of the nation, but also because a major share of the production and distribution facilities for the print and broadcast media happened to have developed there. Even though one might argue that the affairs of government rather than of business and finance are the basic natural resource of journalism today, the fact remains that journalistic manpower is most heavily concentrated along the Northeast seaboard.

Compared with the population as a whole, journalists are overrepresented by 12.2 percent in the Northeast, and are underrepresented in all other regions—by 6.2 percent in the South, 5.1 percent in the North Central region, and .9 percent in the West. As Table 2.2 indicates, however, this concentration is due almost entirely to the contribution of the Middle Atlantic states, which contain 28.8 percent of the journalistic manpower compared with 18.3 percent of the population and 18.1 percent of the labor force. Moreover, although not shown in Table 2.2, 11.2 percent of all journalists in the country work in the New York SMSA (Standard Metropolitan Statistical Area), an area which contains just 5.6 percent of the total population.[4]

While these figures display sizable imbalances in the regional distribution of journalistic manpower, they do not take into account the fact that the major broadcast networks, news magazines, and wire services—news organizations with the greatest national visibility—also tend to be heavily concentrated in the New York area. In terms of national prominence and influence, in other words, the regional imbalances are much greater than indicated in Table 2.2. One illustration of this is the location of the news media which American journalists as a group consider most influential and prestigious. At one point in the interview, respondents were asked which three news organizations they relied on most often in their own work, and which three they considered fairest and most reliable. Although these results will not be discussed fully until a later chapter, it is instructive to note that of the ten organizations named most often in answer to each of these questions, seven were New York-based, and on the criterion of fairness and reliability eight of the top ten were located in the Northeast.

From these two sets of data, then, it is clear that the first prominent feature of journalistic manpower is its concentration both in numbers and in influence in the Northeast, and more specifically in New York City.

That journalistic manpower is also disproportionately concentrated in urban areas is confirmed by the fact that while 33.5 percent of the total population in 1970 lived in places with fewer than 10,000 inhabitants, only 4.0 percent of journalists worked in communities that small (see Table 2.3). Relative to population density, however, journalists are actually more numerous in middle-sized cities than in larger metropolitan centers. For example, cities between 250,000 and 500,000 population contain 15.1 percent of journalists compared with just 6.1 percent of the total population, an overrepresentation of 248:100. Cities with more than a million inhabitants, on the other hand, contain 41.0 percent of journalists and 34.9 percent of the population, an overrepresentation of just 117:100.

This pattern, while surprising in view of the industry's concentration in New York, can be explained by the economies of scale produced by the massive circulations of daily newspapers in the largest metropolitan areas, and the fact that the ratio of editorial manpower to circulation shifts downward as circulation increases. To illustrate this, Table 2.4 shows the median number of full-time editorial personnel per 1,000 circulation employed by daily and weekly newspapers with different levels of circulation. Papers with circulations under 10,000 on the average employ 1.33 editorial staff for each 1,000 circulation, but this average decreases to .34 per 1,000 when circulation goes above 500,000. Large circulation newspapers thus require relatively fewer editorial personnel to reach their readers, and since big circulation newspapers are also located in the largest cities, the result is that there are more journalists per capita in middle-sized cities than in the largest metropolitan centers. In other words, the relationship between community size and the relative density of journalists is curvilinear. A second demographic feature of journalistic manpower in the United States, then, is its heavy concentration within urban areas, and in particular in cities of less than a million inhabitants.

Age and Sex Composition

Table 2.5 reveals that though there are relatively few journalists under the age of twenty-five—just 12.0 percent compared
with 19.0 percent of the civilian labor force—the median age of
journalists is nonetheless 2.7 years younger than that of the
labor force as a whole. Precisely one-third of journalists today
are between twenty-five and thirty-four years of age, and an
actual majority, 56.3 percent, are either in their twenties or
thirties. Compared with the labor force, journalists are substantially overrepresented in the twenty-five to thirty-nine age
group, have proportionate representation in the forty to forty-
four age group, and are underrepresented both in the under
twenty-five and the forty-five-and-over age groups. This rather
remarkable concentration of manpower suggests that people
both enter journalism relatively late and leave it relatively early.
The late entry is perhaps to be expected, and can be accounted
for by the higher-than-average educational attainment of
journalists, and the fact, to be documented in the next chapter,
that a college education is increasingly the norm for entering
the news media. The relative absence of journalists in older age
groups, however, suggests that the field may indeed experience
a considerable exodus of its most highly trained and experienced
manpower. This result is consistent with casual observations
about journalism—that it is a young person's field because news
gathering requires a great deal of physical stamina, that advancement to managerial positions is relatively difficult, that many
journalists become bored with their newsbeats but find it difficult to develop new ones, and that journalists who work under
union or guild contracts achieve their maximum earnings relatively early and become blocked economically if they are not
promoted into managerial positions. Some of these inferences
will be explored later in the analysis of sources of satisfaction
and dissatisfaction in journalism, although it is difficult to test
them directly in a study focused on the incumbents of an occupation rather than on persons who have left it. For the present,
however, the data do confirm that journalistic manpower can be
characterized as youthful.

That journalism is also a young *man*'s field is also clearly evident. Table 2.6 reveals that men in journalism outnumber
women by a ratio of 4 to 1, compared to a ratio of 2 to 1 in the
total full-time labor force. Male-dominated occupational fields
are hardly uncommon in our society, of course, and there are

very few professional or technical fields in which women are represented even at their labor force representation. Nonetheless, the imbalance in news-media journalism is surprising, since writing ability and facility in the manipulation of symbolic content are not popularly associated as masculine rather than feminine interests and skills. Moreover, the sharp imbalance is not found among college students studying journalism. Of 27,886 bachelors' degrees in journalism awarded by American colleges and universities between 1964 and 1971, 38.4 percent were awarded to women,[5] which is just slightly below the proportion of women graduates in all academic fields combined.[6] Moreover, about two-thirds of those who take degrees in English and literature are women.[7] Thus, relatively fewer women are found in the news media than are trained to enter the field. Interestingly, the 1960 census reported that 37.2 percent of reporters and editors were women.[8] Although this figure includes both full-time and part-time reporters and editors, it suggests that the underrepresentation of women in the news media cannot be explained by their general absence from the communications field. Moreover, given national trends in women's participation in the labor force, it is unlikely that the proportion of women in the news media has declined since 1960. At the same time, it is evident that there are not many women in a number of other communications occupations either: in 1960, only 25.4 percent of authors, 23.1 percent of public relations specialists and publicity writers, and 10.4 percent of radio operators were women.[9] What seems most likely is that women with degrees in journalism work either part time in the news media, or full time for media other than newspapers, news magazines, wire services, or radio and television. It is clear that the news media are more heavily represented with men than would be expected given their numbers among journalism and English graduates.

Nonetheless, there is considerable variation in the extent to which the editorial staffs of news organizations are dominated by males. Table 2.7 indicates that the representation of women ranges from a low of 4.8 percent in radio to a high of 30.4 percent in news magazines. In general, women are much rarer in broadcast than in print journalism: 90.9 percent of news and public affairs personnel in radio and television are men, compared with 76.5 percent in newspapers and news magazines. And while the wire services fall in between these figures, their full-time editorial personnel are also predominantly male—by a ratio of 669 to 100.

Although these imbalances are striking, it should be noted that part of the discrepancy in sex ratios between print and broadcast organizations is due to differences in the ways these media define news and departmentalize subject matter. Virtually all daily newspapers, for example, handle news pertaining to women's affairs and interests through separate departments, and personnel within these departments, who are typically women, are considered part of the regular news staff. In broadcast organizations, on the other hand, personnel who handle informational programming for women are not usually defined as news staff. At least a small part of the discrepancy is due to the fact that editorial personnel in women's departments of daily newspapers were included as journalistic manpower in our sampling universe, while their counterparts in broadcast media (where they exist at all) were included only if they were part of the news and public affairs department.

Although full discussion of the division of labor within news organizations will be reserved until Chapter 5, it should be noted here that in addition to differences in overall representation, men and women tend to have very different journalistic functions within the media. There are sharp differences in status, in the types of work they perform, and among those in news gathering, in the types of subject matter with which they deal. Many women, perhaps a quarter, deal only with news traditionally defined as of interest to women—the society page, fashion, and home and family life topics. In view of all these considerations, it is essentially correct and only slightly chauvinistic to label as "manpower" those with journalistic responsibility within the American news media.

Any appraisal of women's participation in the labor force would be incomplete if it did not relate participation to life-cycle stages. Table 2.8 reveals the familiar pattern of depressed labor force participation during the child-rearing years, with the representation of women in journalism dropping to 15.5 percent in the thirty-five to forty-four age group. A marked upswing is then evident which continues until retirement age— although it should be noted that the reversal occurs earlier in the labor force as a whole. In general, however, trends in the representation of women in different stages of the life cycle are similar to those in the labor force as a whole.

The most striking information in Table 2.8 is that women are underrepresented in all age categories. Relative to the labor force, they are most numerous in the fifty-five to sixty-four age group, and least numerous among those over sixty-five—suggesting that very few women have the opportunity (or perhaps the interest) to remain in the news media after retirement age. The more critical underrepresentation, of course, is in the twenty-five to forty-four age range, since the relative absence here would affect the upward mobility of women in news organizations. Just as in other occupational fields, it is from these cohorts that news media recruit their managerial and executive personnel. This factor will be considered further when status differentials within the news media are examined.

Finally, the data presented in this section suggest that in addition to retirement there may be two other periods of manpower attrition from journalism. Among persons in their twenties and thirties, it is clear that many women leave the field to raise families. However, it is also the case among journalists that men are an average of 3.1 years younger than women (median ages of 36.3 and 39.4, respectively), and since this differential is just .3 years in the labor force as a whole,[10] it suggests that a sizable number of men in their forties and fifties may leave journalism, perhaps in response to general problems of upward mobility in the field.

Social Origins

It is a well-documented and widely appreciated fact that the ethnic and racial composition of the American population is not represented proportionately throughout the occupational hierarchy. Not only are the largest racial and ethnic minorities overrepresented in the lower echelons of the occupational status ladder (Blau and Duncan, 1967), but also many groups tend to be concentrated within specific occupations. Even in the popular culture, ethnic minorities are stereotyped with specific lines of work, prominent examples being the Jewish businessman, Chinese restauranteur or laundryman, or Irish policeman.

Although journalists, too, are stereotyped in the popular culture—usually as hard-drinking, isolated, and callous (DeFleur, 1964)—they are not typically stereotyped with an ethnicity. Table 2.9 explains why they are not, for it reveals that journalists come predominantly from the established and dominant cultural groups in the society. Thirty-nine percent of journalists compared with 23.8 percent of the total adult population report Anglo-Saxon origins, and close to two-thirds are of Anglo-Saxon, West European, or Scandinavian descent. East Europeans, Orientals, Spanish-Americans, and blacks, on the other hand, are all underrepresented. The most striking imbalance is for blacks: only 3.9 percent of news-media personnel are black, and this constitutes roughly a third of their representation in the population at large.[11] Moreover, about a third of the blacks in the news media work in the black press, and their representation drops to 2.9 percent when these news organizations are omitted. Spanish-Americans, too, are found in the English-language news media at only a fraction of their population representation: although not reported separately in Table 2.9, 1.1 percent of journalists reported Spanish origins, whereas some 4.7 percent of the total population are of Spanish descent.[12]

One should not interpret these imbalances as evidence of differential occupational preferences among ethnic groups. Although, as Porter (1965, p. 74) notes, some tightly knit ethnic minorities encourage certain kinds of occupational choice and discourage others, there is no reason to suspect that these kinds of influences operate with regard to journalism. What these data reflect better is the fact that in virtually any society those in charge of mass communications tend to come from the same social strata as those in control of the economic and political systems. The patterns displayed here confirm that the American news media are no exception to this.

One other consideration in this regard is that journalism has a long-standing history in our society, and in earlier periods the dominant ethnic affiliation of its practitioners was in all likelihood more substantially "WASP" than today. In this sense, journalism is an example of what Hughes (1969, p. 453) identified as "historic occupations"—fields which have a "strong sense of identity and continuity, a galaxy of historic founders, innovators and other heroes . . . and a wealth of remembered historic or legendary events which justify its present claims." The assimilation of minorities would be expected to occur slowly in occupations of this type, and it is perhaps not surprising then that American newsmen today are overwhelmingly white and come from the cultural groups which have been in the country the longest.

Given this pattern of ethnic heritage, it is also not surprising to find that journalists come from substantial socioeconomic beginnings as well. Table 2.10 reveals that nearly half of the respondents' fathers (48.8 percent) were employed in professional or managerial occupations, and that 61.9 percent were in the white-collar sector of the labor force. The degree of relative economic advantage this represents can be appreciated by the fact that in 1950 only 18.3 percent of the labor force worked in professional or managerial occupations, and even today the number is just 25.2 percent.[13] Table 2.10 also shows that the occupational origins of journalists are closely comparable to those of self-employed professional males, and that they are considerably higher than those of salaried professionals. The degree of similarity between journalists' origins and those of self-employed professionals is .857, while between journalists and salaried professionals, it is .785.[14] Thus, even though journalists themselves are a salaried occupational group, their social origins resemble more those of solo professionals, an economically higher occupational stratum.

It is also noteworthy that just 4.5 percent of journalists have fathers who are farmers, a rate less than half that for both groups of professionals in 1962. Although information is not available on the sizes of communities in which members of the sample grew up,[15] it is clear that very few come from rural beginnings. Just as the places journalists work are disproportionately urban, so it would appear are the places from which they come.

Although not reported separately in the table, 6.7 percent of our respondents indicated that their fathers had worked in the news media, while the fathers of another 3.2 percent had been employed in other branches of the communications industry. Intergenerational occupation inheritance is therefore characteristic of no more than about 10 percent of practitioners in the field today. Although this rate is considerably higher than would be predicted by chance,[16] the same could probably be said for many if not most other occupations. In general, occupational succession tends to be highest in self-employed lines of work—the solo professions, farmers, and proprietors. For example, Blau and Duncan (1967, p. 39) report that in 1962 the fathers of 16.3 percent of proprietors and as many as 82.0 percent of farmers had had the same occupations. Occupational succession in journalism, then, is not nearly as prevalent as in some other lines of work.

Journalists do, however, start out from relatively advantaged positions in the socioeconomic hierarchy, and the field cannot be characterized as one which recruits substantial numbers of persons who are upwardly mobile from the working class. If craftsmen and foremen are added to the white-collar group to represent middle-class origins, then as many as 78.5 percent of those currently employed in the news media could be said to have started out from middle- or upper-middle-class beginnings.

Summary

A preliminary mapping of the characteristics of editorial manpower in American journalism reveals prominent departures from proportionate representation along geographic and demographic dimensions. First of all, American journalists are heavily concentrated within the print media, and despite the influence of broadcast media as information carriers in contemporary America, only 20.2 percent of American newsmen are employed within radio and television. Moreover, although American news institutions may well be the most localized in the world (Bagdikian, 1971, p. 69), working newsmen in the United States are disproportionately concentrated within large urban places and within the eastern seaboard region. American journalists also tend to be young, male, and from solid middle- or upper-middle-class social backgrounds, but in these terms they probably resemble their counterparts in other industrialized nations.[17]

While the relation of these manpower characteristics to the nature of mass news in America is beyond the legitimate scope of the present analysis, one cannot but be struck by certain parallels between the classes of phenomena which become news topics in our society, and the characteristics of those who gather and edit news. News is ultimately what newsmen make it, and what finds its way into the news system is by necessity a reflection of where news is gathered and what those who gather it define as newsworthy. It is perhaps more than accidental, then, that affairs and events emanating from urban places tend to dominate American news; that news in large measure reflects men's rather than women's definitions of newsworthiness; and that the affairs of established groups in the society are virtually always defined as more newsworthy than those of minorities and disadvantaged groups. Attention is now turned to the nature of journalists' formal education and training.

Notes

1. Source: U.S. Bureau of the Census, *Statistical Abstract of the United States.* Eighty-fourth edition. U.S. Government Printing Office, Washington, D.C., 1963. (Hereafter cited as U.S. Bureau of the Census, 1963b.)

2. Blumler and Madge (undated, p. 30) report a 1966 British survey as showing that 48 percent of television owners rely more on television than on newspapers, while 23 percent rely more on the press, and 29 percent rely equally on the two sources.

3. In a series of national surveys in the late fifties and early sixties, Roper (1965) found that between 1959 and 1961, television had surpassed newspapers as the most credible information source among the four major media—newspapers, television, magazines, and radio.

4. In 1970, the New York SMSA contained 11,529,000 of a total population of 203,212,000. Source: U.S. Bureau of the Census, *Statistical Abstract of the United States.* Ninety-second edition. U.S. Government Printing Office, Washington, D.C., 1971. (Hereafter cited as U.S. Bureau of the Census, 1971.)

5. Source: The Newspaper Fund, "Where They Went to Work, 1964-68," Princeton, undated, and 1969, 1970, and 1971 supplements.

6. In 1969, 41.9 percent of 770,000 bachelors and first professional degrees awarded by American colleges and universities went to women. Source: U.S. Bureau of the Census, 1971, Table 204, p. 130.

7. *Ibid.*

8. Source: U.S. Bureau of the Census, 1963b, Table 305, p. 232.

9. *Ibid.*

10. In 1970, the median ages of men and women in the total labor force eighteen and over were 38.5 and 38.8 years, respectively. Source: U.S. Bureau of the Census, 1971, Table 328, p. 211. In just the civilian labor force as a whole, men are slightly older than women, the median ages for November, 1971, being 39.3 and 38.8 years, respectively. Source: U.S. Department of Labor, *Employment and Earnings* 18, No. 6 (December), U.S. Government Printing Office, Washington, D.C., 1971, Table A-3, p. 29. (Hereafter cited as U.S. Department of Labor, 1971.)

11. Figures differ on the number of blacks in the American population, and it is widely acknowledged that black males have for decades been underenumerated in the census. The national survey figures reported in Table 2.9 set the number at 14.9 percent of the 1967 population, but most official estimates are lower. Figures for 1970 report the black population as 11.2 percent of the total, and 1971 labor force statistics report the black labor force at 11.0 percent. Sources: U.S. Bureau of the Census, 1971, Table 27, p. 27, and U.S. Department of Labor, 1971, Table A-4, p. 31.

12. Source: U.S. Bureau of the Census, 1971, Table 30, p. 29.

13. Source: *ibid.*, Table 347, p. 222.

14. The measure employed is the index of similarity, which indicates as a proportion the degree to which two percentage distributions are identical.

15. Information on their regional origins is available, however, and will be discussed under patterns of geographic mobility in Chapter 4.

16. In 1970, just 1.8 percent of the labor force was employed in the

printing and publishing industry or in radio and television broadcasting. Source: U.S. Bureau of the Census, 1971, Table 344, p. 218.

17. In a study of editorial personnel in four Polish newspapers, for example, Aleksander Matejko (1970, p. 173) reports that 75 percent were men, 80 percent belonged to the intelligentsia by background, and only 20 percent were aged forty-five or older.

3

The Education and Training of Journalists

While it would be both redundant and inappropriate to ask incumbents of most professional groups what they had studied in school, and whether or not they had graduated from college, such information is far from obvious in the case of journalists. Indeed, it is a continuing dilemma for those who would claim for journalism status as a profession that the field has no single set of procedures or requirements for certifying its practitioners. One does not need a college degree to work as a journalist, and there is no other specific credential, license, or certificate necessary to enter the field. Moreover, as shall be confirmed later, there is little agreement among those currently in the field as to how specifically one should go about becoming a journalist.

Years of Schooling

Yet as an aggregate journalists do go to college, a majority hold college degrees, and a few end up with advanced degrees. Table 3.1 reveals that 86.0 percent of contemporary newsmen have attended college for one or more years, 58.2 percent are college graduates, 18.6 percent have pursued some graduate study, and 8.1 percent hold graduate degrees. The most important feature about these figures is the heterogeneity of educational backgrounds they reveal, for while graduation from college may be the modal educational attainment in journalism, the field is also one in which there are sizable minorities who have both never been to college and who have gone on to obtain higher degrees. Very few other occupations in our society, and particularly those generally considered as professions, are characterized by such pronounced extremes. This characteristic can be cited as a prominent feature of contemporary American journalism.

At the same time, this diversity is probably not a stable feature of the field, for Table 3.1 also suggests that the average educational attainment of journalists has been increasing steadily over recent decades. For example, among media personnel now aged fifty-five or older, just 45.5 percent hold college degrees, but the number increases to 56.0 percent in the forty-five to fifty-four age group, and to 64.0 percent among those between twenty-five and forty-four. The fact that just 50.1 percent of those in the youngest age group are college graduates should not be interpreted as a downward trend since many of these persons are undoubtedly in the process of completing their formal education. The figure is instructive, nonetheless, for it indicates that even today substantial numbers of persons enter journalism before completing their formal education. And while it is not strictly possible to project just how many persons in the youngest cohort could be expected to complete college, the age group does contain a sizable proportion (44.4 percent) who have started but not completed college. If that proportion were eventually reduced to the level currently found in the twenty-five to thirty-four age group, the percentage of college graduates would rise to slightly over two-thirds. In spite of the lower rates of college completion among those under twenty-five, then, the data on the whole suggest that degree holding is more and more becoming the educational norm in American journalism.

At the other end of the continuum, newsmen with no college training at all would appear to be becoming increasingly rare. Moving across the five age groups from oldest to youngest, Table 3.1 indicates that the numbers with high school graduation or less as their highest educational attainment decline continuously from 32.7 to 5.5 percent, with the most sizable drop occurring between the forty-five to fifty-four and fifty-five-and-older age groups. This pattern suggests that a sharp upswing in rates of college attendance occurred around the end of World War II, and that the trend toward increased college attendance has continued ever since.

Variation among Media

Although graduation from college may well be becoming the standard for employment in American journalism, news organizations of different types vary markedly in the numbers of college graduates they employ. Table 3.2 reveals that college graduates are extremely numerous in the news magazines and wire services, are found somewhat more frequently than not in daily newspapers and television, but are a minority among news personnel in weekly newspapers and radio. In addition, although the ranking indicated in the table does not discriminate perfectly between print and broadcast sectors of the media, overall there are 11.7 percent more college graduates working in print than in broadcast journalism. Finally, the table indicates that within the broadcast sector, levels of degree holding are considerably higher among those employed by the networks than among those who work for independent or network-affiliated stations.

Although these differences among media are striking, the variance can in large part be accounted for by the fact that degree holding also varies markedly within communities and news organizations of different sizes. Table 3.3 illustrates these relationships, and shows that degree holding practically doubles as one moves from communities of under 10,000 to cities of a half-million or more, and similarly, as one moves from news organizations which employ ten or fewer editorial employees to those employing 100 or more. Although larger news organizations tend to be located in larger cities,[1] additional analysis revealed that the overall educational level of a news staff was independently related to both factors, although it was slightly stronger with city size than organization size.[2]

These relationships suggest that the very high percentages of college graduates in news magazines and wire services, and the low percentages in weekly newspapers and radio can be interpreted largely as a function of either organization size or of the types of locales in which these news organizations typically function. Both national news magazines and wire services, for example, concentrate their editorial and news-gathering resources in large population centers, and tend to rely on "stringers," correspondents on assignment, or other news media for the flow of news from smaller population centers. Weekly newspapers, on the other hand, are both smaller in size and relatively more numerous in smaller cities and towns, and while there are weeklies in urban and suburban communities, too, a majority of full-time manpower in this sector of the news industry (77.0 percent) works in cities and towns of under 50,000. Moreover, more radio than television news personnel work in population centers as small as 50,000 (30.1 compared with 10.3 percent). It is these tendencies, then, which explain the extremely pronounced differences in the educational attainment of journalists working in different media.

Table 3.4 summarizes the joint relationship of population density and media type with the educational attainment of journalists, and shows clearly that even though differences between print and broadcast journalists are found in cities of all sizes, more variation in degree holding is explained by city size than by media sector. Insufficient sample sizes preclude showing these relationships for all six categories of media, but the table does confirm that in cities of over 500,000, the number of college graduates working in dailies and in television closely approximates the overall levels found in news magazines and wire services. The data confirm, then, that educational norms for employment in the news media are more a function of size of community than type of news organization.

Regional Differences

Table 3.5 reveals a surprising consistency in the percentages of college graduates working in the nine regions. Although college graduates are most numerous in the Pacific and Middle Atlantic regions and least numerous in the New England, West North Central, and West South Central states, the overall range in these figures is less than 10 percent. Sharp regional differences are evident, however, in the academic ratings of the schools from which journalists graduated. As a measure of academic quality, colleges and universities were classified on the basis of selectivity ratings listed in a national directory of American colleges and universities compiled by Cass and Birnbaum (1970). These ratings differentiate schools on criteria such as the percentage of applicants accepted, the scores of entering freshmen on national achievement tests, and a variety of other statistical measures of the scholastic potential of the student body. According to the editors of the directory these measures are good indicators of the academic quality of a school since, as they argue, a college can never be much better than its student body and is not likely to be much worse. In any event, colleges and universities were classified into one of six categories ranging from "the most selective schools in the country" to those "not selective at all." Rather than report the full distribution on these measures, it is perhaps sufficient to note simply that the sample contained newsmen from all six categories of schools, and that 10.7 percent attended colleges in the most exclusive category while 29.2 percent graduated from those rated as nonselective.

As a summary measure, Table 3.5 reports the percentages in the nine regions who graduated from schools rated in the top four categories of the six, the dividing point between schools described as "selective" and "very selective." In the sample as a whole, 42.9 percent had attended schools in the upper four categories, but the table indicates that the percentages are much higher among those working on the eastern seaboard and, in particular, in the Middle Atlantic region. On the other hand, very few graduates from highly rated colleges work in the deep South or in the Southwest, and there are practically none in the sparsely populated mountain states. The discrepancies on this measure provide further evidence of regional stratification within the field. The hegemony of the eastern seaboard in American journalism is thus reflected not only by the overall size of the manpower pool in the East, but also by the fact that the region is able to attract graduates from schools judged qualitatively superior in national ratings.

Fields of Study in College and Graduate School

The patterns described in the foregoing section suggest a major division between those who start their careers with a traditional type of apprenticeship experience, and those who enter journalism with college training. Although the effects of these entry paths into the field remain to be investigated, this division can be anticipated as a potential source of differentiation and segmentation within the occupation. One "effect" already evident, for example, is on the size of community in which journalists work.

In addition to the amount of formal schooling, journalists also differ in the kind of training they receive, and a second prominent division within the field is between those who study journalism or other communications specialties in college and those who major in other fields. Table 3.6 reviews this diversity by presenting a detailed enumeration of the subjects studied in college and graduate school by the 58.2 percent of journalists who graduated from college and the 18.6 percent who pursued graduate studies after receiving the baccalaureate.[3] The table shows the percentages of all journalists with preparation in specific fields, and the overall distribution of subjects studied at each level.

Table 3.6 indicates that formal training in journalism is by no means typical among practicing newsmen. Although journalism represents the modal field of concentration at both undergraduate and graduate levels, journalism majors are outnumbered about 2 to 1 by persons with other types of college training. Moreover, within the sample as a whole, just 22.6 percent hold B.A. degrees and just 6.9 percent pursued graduate studies in journalism. All together, 27.0 percent of practicing journalists studied journalism at one level or the other.[4]

A remarkable feature about this figure is that it closely approximates the number of journalism graduates who enter the news media. Data compiled by the Newspaper Fund (1971, p. 4), for example, show that just 25.2 percent of journalism graduates in 1971 found employment in the news media. Although these processes are entirely distinct and the similarity in the rates is purely accidental, the figures in combination confirm that formal training in journalism is neither a necessary nor sufficient criterion for entry into the news media: most working journalists were not trained in journalism in school, and most of those trained in journalism in college do not enter the news media.

At the same time, considerably more newsmen studied journalism than any other specific subject matter: 34.2 percent of college majors were in journalism compared to 22.9 percent in English, literature, and creative writing, 9.7 percent in history, and 7.5 percent in political science or government, the next three most frequently studied fields. At the graduate level, these same four fields are again the most frequent areas of concentration, although proportionately fewer studied English at the graduate level, and slightly more studied political science and government.

One clear difference between journalists' undergraduate and graduate training is in the balance between academic and professional concentrations. At the undergraduate level, 54.4 percent of all majors were in academic fields, and 46.6 percent were in professional or vocational fields (34.2 percent in journalism, 7.5 percent in radio-TV or other communication specialties, and 5.0 percent in other professional and vocational fields).

At the graduate level, on the other hand, 58.0 percent of majors were in professional curricula and just 42.0 percent were in academic. While this pattern is by no means unusual and would characterize incumbents of many other occupations and professions, an interesting feature in the present case is that the additional numbers with professional training at the graduate level are not made up of persons who studied journalism. Indeed, almost precisely the same proportion studied journalism at the graduate level as at the undergraduate, and the added numbers come primarily from persons whose professional training was not in the communications field at all. Of all journalists with graduate training, it would appear that as many as 13.6 percent were preparing to enter occupations other than journalism, teaching and law being the most frequent.

These patterns further illustrate the high degree of educational diversity among journalists. Although journalism and English, as expected, are the most frequent types of undergraduate preparation newsmen get, the news media contain large numbers of persons whose formal preparation was in other fields. Moreover, while the M.A. in journalism may well represent the official professional degree in the field, a majority of the newsmen who studied for higher degrees were registered in programs other than journalism. Journalism is clearly an occupation which attracts persons from a variety of backgrounds. Given the heterogeneity of educational backgrounds, it is also likely that fairly sizable numbers entered the field relatively late in their careers, perhaps even after becoming established in other occupations.

Trends over Time

Table 3.7 shows the major fields of study of those who received college or graduate degrees during three time periods, and reveals several important changes in journalists' education during recent decades. Considering undergraduate fields first, it is clear that journalism majors are more numerous among those who attended college in the period between 1945 and 1959 than among those who went either earlier or later. The percentages of journalism graduates jump from 23.6 to 42.5 percent following World War II, but then slip back to 32.0 percent after 1960. By comparison other communication programs show a continuous increase over these periods, although the recency of college-level programs in these fields (radio-TV, communications, public relations, advertising) is evidenced by the fact that only .8 percent of degrees received prior to 1945 were in one of these specialties. Thus, it is only the lower prevalence of journalism majors since 1960 that produces the overall decline in the number of newsmen with professional degrees. A more detailed analysis would pinpoint the decline of journalism majors at just about the 1960 cohort of college graduates: 44.5 percent who graduated between 1955 and 1959 majored in journalism, compared with 31.8 percent between 1960 and 1964.

Prior to World War II, most journalists who attended college majored in English, history, philosophy, or modern or classical languages. In total, degrees in the humanities make up 55.1 percent of all college degrees earned by journalists prior to 1945, with over a third (35.4 percent) in English alone. Before 1945, academic degrees were much more common than professional degrees, and more newsmen had studied English than journalism.

Following World War II a shift occurred between the fields of English and journalism: whereas journalism majors are outnumbered by 11.8 percent by English majors among those who graduated before 1945, they are 20.6 percent more numerous among those who went to college during the late 1940s and 1950s. More generally, all academic fields except the social sciences had proportionately fewer graduates in the immediate postwar period, and the representation of arts and science majors, excluding the social sciences, dropped from 61.1 to 33.3 percent. Social science majors, on the other hand, increased in number from 7.9 to 12.0 percent over this same period. After World War II, then, persons preparing to enter the news media were less likely to major in the humanities, more likely to study the social sciences, and much more likely to enroll in professional programs leading to degrees in journalism or other communication specialties.

As noted in the previous discussion, newsmen who graduated from college more recently than 1960 are less likely (by 10.5 percent) to have majored in journalism than those graduating during the prior decade and a half. Since 1960, the fields of preparation which have become more prevalent are political science and government (by 4.0 percent), history (by 3.7 percent), and communication specialties other than journalism (by

3.6 percent). Although these shifts have been gradual rather than sharp, it is noteworthy that since 1960, more journalists have earned college degrees in political science and history (combined) than in English. The renewed interest in liberal arts training in college, then, has not meant a heavier recruitment of English majors into the news media: indeed, English majors have become 1.2 percent fewer since 1960 while ever since the end of the war the media have increasingly recruited persons with college degrees in political science and government. This latter trend would appear still to be in ascendancy since among those who graduated from college since 1965, 11.3 percent majored in political science.

Finally, it should be noted that the number of persons with undergraduate degrees in "other fields," that is, professional or vocational specialties other than in the communications field, are relatively fewer among the more recent cohorts of graduates. Whether this reflects a trend toward declining recruitment by the media of persons from other occupations is not altogether clear, however, for it would also be the case that late career recruitment into journalism would not yet be complete among more recent college graduates. In either case, the shift is only a slight one.

Most of these same trends are paralleled in the data on graduate degrees: advanced degrees in journalism are most numerous among persons who graduated between 1945 and 1959; degrees in political science and in media specialties other than journalism increase in number over time; and degrees in the humanities (other than history) and in other professional and vocational fields are less common among more recent cohorts of graduates.

Over and above these similarities, the data in Table 3.7 indicate several discrepancies between undergraduate and graduate *degrees* which were not evident in the earlier comparison of *fields of concentration* at the two levels. For example, Table 3.7 shows that in all three time periods proportionately more advanced than baccalaureate degrees were in journalism. Of all graduate degrees earned, in fact, nearly half (47.5 percent) were in journalism,[5] compared with just 34.2 percent of all first college degrees. Moreover, the fact that just 34.9 percent of all *fields* of graduate study were in journalism (Table 3.6) suggests that it is not uncommon for the news media to recruit personnel who begin but do not complete graduate studies in programs other than journalism. Or stated differently, it would suggest that prospective newsmen are more likely to complete their graduate studies if they are in journalism programs than if they are seeking degrees in other fields. Although not shown in Table 3.7, the tendency to drop out of graduate school and enter the news media was particularly true of those in social science graduate programs: 17.3 percent of all fields of graduate study compared with just 7.8 percent of all graduate degrees were in the social sciences. Defectors from graduate programs in the social sciences thus constitute a not unimportant recruiting source of journalistic manpower.

To conclude this section, three distinct periods of news-media recruitment may be identified. First, prior to 1945, the most typical college recruit was one whose preparation was in English or the humanities. In spite of the rapid growth in journalism schools in the United States during the second and third decades of this century (Sutton, 1945, p. 20), the data suggest that the full impact of this growth was not realized in news-media recruitment until after World War II. Second, the period from the end of the war until about 1960 can be identified as one in which the media recruited heavily from graduates of journalism schools. Finally, the premium on journalism graduates appears to have leveled off around 1960, and since that time the media have recruited more substantially among those with liberal arts backgrounds—and in particular those with backgrounds in political science and history. Given the nature of these changes, media recruitment during the prewar era could be said to have emphasized literary training and skills, during the immediate postwar era professional and technical training in journalism, and during the current era knowledge and understanding of the social and political order.

Prescribed Courses of Study

Although few newsmen today deny the importance of college training for persons aspiring to enter the news media (only 10.1 percent felt it was not necessary to attend college), there is little consensus among practitioners in the field as to what type of college training best prepares one for employment in the news media. As indicated by Table 3.8, fewer than half of the sample recommended any single field of study, four fields (liberal arts, the social sciences, English, and journalism) were mentioned by between 30 and 40 percent, and fewer than 10 percent cited any other specific type of background or training.

Table 3.8 also reveals that a liberal arts background was the type of preparation most often recommended by practicing journalists, and that more newsmen recommended background in the social sciences and in English than in journalism. In total, fewer than a third (31.1 percent) endorsed professional training in journalism, and this coupled with the fact that just 3.7 percent recommended professional programs in other communication specialties confirms that most journalists today judge a substantive academic background preferable to professional training as preparation for a career in the media. Table 3.8 indicates that this was the case for journalism school graduates as well as others.

Compared with persons holding degrees in other fields, journalism graduates were 9.3 percent more likely to recommend the social sciences, 8.6 percent more likely to endorse journalism, and slightly less likely to recommend preparation in English or straight liberal arts. Newsmen without college degrees at all, on the other hand, were more likely than either other group to recommend English as the best preparation, and were much less likely to mention either the liberal arts or the social sciences. These data would suggest that some newsmen trained in journalism may experience difficulty in writing about complex social phenomena, while those without college degrees may feel somewhat deficient in their facility with the language. It is clear in any event that the types of educational background journalists recommend are often different from what they themselves have obtained.

Opinions regarding the best type of preparation for employment in the news media also vary markedly according to the sector of the news media in which one is employed. The relevant data are presented in Table 3.9, and can be summarized as follows: first, broad exposure to the liberal arts is much more salient to those working in news magazines and in the wire services; second, journalism, somewhat surprisingly, is endorsed most often by broadcast journalists—and is cited only rarely by those who work for news magazines; third, preparation in English is recommended most frequently by those in weekly newspapers, and least often by those in radio and television; fourth, there is little variation in the endorsement of social science training, although those in magazine journalism mention it somewhat more frequently; and finally, broadcast journalists are the ones most likely to recommend training in communication fields other than journalism—which is perhaps not surprising given that programs in radio-TV and speech fall within this category.

More generally, the data in Table 3.9 suggest that journalists in various media differ in the emphasis they assign to academic and professional training as background for the news media. This variation is vividly demonstrated in the following figures, which present as a summary measure of the salience of professional training the percentage of total mentions which were for either journalism or other communication specialties:

Radio	35.6
Television	33.1
Weekly newspapers	21.6
Daily newspapers	20.6
Wire services	16.2
News magazines	5.8

It is clear, then, that the journalists most likely to endorse professional training work within the broadcast media, while those who most often recommend substantive preparation are located in the news magazines and wire services.

One interpretation of these discrepancies is that they reflect basic differences in the types of journalistic skills emphasized within different media sectors. Within the broadcast media, for example, newsmen work under severe time constraints both in gathering news and in presenting it. The broadcast journalist must develop news stories quickly, present them concisely, and in addition, be skilled in the verbal presentation of information. In view of these kinds of demands, it is understandable that training in journalism, with its emphasis on technique and form, would be seen as relevant preparation. Magazine journalism, on the other hand, demands rather different journalistic skills. Since news magazines do not for the most part deal with breaking news and because the periodicity between editions is greater, the magazine journalist does not face the same time and space contraints as his counterpart in broadcast journalism. Evidence of this is given by the fact that of journalists in the six types of media, those in news magazines were least likely to report insufficient time to prepare news stories adequately, while newsmen in television were the most likely to do so: 93.0 percent of television newsmen compared with 67.9 percent in the news magazines reported that deadlines negatively affected the adequacy of their work. In magazine journalism, on the other hand, the newsman is called upon to report news in greater depth and to report it within a context and background, expectations which would make a broad substantive background more appropriate to the work task. The types of training emphasized by broadcast and magazine journalists, then, may very well be consistent with the journalistic responsibilities one is most likely to encounter within these media.

From this same perspective, however, it is surprising that so few newsmen in the wire services recommended a journalism curriculum as suitable preparation for the news media. Journalists in the wire services also work under severe deadline pressures, do straight rather than interpretive reporting, and for the most part are expected to follow the news-writing style taught in journalism schools (Emery, Ault, and Agee, 1970). At the same time, however, press-association newsmen are called upon to cover a wider variety of news stories than their counterparts in other media. Dunn (1969, p. 4), for example, comparing newspaper and press association reporters assigned to state government beats, notes that newspaper reporters generally cover the state government only while the press-association reporters in addition have responsibility for all other news emanating from the area. Moreover, wire-service journalists work on a considerably larger volume of news stories per week than do other newsmen: in the present study press-association newsmen reported working on an average (median) of 42.2 stories per week, compared with 26.8 in radio, 14.1 in television, 12.7 in daily newspapers, 9.7 in weeklies, and 3.6 in the news magazines. It is possible, then, that because of the relatively greater volume and variety of his assignments, the wire-service journalist is more conscious of the substantive than technical demands of his job.

This section is concluded by considering an anomaly. Table 3.10 orders the six media sectors by the percentage of newsmen working in them who hold degrees in journalism, and then reproduces from Table 3.9 the percentages who recommended journalism as suitable preparation for entering the media. This table indicates that journalism graduates are most numerous in the wire services, and are more common on newspapers, both daily and weekly, than in either of the broadcast media. The anomalous aspect of these figures is that with the exception of news magazines, where both the numbers of journalism graduates and the numbers who recommend training in journalism are low, the rank ordering of the two sets of figures is completely reversed. In the media where journalism graduates are most numerous, in other words, newsmen are less likely to recommend training in journalism, and vice versa. The magnitude of these discrepancies is illustrated in the right-hand column of the table. In three media sectors, radio, television, and weekly newspapers, many more recommend training in journalism than have obtained it themselves. In the wire services, on the other hand, the reverse is true, and it is only in daily newspapers and news magazines that the figures are balanced.

These discrepancies are revealing, and suggest that both the wire services and broadcast media have tended to recruit editorial personnel whose preparation is somewhat out of keeping with the journalistic demands one is likely to encounter within those media. More generally, the result constitutes additional evidence of the lack of consensus in the field regarding how journalists should be trained.

The Continuing Education of Journalists

Although most journalists terminate their experiences with formal education when they enter the labor force, just over a third—35.7 percent—said they had participated in some type of structured educative activity subsequent to entering the news media. A total of 29.5 percent reported taking one or more formal courses; 5.9 percent had had in-service training; and 1.6 percent said they had held a mid-career journalism fellowship.[6] These levels of educative participation, though impressive, may nonetheless be lower than in the adult population as a whole: in a recent study of the educational behavior of American adults, for example, one of the present authors found that 47 percent of persons twenty-one and over had engaged in structured learning pursuits at some time since leaving school (Johnstone and Rivera, 1965, p. 128). Even though more comprehensive measures of educative behavior were used in the earlier study than in the present one, it would appear that journalists as a group are not particularly heavy pursuers of continuing education. That is not to say that newsmen are not heavily involved in informal learning: indeed, in simply carrying out day-to-day news assignments, many are continuously involved in the systematic acquisition of new knowledge and information.

Table 3.11 presents a breakdown of the formal educative pursuits reported by newsmen, and indicates a fairly even balance between vocationally oriented topics and conventional academic subjects—although slightly more had studied the latter than the former. As might be anticipated, however, training in journalistic skills such as news analysis, copy editing, reporting, radio script writing, or news film editing topped the list, with some 12.7 percent of the sample reporting courses, workshops, seminars, or clinics in one or more of these fields. In addition, some 1.9 percent had taken management training courses, and 5.1 percent reported a variety of other vocationally relevant subjects and skills, such as photography, shorthand, or public relations.

In the academic field only two types of subject matter were reported with any meaningful frequency—courses in English, literature, and creative writing (by 7.0 percent), and in politics, government, and public affairs (by 4.4 percent). A total of 9.4 percent reported courses distributed among a variety of other academic fields.

Finally, it should be noted that very few newsmen (only 2.5 percent) had been active in any of the nonvocational and non-academic types of adult education pursuits so prevalent in the population at large—areas such as hobbies, recreations, home and family life subjects, or "personal development" courses.

Although journalists are not breaking down the doors at American evening colleges and adult education centers, over half of the total sample admitted there was some type of additional training, study, or refresher course that would be useful to them in their work, and a majority in all age groups except those fifty-five and older identified a subject or skill they would like to know more about or would like to be able to perform better. Table 3.12 lists all subjects and skills mentioned by at least 1.5 percent of the sample, the equivalent of approximately 1,000 working newsmen in the country at large. General courses in journalism are seen to top this list of perceived learning needs, being mentioned by 10.1 percent of the sample. In addition, a total of 12.0 percent (not aggregated in Table 3.12) mentioned one or another of a variety of specific vocational topics or skills, including news analysis, shorthand, photography, reporting, editing, layout, and cinematography; and some 6.0 percent mentioned general studies in other communication fields, such as radio-TV, advertising, and public relations.

Table 3.12 also reveals that several conventional academic disciplines were mentioned by small groups of journalists, most notably political science and government, English, history, economics, law, and business. What is not evident from these figures, however, is that in the aggregate academic subjects were cited more frequently than vocational and technical subjects and skills. Of the total topics mentioned, 52.9 percent were academic subjects, 39.7 percent were professional or vocational topics, and 7.4 percent were neither. This balance is thus consistent with the overall experiences of newsmen in continuing education, and in general with the types of preparation they recommend for young persons planning to enter the news media.

Summary

While thirty years ago it was not at all uncommon for persons to enter the news media directly out of high school, today this type of "apprenticeship" route into the field is rare. Since World War II the news media have increasingly restricted their recruitment to persons with college background, and current indications are that this practice will continue and increase. Today older journalists have had less formal schooling than their juniors, but this differential will become less pronounced as those in the oldest age groups are replaced by succeeding cohorts.

A number of shifts may also be observed in recent years in the types of college graduates being recruited into the news media. Prior to World War II, aspirant journalists who went to college were likely to have taken degrees in English and the humanities. Beginning about the end of the war, however, this practice changed and the media began to recruit heavily from professional journalism schools. More recently, since about 1960, the media have once again sought out liberal arts graduates, but this time among those with preparation in history and the social sciences rather than English. All in all, a high degree of cohort differentiation characterizes contemporary American newsmen: those who have been in the field the longest may not have attended college at all—and if they did were likely to have focused on developing literary skills; those in the middle stages of their careers are likely to have been professionally trained; and those just starting out are most likely to be liberal arts graduates and social science majors.

Although journalists on the whole recommend the same types of training they themselves obtained, it is interesting that there are substantial numbers who do not. This tendency is particularly noticeable in the broadcast media, where many more newsmen recommend training in journalism than obtained it themselves, and in the wire services, where the reverse is true. More generally, journalists are divided between those advocating subject matter specialization and those who recommend preparation in a professional curriculum, and differences of opinion in this regard seem to be linked to the sector of the media in which a journalist works. These discrepancies probably reflect differences in the kinds of journalistic demands peculiar to various sectors of the news industry.

In overview, journalism in the United States is an occupational field with diverse entry routes. As such, one might well anticipate a high level of differentiation and segmentation among journalists on other issues—such as work norms and practices, standards of journalistic excellence, and definitions of professional responsibility. At this point, however, attention is turned to the nature of careers in journalism, beginning with decisions to enter the field, and turning then to patterns of geographic, job, and professional mobility.

Notes

1. The correlation (Pearson) between city cize and size of editorial staff was .615.

2. At the zero-order level, both city size and organization size show moderate positive relationships with overall years of schooling ($r = .305$ and $r = .258$, respectively). The two partial relationships are also positive: the partial correlation between city size and years of schooling, controlling for organization size, was .184, while between organization size and years of schooling, controlling for city size, it was .105.

3. Information was not obtained on subjects studied by those who attended but did not graduate from college. For undergraduate study, therefore, the table reports only the curricula of those with completed majors.

4. Some 2.5 percent majored in journalism at both levels.

5. Not shown in Table 3.7.

6. Some 1.3 percent had participated in more than one of these types of endeavors.

4
Careers in Journalism

Up to this point we have dealt with the characteristics of journalists from a static perspective: their numbers, location, background and personal characteristics, education, and training. We will now consider the nature of careers in journalism, and following Glaser's (1968, p. 1) definition of an "occupational career" will be concerned with the patterned paths of organizational, social, and geographic mobility journalists follow in pursuing their vocation.

Several aspects of journalists' careers are discussed in this chapter. The first section focuses on decisions to enter journalism, and links the timing of such decisions both with socioeconomic factors and with the amount and type of education obtained. Entry paths into the news media are then described, and following this, levels of job mobility are estimated for journalists in various career stages. A detailed analysis of the flow of manpower within the news media is then presented, and the chapter concludes by tracing the migratory routes newsmen follow when they change jobs. Although job functions are also an important element in an analysis of work careers, discussion of this topic will be postponed until the next chapter.

Decisions to Enter Journalism

Although the dynamics of occupational choice in our society are not fully understood, vocational decisions are thought to be made in one of two ways. The first is where persons settle on a precise occupation relatively early in life, and then direct their education and training to the specific requirements in question. In contrast to this is a pattern in which decisions about schooling, such as going to college, are made first, and the selection of a specific occupation is made as the individual progressively narrows down his alternatives. For most persons, educational and occupational decisions are closely interrelated: in the former case vocational goals determine education and training, and in the latter, the process is reversed. Sharp changes of occupational direction in later life are by comparison rare.

Table 4.1 reveals that journalism contains sizable numbers of both early and late choosers. Although the median age of decisions to enter the field was 19.0 years, one in ten had decided before the teen years, while as many as 17.5 percent did not decide until after their twenty-fifth birthday. The principal periods of decision making, however, are the years between thirteen and twenty-four, and most commonly in the seventeen to twenty period. These figures represent further evidence of the diversity of entry paths into journalism: the fact that substantial numbers made entry decisions in the high school years, the college years, *and* the early twenties shows the absence of any common period of initial commitment. Careers in newsmedia journalism are clearly not dependent on early decision making, as are, for example, careers in medicine, where one's chances of entry can be at least negatively determined by early curriculum decisions. Career beginnings in journalism thus appear about as varied as the educational backgrounds of practitioners, although on balance the field can perhaps accurately be labeled a late-decision field.

Although few contemporary newsmen started out from lower-class origins, the sample does contain persons from sufficiently varied backgrounds to allow us to assess the influence of economic origins on career beginnings. Table 4.1 therefore subdivides the sample into three groupings based on the prestige rankings of fathers' occupations,[1] and indicates the ages at which persons in each group made up their minds to enter the communications field. Although the differences are not pronounced, journalists from more advantaged backgrounds did tend to make later occupational decisions, the median ages being 18.8, 18.9, and 19.4 years, respectively, moving up the status ladder. Closer inspection of the table reveals that the relationship is not simply monotonic, however, since persons in the lowest quartile of the distribution were more likely than those in the highest quartile to make decisions both during the high school years (thirteen to sixteen) *and* after the age of twenty-five. The relatively later decisions of persons from the more advantaged backgrounds, then, is entirely a function of their propensity to make decisions during the early twenties: those deciding later than this were disproportionately from the lower echelons of the socioeconomic ladder.

Before pursuing this topic further, it should be noted that journalists whose fathers were employed in the news media made somewhat earlier career decisions than would be predicted by their socioeconomic background. Although not identified separately in Table 4.1, 20.1 percent of this group made career decisions before the teen years, and 41.5 percent had done so before the age of seventeen. Since virtually all news-media job titles fall within the upper quartile of the distribution,[2] this constitutes a considerable departure from expectation, and can probably be attributed to the influence of early exposure to occupational role models.

More generally, the patterns revealed in Table 4.1 can be accounted for by the relationship between social background and schooling. As in the population as a whole, a positive relationship was found in the sample between socioeconomic background and the amount of formal schooling obtained. The correlation (Pearson) between years of schooling and father's occupational prestige was .155, and Part A of Table 4.2 shows that the percentages of newsmen with college degrees, graduate training, and graduate degrees all increase as one moves up the socioeconomic hierarchy. The specific effects of socioeconomic origins on educational attainment are isolated in Part B of the table, which indicates the transition probabilities between levels—the proportion continuing their schooling from one level to the next higher level. For example, the probability of a high school graduate from the lowest quartile entering college was .827, while the chances of his middle- or upper-group counterpart doing so were .885 and .922, respectively. The net impact of background on entering college is thus .095, and the right-hand column of figures isolates these effects at each transition stage. These figures pinpoint three main effects of social background: first, on the chances of completing college once one has entered; second, on the chances of entering college in the first place; and third, on the chances of entering graduate school once one has obtained a college degree.

Part B of the table also highlights a number of more general parameters regarding the education of journalists. For example, it shows that while journalists' chances of entering college are very high (about eight or nine in ten), their chances of entering graduate school are much lower (about three in ten); or similarly, that the probability of remaining in college until graduation is considerably greater than the probability of pursuing graduate study through to an advanced degree.

The main conclusion from this section of the analysis, however, is that a newsman's educational attainment is indeed influenced by his social origins, and that socioeconomic background has its most important effect on one's chances of completing college. The reason that persons from more substantial backgrounds make later occupational decisions is that they are more likely to attend college and more likely to remain there until they graduate. Since journalism is not a field which requires early commitment, firm entry decisions among college students can be postponed until just before graduation—or even later for that matter.

Another way in which social origins affect journalists' education is that those from higher status backgrounds are more likely to attend highly selective colleges and universities. The correlation between father's occupational prestige and college selectivity was found to be .176, a modest though statistically significant relationship. The most immediate significance of this fact is that the type of college a person attends has a bearing on the curriculum he is likely to pursue. For example, a moderate negative relationship ($r = -.247$) was found between college selectivity and majoring in journalism.[3] In other words, persons attending more selective schools were less likely to take journalism and more likely to major in an academic discipline. This relationship may reflect the fact that professional and vocational programs developed primarily in the public rather than private sector of American higher education, where entrance criteria have traditionally been more open. In addition, it was found that the propensity to major in journalism is more strongly related to the type of institution attended than to socioeconomic background, since the correlation between background and college major was just $-.078$.[4] Choices of majors among college students destined to end up in the news media, then, can perhaps be said to be influenced more by the programs available where one attends college than by predispositions linked to social class.

Although early career commitment was negatively related to the amount of formal schooling obtained ($r = -.071$), it should be noted that journalists who coupled career plans with decisions to go to college were more likely to become journalism majors: the correlation between age of commitment to the field and selection of journalism as a major was −.229. Early decisions to enter the communications field thus direct persons *either* to seek employment immediately following high school *or* to enter professional programs in college. Among college-trained journalists, then, it is only those who pursue an academic curriculum who postpone making specific occupational commitments. These processes, although intuitively obvious, constitute important realities of the early stages of journalism careers.

To sum up, Figure 4.1 illustrates the principal ways in which socioeconomic origins have a bearing on journalists' career beginnings. First, socioeconomic background influences the overall level of schooling one is likely to obtain, by affecting one's chances of entering college, completing college, and entering graduate school. And second, social origins have a direct bearing on the type of college one attends, those from more prosperous beginnings finding their way into more selective and presumably qualitatively superior institutions. An important consequence of this latter propensity, in turn, is that persons who attend more selective schools are likely to obtain substantive background rather than professional preparation for entering the news media.

Entry into the News Media

Since complete job histories were collected from all respondents, it is possible to isolate a number of different aspects of the careers of journalists—how they enter the news media, their propensity to change employers, the sequences of organizations they work for in arriving at their current locations, and the migratory routes they follow when they change their employment. Since the study is restricted to journalists in the news media, of course, it is not possible to report anything at all about the careers of those who leave news-media journalism for other spheres of employment. Moreover, the fact that the sample includes persons in all stages of their careers means that the data are necessarily more complete in delimiting early rather than late phases of journalists' careers. In spite of these limitations, however, several important dimensions of careers in journalism can be reconstructed or estimated from these job histories.

To begin, Table 4.3 describes the locations of all first jobs held by journalists, and as such indicates the directness with which persons found their way into the news media. Excluding the 6.7 percent of the sample whose first full-time employment was in the armed forces, the table reveals that 70.0 percent made direct transitions from school to the news media, while 30.0 percent held first jobs in other settings. This latter figure is made up of 20.0 percent who were employed first in sectors of private industry other than the news media, while the other 10.0 percent were distributed across a variety of settings— educational institutions, government, other nonprofit institutions, and self-employed enterprises. Although it is not clear whether these figures represent an unusually direct or indirect recruitment pattern for an occupation, it is clear at least that substantial numbers of those who eventually work in the news media do not start out there.

Table 4.3 also reveals that both the amount of formal schooling completed and the type of college training obtained have a bearing on the directness of recruitment into the media: journalists with college degrees were 12.5 percent more likely than nongraduates to have entered the news media directly,[5] and college graduates who majored in journalism made direct transitions 10.9 percent more often than those majoring in other fields. Thus, even though just a minority of those who obtain journalism degrees enter the news media at all (Newspaper Fund, 1971, p. 4), four-fifths of those who do are recruited immediately after they leave school rather than later. These propensities thus result in the following paradox: looking forward in time one would say that becoming a journalism graduate establishes only about a .25 probability of entry into the news media; looking backward over the careers of established journalists, on the other hand, one could conclude that an early decision to enter the communications field coupled with a decision to go to college and major in journalism consti tutes the most direct route of entry into news-media journalism.

Since most American newsmen work for daily newspapers, it is not surprising to learn from Table 4.4 that a majority of those who entered the media directly out of school went to work for dailies. To properly interpret these figures, it is necessary to compare the distribution of entry locations with the current distribution of manpower in the field. Table 4.4 summarizes these comparisons by reporting for each sector the ratio of

current share of manpower to the share recruited directly from
school—a crude index of net manpower gains (or losses) over
time. Even though 58.2 percent of all raw recruits entered
dailies, the results indicate that this is just slightly less than the
current share employed in that sector.[6] In other words, daily
newspapers tend to hire just about their proportionate share of
fresh recruits to the media. In contrast, television's current
share of manpower is substantially higher than its share of fresh
recruits, while radio's is much lower. Radio, in fact, retains only
about half of the young people it recruits. These patterns reflect
the fact that employment opportunities in television have
developed in sizable numbers only during the past twenty or
twenty-five years, and also suggest that television has recruited
heavily from radio.

Table 4.4 also reveals that proportionately more newsmen
currently work for weekly papers than started out there, a
result which is somewhat more surprising since it is often
thought that weeklies serve as training grounds for newsmen en
route to other sectors of the news industry. In this regard, however, it should be pointed out that the dynamics of manpower
flow in the news media are more complex than represented in
this table, and involve three rather than two recruitment
sources—recruitment directly from schools and colleges, from
other news organizations, and from other sectors of the labor
force. The degree to which news organizations utilize these various sources of manpower will be clarified later in the chapter.

Finally, Table 4.4 indicates that fewer newsmen end up working in the wire services than start out in that sector, although
the net loss (.05) is a fairly modest one. More substantial losses
(.16) are evident for news magazines, however, which may in
part reflect the declining economic viability of mass-circulation
news magazines in recent years. All in all, however, it is radio
which in recent decades has suffered the most significant net
loss of the young journalists it has recruited.

Persons who enter the news media from other sectors of the
civilian labor force come from a variety of occupations, but
much more often from white-collar than blue-collar lines of
work. Table 4.5 reveals that more than four-fifths of this group
(82.2 percent) held their most recent employment in the white-
collar sector of the labor force—31.4 percent entering from
professional and technical occupations, and 24.4 percent from
jobs classified in the managerial or administrative census

categories. Although not shown in the table, the single most frequently held occupation prior to entering the news media was teaching, by 11.6 percent, while another 2.4 percent had been educational administrators. Apart from this group, however, there was no sizable concentration from any single occupational category: the group included accountants, clergymen, social workers, technicians, a lawyer, librarian, musician, computer programmer, electrical engineer, statistician, dietician, funeral director, and various and sundry salesmen, office managers, and clerks. Those coming from blue-collar jobs included machinists and mechanics, a carpenter, a brickmason, a taxi driver, a janitor, and several policemen and firemen. What is perhaps most notable about this group is that very few had been previously employed in occupations in which they would have performed editorial or quasi-journalistic functions: only 11.3 percent had worked previously as writers, in public relations, or in advertising. By and large, then, late media entrants are very predominantly persons who are changing their fields of work and not simply their occupational situses.

To conclude this section, it would also appear that late entrants on the whole improve their socioeconomic standing when they enter the news media. Compared with prestige scores of 51 for reporters and editors, Table 4.5 indicates average (mean) standings of 43.9 for jobs held most recently, and 35.8 for jobs held prior to that. Even though late entrants tend to come from professional and managerial ranks, they do not typically experience downward—or even lateral—social mobility when they enter the news media: most are in fact upwardly mobile.

Job Mobility

Work histories can be examined from at least three perspectives: first, vertical mobility, the extent to which persons change their status or economic position over time; second, spatial mobility (or motility), the migratory paths people follow when pursuing a particular line of work; and third, job stability, the number of times incumbents of an occupation change jobs and employers, and the length of time they spend in successive employments.

In the present section, we will examine the last of these three processes by looking at the frequency with which newsmen change employers, and the types of organizational shifts involved in these changes. Little hard data currently exists from which to formulate expectations regarding these aspects of journalism careers, and what available evidence there is would appear to be contradictory. For example, it has been noted (Breed, 1950, p. 126) that journalists, at least those in daily newspapers, very rarely are fired; yet prevailing imagery seems to be that newsmen move from job to job more often than incumbents of occupations of comparable status—imagery which may stem in part from the fact that some newsmen travel frequently in carrying out their work, and in part from the attention the media give when news organizations go out of business. In addition, of course, available biographical data on the Washington press corps (Rosten, 1937; Rivers, 1962) suggest quite complex career patterns among veteran elites in the field.

In the sample as a whole, a majority (60.1 percent) reported working previously for one or more different news organizations, slightly over a third (34.7 percent) reported two or more previous media employers, and one in five (20.1 percent) reported three or more. The average (mean) for the sample as a whole was 1.32 previous media employers, and 2.14 previous employers in total. In general, it is more common than not for American newsmen to shift employers at least once during their careers in the news media, though the number one would classify as highly mobile may well be only a minority. Although one veteran newsman reported working for seventeen different news organizations, only 4.7 percent had worked for five or more.

Two characteristics of work histories complicate the task of measuring job mobility. On the one hand, the longer people work the more chances they accumulate to change their employment, and as a result the total number of job moves people make increases with time spent in the labor force. At the same time, however, it is also more common for people to change jobs during the early rather than late stages of their careers (Form and Miller, 1949). In combination, these two tendencies mean that over time the probability that a given person will have changed jobs at least once goes up, while the probability that he or she will do so again goes down.

One manifestation of this latter phenomenon is that the length of time a person remains with the same employer increases over successive career stages, a feature which can be observed, at least indirectly, in the job histories of journalists. Working from current employment backward, for example, Table 4.6 reveals a clear-cut gradient of tenures, with jobs held in the more distant past being of briefer and briefer duration. It should be noted, of course, that the temporal categories used here combine persons who are in quite varying stages of their careers: for some, "current" employers would be "first" employers, while for others, second, third, fourth, or even "ultimate" employers.[7] Nonetheless, the results are consistent with the generalization that as work histories progress, employment becomes more stable.

The parameters of job mobility within an occupation are best estimated from completed work histories, ideally by following a cohort of recruits through all career stages. Although this type of analysis cannot be carried out in the present study, it is possible to subject the sample to a synthetic cohort analysis and to compare the mobility of persons with differing amounts of experience in the field. At this point, three measures of job mobility will be examined among journalists who have been employed in the news media for varying periods: first, the percentage who have changed media jobs at least once, an indicator of the cumulative prevalence of job mobility over time; second, the mean number of previous jobs held, a measure of the cumulative incidence of job changing; and third, estimates of the annual rates of job mobility at specific career stages—obtained by comparing the total job moves accumulated by a cohort with the total accumulated by the cohort immediately following it.

Table 4.7 reports these three measures for the sample as a whole. Turning first to the figures in the left-hand column, it is evident that most American newsmen change their jobs at least once within their first three or four years in the news media. The figures indicate that about 10 percent change jobs during the first year, more than a quarter have done so after two years, almost half after three years, and a clear majority after four years. The figures continue to rise to 81.6 percent among the sixteen to twenty year group, suggesting that *eventually* slightly more than four journalists in five will change the organizations for which they work. Interestingly, the figures tail off for the two most senior groups, an outcome which requires explanation since it would be a logical impossibility in the analysis of a real cohort. Two possibilities seem most likely in accounting for this anomaly. First, rates of job mobility among journalists may have increased during recent decades, and younger newsmen today may simply change jobs more frequently than their seniors did at similar career stages. As such, the results may reflect generally elevated rates of job mobility within the labor force as a whole. A second possibility is that younger journalists differ from veterans in characteristics which have a bearing on mobility: younger newsmen, for example, are more likely than their elders to hold college degrees, and this fact may mean that they command a more favorable position in the media job market than their elders did at the same career stage. A test of this possibility among veteran newsmen proved negative, however, since it turned out that among cohorts with twenty or more years of experience, 67.3 percent of college graduates and 70.1 percent of nongraduates had had previous media employers. In view of this, the inversion of the trend line may well mean that rates of job mobility in journalism are higher today than they were around 1950.

From the second column of figures in Table 4.7, it is evident that the averages for total job changes follow a similar pattern: the numbers rise continuously through the first twenty years, and then decline. At their peak, however, the averages remain slightly below two job changes per person.

It should be emphasized that where the first measure charted the number of different *persons* who have changed jobs, the second averages both initial and subsequent job changes. From the figures in the two columns, it is evident that during the first year all job changes are first job changes, since the values are the same. After two years of media experience, however, approximately a tenth of the moves involve people leaving second jobs $(.315 - .284/.315 = .101)$, a departure rate almost identical to the number leaving first jobs after one year. Although these functions cannot be traced further, they suggest a consistent manpower turnover of about 10 percent following the first year of employment with a news organization.

Together these two columns of figures illustrate how mobility experiences accumulate over time. The figures in the third column of Table 4.7, on the other hand, estimate the annual turnover rates at specific career stages, and as such offer a test of the premise that as careers in journalism progress the chances decline that newsmen will change their jobs during any specific year. What the results show, however, are accelerating rates of mobility through the first three years of employment, a dramatic decline between the third and fourth year, and (with one inversion) continuously declining rates after that. Although both the assumptions of synthetic cohort analysis and high sampling variability weaken the confidence which can be placed in the absolute levels of turnover described here, it is clear nonetheless that substantial numbers of newsmen leave their jobs during their third year of employment. Taken at face value, the data suggest that mobility rates double between the first and second years, double again between the second and third years, and then fall off sharply.

It should be noted, finally, that because of the inversion of the trend line in the second column of figures, the annual mobility rates after twenty years in the media would be estimated as zero—or actually as negative functions—from the approach being followed here. While the actual rates of job mobility during later stages of careers in journalism in all likelihood are *close* to zero, this fact can be neither confirmed nor negated from the data.

To expand this discussion, Figures 4.2 through 4.4 chart the three mobility functions separately for persons in the print and broadcast sectors of the industry. Although the actual procedure followed here was to classify respondents according to the sector in which they were employed at the time of the interview, the results reflect typical mobility patterns in the two sectors since it is rare for newsmen to move across these sectors when they change jobs. As will be confirmed in the next section, fewer than 5 percent of the interorganizational moves journalists make are shifts from broadcast media to print, or vice versa.

On all three measures, the graphs reveal much higher rates of job mobility within the broadcast sector. Figure 4.2 shows, first, that within all tenure groupings more broadcast newsmen than print had changed jobs at least once, and in addition, that *all* veteran broadcasters reported previous employers. Thus, it is only within the print sector that veteran journalists are less likely than their juniors to have worked for a different news organization at some point in the past. Moreover, the discrepancy in this regard is fairly dramatic. More than a third (35.0 percent) of all print journalists with twenty or more years of experience have spent their entire professional careers with the same news organizations: not a single broadcast journalist with that much experience reported a similar career. This discrepancy will become less pronounced in the future, but it can nevertheless be concluded that life-long loyalty to the same news organization is uniquely a characteristic of print journalism.

Broadcast newsmen are not only more likely to leave the news organizations they start out with, but are also more likely to make subsequent job changes as well. This is confirmed in Figure 4.3 by the progressively widening gap over time in the average number of previous jobs held. Inspection of the levels of these figures, moreover, indicates that at each career stage broadcast newsmen have changed jobs roughly twice as frequently as their print-media counterparts. Among those with more than twenty-five years of experience, the gap is actually wider than two to one, since broadcasters in that group reported an average of 3.9 previous jobs compared to 1.6 for print newsmen.

The widening gap in cumulative career moves is due to the fact that at each specific career stage annual rates of job mobility are higher within broadcast journalism. Although the trend line for broadcasters in Figure 4.3 is somewhat unstable—probably because of small sample sizes—there is not a single career period during which it could be said that print newsmen move as frequently as broadcasters. At the same time, the two career patterns do have similar shapes, and in both sectors, rates of job mobility accelerate during the first few years of employment, and decline thereafter.

On the basis of the varied evidence reviewed in this section, it can be concluded that careers in broadcast journalism are characterized by a much higher frequency of job movement than careers in print journalism. The image of the journalist as rootless and continuously on the move is therefore much more apt for one sector of the industry than the other. In this respect, contemporary broadcast newsmen seem to resemble the oldtime tramp newspapermen who floated from job to job.

Interorganizational Mobility

Next the types of organizational shifts journalists make when they change employers will be examined. Table 4.8 aggregates the total job changes involving a move from one news organization to another, and shows the proportion of the total falling within the thirty-six possible types of moves. Thus, of all previous moves between news organizations which were reported by the respondents, 38.79 percent were moves from daily newspapers to other dailies, .92 percent were moves from dailies to television, and no one at all reported moving from television to a weekly newspaper. This table contains a great deal of information, and its contents will be discussed under four headings: first, the net manpower gains and losses for specific types of organizations; second, levels of intra- and intersector job mobility; third, relatively common and relatively rare exchange routes; and finally, the degree of balance or imbalance in exchanges between specific pairs of news organizations.

(1). *Net gains and losses.* Comparisons of the values in the right-hand column and bottom row of the table provide evidence as to the net gains or losses realized by specific news organizations in their total exchanges of manpower with other media. The ratio of total recruitment to total departures constitutes a direct measure of net gain or loss, and calculation of these measures results in the following values for the six types of media:

Television	1.47
Wire services	1.09
Daily newspapers	1.03
News magazines	.95
Weekly newspapers	.91
Radio	.80

These ratios show both similarities and differences from those reported in Table 4.4 comparing current share of manpower with the share of fresh media recruits. Once again, television realizes the largest net gains, radio suffers the heaviest net losses, daily newspapers gain slightly, and news magazines experience net losses. The figures for wire services and for weekly newspapers are reversed from the earlier patterns, however: the wire services gain from intermedia manpower exchanges while weeklies lose, both by just under 10 percent. These reversals can be accounted for by the fact that media differ in the sources they recruit from, some recruiting more heavily than others from persons already employed by news organizations. Although full discussion of these patterns will be reserved until the next section in this chapter, it should be noted here that weeklies are less likely than wire services to recruit *either* from other news media *or* directly out of school, and are more likely to hire personnel employed outside the news media. As a result, weeklies gain personnel over time but lose in exchanges with other media—while the wire services show the reverse pattern.

More generally, it can be concluded from this analysis that when news-media journalists change their employers, they are on the whole attracted toward jobs in television, the wire services, and daily newspapers, and away from jobs in news magazines, weekly papers, and radio.

(2). *Intra- and inter-sector mobility.* Summing the proportions along the diagonal of Table 4.8 reveals that .6481 of all job changes were exchanges between the same kinds of news organizations. When newsmen change jobs, about two-thirds of the time they take new jobs in the same types of organizations they leave. Moreover, if news organizations are regrouped into broader categories, print and broadcast media, the level of intra-sector mobility is much higher. Excluding the wire services and recalculating the figures reveals that 67.1 percent of all moves were within print media, 28.6 percent were within broadcast media, and only 4.3 percent were between sectors—2.0 percent from print media to broadcast, and 2.3 percent from broadcast to print. All in all, then, over 95 percent of all job changes by journalists take place within the same broad media sectors, and it is extremely rare for newsmen to shift sectors. It might be added that when journalists leave wire service jobs, 79.1 percent move into the print sector, 6.9 percent go to radio or television, and 14.5 percent take jobs with other press services.

(3). *Common and rare mobility paths.* In order to evaluate the volume of specific interorganizational shifts, it is necessary to take into account the relative sizes of the different categories of media. Table 4.9 therefore presents as ratio values the actual mobility between organizations divided by the mobility which would be expected if journalists made simply random moves between news organizations.[8] In this table values greater than 1.00 indicate paths traveled more often than chance, and values less than 1.00 routes followed at less than chance expectation.

Table 4.9 reveals, first, that although all types of *intra*-organizational job changes are overrepresented, this type of recruitment is relatively most frequent within news magazines and television (8.82 and 5.70 times higher, respectively, than chance) and is lowest within daily newspapers (1.49 times greater than chance). One interpretation of these discrepancies is that the journalistic skills required in television and in news magazines are more specialized than those required in other media, thus decreasing the likelihood that personnel with appropriate experience will be located in other types of news organizations. By the same logic, dailies perhaps make the fewest demands in terms of specific types of prior experience.

Table 4.9 also identifies many exchange routes which are used only rarely, if indeed at all. Four types of exchanges were not reported at all: none of the 1,313 journalists interviewed reported *ever* leaving a news magazine to take a job in radio (or vice versa), and there were no exchanges in either direction between television and weekly newspapers. In addition, many other exchanges, in particular those involving moves between the print and broadcast sectors, occurred much less frequently than would be expected by chance. For example, moves from dailies to radio were observed at just .08 of their expected frequency, and from radio to dailies at just .11 the chance expectation. No mobility paths between print and broadcast media were reported with even chance frequency, although exchanges between news magazines and television would appear to be less rare than most.

Information is also available on the *inter*organizational paths within broad media sectors which are most likely to be followed. Three of these were reported at more than twice their expected frequency—moves from wire services to news magazines, from radio to television, and from news magazines to weeklies; and three others had been taken between 25 and 50 percent more often than chance would predict—moves from television to radio; from dailies to news magazines; and from dailies to wire services. Finally, it should be noted that only three interorganizational paths within broad media sectors were utilized less frequently than chance—moves from news magazines to dailies, from dailies to weeklies, and from weeklies to news magazines.

In terms of actual numbers, however, a limited number of exchange routes dominate the paths newsmen follow when they switch media. Counting job moves in both directions these changes, in order of volume of manpower flow, are between (a) dailies and weeklies, (b) radio and television, (c) dailies and wire services, (d) dailies and news magazines, and (e) dailies and radio. Together these exchanges account for 30.5 percent of all job changes, and 86.4 percent of job changes which involve news organizations of different types.

(4). *Balanced and imbalanced exchanges.* To conclude this section, Figure 4.5 illustrates the degree of balance or imbalance in the five most common intermedia exchange routes. This mapping locates daily newspapers at the focal point of manpower exchanges among the media, and indicates that dailies, though they may gain more personnel than they lose, function primarily as sources of manpower for some types of news organizations. Dailies gain fairly substantially in personnel exchanges with weeklies and with radio, but lose manpower to the news magazines and the wire services—though just slightly so in the latter case. It should also be added that personnel exchanges between dailies and television, though rare, favor television by a wide (68 to 32) margin.

The most imbalanced manpower flow of all, however, occurs within the broadcast sector, where 73 percent of the total job shifts are into television. Radio thus loses heavily in exchanges with both television and dailies, and it could be added that radio also loses (by a 39 to 61 margin) in its rare exchanges with weeklies and wire services.

Although the bulk of job mobility within journalism consists of moves within the same media, these imbalances suggest certain regularized routes of interorganizational mobility. Within the print sector, weeklies appear to serve as training grounds for dailies, which in turn send experienced manpower to news magazines and the wire services. And within the broadcast sector, television is clearly dominant over radio.

Overall Recruitment Sources

As an addendum to this discussion, Table 4.10 provides an overview of the sources American news media utilize when recruiting editorial personnel. This table structures the data from the perspective of the recruiting institution rather than the individual journalist, and aggregates the total number of instances in which members of the sample reported taking jobs in news organizations of each type.[9] The table shows the percentages recruited directly out of school, from other news organizations, and from other occupational spheres.

Of initial interest here is the fact that almost half of the aggregated recruitment (47.1 percent) involved shifts of experienced newsmen. This, coupled with the fact that 22.5 percent of all recruits were entering the news media from other labor force situses, means that in total the American news media are much more likely to fill staff openings with experienced personnel than they are to hire, train, and promote their own raw recruits.

While this tendency is true for all categories of media, Table 4.10 does reveal variations in recruitment sources among news organizations of different types. Thus television recruits a substantial majority (63.8 percent) of its personnel from other news organizations, and is considerably less likely than other media to hire persons entering the labor force for the first time. Radio and the wire services also show a relatively strong propensity to recruit experienced journalists. News magazines, on the other hand, recruit almost as many inexperienced as veteran newsmen, while weekly papers are more likely than other media to recruit from elsewhere in the experienced labor force. Weeklies, in fact, recruit slightly more often from other occupations than they do from schools, and this fact explains how it is possible for weeklies to increase their total share of manpower over time but lose in manpower exchanges with other news organizations. The personnel weeklies lose to other media they more than compensate for by their recruitment of persons entering journalism from other lines of work.

In general, then, different news organizations do utilize different recruitment sources. Broadcast media are more likely than print to hire journalists with prior experience, and print media are more likely than broadcast to offer employment to persons entering the media relatively late in their careers. Although their overall share of manpower is small, news magazines are the sector most likely to hire fresh recruits to journalism, and this result coupled with information presented earlier suggests that news magazines either hire and train young college graduates or recruit experienced manpower away from daily newspapers. Finally, it could be concluded that persons who enter news-media journalism relatively late find it easiest to do so via weekly newspapers.

Geographic Mobility

Although it cannot be readily determined whether the patterns of job mobility exhibited by journalists are typical or atypical, comparative data can be introduced against which to evaluate the geographic mobility of journalists. Table 4.11 compares the migratory habits of newsmen with estimates for the labor force as a whole obtained by the Survey Research Center of the University of Michigan in 1962, and reported by Lansing and Mueller (1967, p. 35). In addition to providing information on the origins and current locations of newsmen and household heads, this table shows the numbers who have migrated from region to region, and who, at the time they were interviewed, were employed in the same region in which they were born.

(1). *Origins.* Comparisons of the right-hand columns of Table 4.11 indicate fairly substantial discrepancies in the birthplaces of journalists and the labor force at large. These imbalances are expressed most directly as ratios of the number of newsmen born in a given region to the number of household heads born there, and the values are as follows: 1.76 for the Northeast; 1.47 for the West; .99 for the North Central region; .62 for the South; and .36 for countries other than the United States. Thus, both the Northeast and the West supply more newsmen than they would be expected to, the North Central region produces a proportionate share, and there are underrepresentations of both southern-born and foreign-born newsmen. It is evident, then, that the Northeast not only *employs* a disproportionate share of the working press of the nation, but in addition, *supplies* more than its share.

In total, just 2.9 percent of those employed currently in the English-language news media in the United States are foreign-born, and it might be added that of these 1.7 percent come from Canada, Britain, or other English-speaking countries. These figures thus reinforce the conclusion from Chapter 2 that newsmen are drawn primarily from national groups which have been resident on the continent the longest.

(2). *Rates of migration.* Just as in the labor force as a whole, most journalists (about 70 percent) work in the same regions in which they were born. Summing the proportions *off* the diagonals in Table 4.11 reveals that only .294 of newsmen and .278 of household heads were born outside the regions in which they were working at the time they were interviewed. While this suggests that the motility of newsmen is fairly conventional, it should be noted that the discrepancy between the two groups widens when foreign-born are excluded from the comparison. Among just the United States born, 27.3 percent of journalists compared with 21.5 percent of heads of households had migrated from other parts of the country. All in all, then, it is perhaps fair to conclude that journalism is an occupation marked by relatively high rates of geographic mobility.

(3). *Regional gains and losses.* While direct comparisons of the row and column totals in Table 4.11 yield crude estimates of regional gains and losses due to migration, standardized measures of this movement can be obtained by dividing the total in-migration to a region by the total out-migration. The resulting migration ratios are as follows:

	Journalists	Household Heads
Northeast	1.00	.62
North Central	.37	.62
South	1.46	.63
West	2.70	13.00

These values illustrate clearly how the migratory habits of journalists differ from those of the population as a whole. The data for household heads reveal the familiar pattern of population movement to the West, and indicate almost identical losses of manpower, proportionately, from the other three regions. For journalists, however, the patterns are quite different. First of all, the Northeast does not lose manpower from migration, and attracts the same number of in-migrants as it loses native sons. The North Central region, on the other hand, suffers a much heavier attrition than would be predicted, and thus supplies the rest of the country with many more journalists than it is able to attract. Somewhat surprisingly, the South ends up with a net gain in journalistic manpower, an outcome perhaps due in part to the presence of the nation's capital in that region, and in part to the fact that the region supplies so few newsmen to begin with. Finally, the West nets substantial gains from migration, though it should be emphasized that westerly migration is by no means as pronounced among journalists as it is in the labor force as a whole: whereas the general flow of manpower into the West exceeds out-migration by a factor of 13:1, among journalists the imbalance is less than 3:1.

At this point it should be noted that despite heavy out-migration, the North Central region plays a major role in the professional training of journalists. In fact, more newsmen obtained journalism degrees in the Midwest than in any other region. Table 4.12 shows that a substantial majority (66.9 percent) of those with journalism degrees graduated from colleges and universities located in the Midwest or the South, and the figures in the right-hand column make it clear that this concentration is not unique to journalism graduates who have entered the news media: 68.4 percent of *all* baccalaureate and advanced degrees in journalism awarded in 1970 to 1971 were from schools in these regions. By comparison, those with degrees in other fields were much more likely to have graduated from institutions in the Northeast. These patterns reflect the role land-grant universities have played in the development of journalism education in the United States, and suggest that the impact of those developments persists even today. It is somewhat anomalous, nonetheless, that the region of the country which has produced the largest numbers of professionally trained newsmen is also the region which has lost the largest numbers of its native-born products via out-migration.

While the results presented earlier confirm that the migratory habits of journalists differ from those of the labor force as a whole, they do not indicate precise directions of job mobility within the news industry since some undetermined portion of the overall movement would have occurred prior to the time that respondents entered the labor force. A more direct appraisal of geographic mobility among newsmen, then, is obtained by focusing on the origins and destinations of those who are changing jobs. These data were therefore aggregated, and each previous job change within the United States was charted in terms of regional origins and destinations. Migration ratios were then computed for each of the nine subregions of the country, and these values are reported in Table 4.13.

Before commenting on these results, it should be reported that most job mobility is intra- rather than inter-regional: 73.9 percent of all previous changes of employment reported by the sample took place within subregions, and 80.7 percent of all moves were within the four principal regions. In other words, job mobility does not necessarily imply geographic mobility. Although data were not preserved on specific origins and destinations within regions, it is likely that a sizable percentage of job changes took place within the same cities or counties.

Table 4.13 reveals several dimensions of manpower flow which were not visible in Table 4.11. Within the Northeast, for example, there is a substantial flow of manpower into the Middle Atlantic states and out of New England: and similarly, the South Atlantic subregion gains journalists while the deep

South (the East South Central region) loses them. More important, Table 4.13 shows that when newsmen do migrate, they do
not follow the predominantly westerly path of the labor force
as a whole. It is the Middle Atlantic subregion which has the
most favorable migration ratio, and these states attract substantially more newsmen than they lose. To be sure, the Pacific and
mountain regions also recruit more experienced newsmen than
they lose, but migration West is superseded by migration East.
Only one other subregion, the South Atlantic, shows a favorable
net balance, and this result may again be due primarily to the
influx of experienced journalists into Washington, D.C. All
other subregions, then, function more as suppliers than recruit-
ers of experienced manpower, though it should be acknowledged that the East Central states, both North and South, just
about break even. There are three areas of the country, however, which have experienced a heavy outward flow of editorial
personnel in recent years: these, ordered by the magnitude of
proportionate losses, are (a) the West North Central region—
North and South Dakota, Nebraska, Kansas, Minnesota, Iowa,
and Missouri; (b) the New England states—Maine, Vermont,
New Hampshire, Massachusetts, Rhode Island, and Connecti-
cut; and (c) the West South Central states—Oklahoma, Arkan-
sas, Texas, and Louisiana.

In overview, journalistic manpower in the United States
migrates away from the interior of the country toward the two
coastal regions. All maritime areas except New England attract
journalists, and all interior regions except the Mountain states
lose them. It is clear also that the prevalent westerly flow of the
United States population is superseded within journalism by
substantial migration to the Middle Atlantic states, the heart of
the United States news industry. While most migrating Americans are pulled westward, journalists are pulled toward the East
and the West at the same time.

As a footnote to this discussion, it should be emphasized
that these migratory patterns reflect the areal distribution of
economic opportunities within American journalism. Although
newsmen's incomes will not be reviewed in full until Chapter 8,
it is noteworthy that the correlation (Spearman rank-order)
between net migration and median income for the nine subregions was .52. Just as in the labor force as a whole, journalists
migrate to the areas of the county where their opportunities for
economic advancement are the greatest.

Summary

Careers in news-media journalism are marked by an absence of common beginning points or fixed entry routes. There are several different paths into journalism: one can decide to enter the field relatively early in life or relatively late; one can opt for professional training in college or for a broad substantive background; and one can enter the news media right out of school or work first in some other occupation. Perhaps because of the variety of options available, journalism on the whole can be described as a late-entry field.

These patterns of career beginnings are not without their social structural roots. From the evidence reviewed in this chapter, it is clear that newsmen from higher socioeconomic backgrounds went further in their schooling, and in addition, attended more selective colleges and universities—where in turn they were less likely to end up in professional training programs. These propensities have the net effect of channeling persons from higher economic backgrounds into academic majors in college and those from less affluent beginnings into journalism programs.

Journalists are more migratory than the average American worker, and it can probably be concluded, therefore, that the field is one which is characterized by high levels of job mobility. Organizational mobility may be higher in the field today than it has been in the past, since it was found that more newsmen in late career stages than in the middle of their careers had spent their entire professional histories with the same news organizations. Since in the labor force at large mobility is positively associated with level of schooling (Lansing and Mueller, 1967, p. 45), one would be inclined to interpret this trend as a by-product of rising levels of education in journalism. This interpretation was not substantiated in the analysis, however, and the trend may therefore reflect general increases of mobility within American society.

While life-long loyalty to the same organization may be becoming extinct in the news industry generally, it is already an unknown career pattern in broadcast journalism. Broadcast newsmen change jobs much more frequently than do their counterparts in print journalism, and they do so continuously throughout their careers. Explanations for this difference were not explored in the analysis, but it is likely that the discrepancy is related more to industry characteristics than to characteristics of the personnel employed in the two sectors. Broadcast organizations appear to engage in much more aggressive recruiting practices than print organizations, for example, since they are more likely to recruit experienced manpower away from other news organizations. Further support for this interpretation comes from the fact that 84.2 percent of broadcast newsmen compared with just 50.9 percent of those in the print sector reported they had had job feelers from other news organizations during the twelve-month period prior to the study. Broadcast journalism can still be regarded as an expanding industry, of course, and the elevated rates of labor turnover in the broadcast sector may therefore be largely a temporary phenomenon reflecting general patterns of labor mobility in young and expanding industries.

It is also noteworthy that there is little manpower flow between the two sectors. It is rare for newsmen to switch from print journalism to broadcast, or vice versa. Most job changes, in fact, occur within the same types of news organizations, although some movement takes place between dailies and weeklies, and between radio and television. Within broadcast journalism, the dominant mobility route is from radio to television. Outside the broadcast sector, mobility paths are more complex, with dailies recruiting from weeklies, and news magazines and the wire services from dailies.

While journalists are more mobile geographically than persons in most occupations, the direction of their movement differs noticeably from the dominant direction followed by the labor force at large. Because the United States news industry is centered along the East coast megalopolis, migrating newsmen are attracted primarily to the East, though many do migrate West. On the whole, then, experienced manpower in American journalism gravitates away from the interior of the country and toward the two coastal regions.

The topics reviewed in this chapter by no means exhaust the perspectives from which careers in journalism can be examined. Attention is now turned to how job functions and journalistic responsibilities change over the course of careers.

Notes

1. The ratings used were those developed by Reiss, *et al.* (1961). The table compares persons in the upper and lower quartiles on this distribution with those in the middle half. Persons in the lowest quartile are not

necessarily of "lower class" origins, and a more appropriate label might be "lower middle class." The fathers' occupations classified in this group have prestige ratings between 15 and 40, and the mean score, 31.4, is equivalent to the status of butchers, piano tuners, roofers, and some craftsmen. Scores in the middle group range between 41 and 50, with a mean of 47.1, which is equivalent to the status of insurance agents and technicians. The upper quartile contains a mixture of professional and managerial backgrounds, with scores ranging from 51 to 82. The mean for this group, 63.0, is the level of prestige the public accords optometrists, pharmacists, hospital administrators, and secondary school teachers. In later sections of the analysis these scores will be used as a continuous variable for purposes of correlation and regression analysis.

2. Editors, reporters, writers, and radio and television announcers all receive occupational prestige scores of 51, which places them at the bottom rung of the upper quartile.

3. In this calculation college major is treated as a dummy variable: journalism majors are given a score of 1 and all other majors a score of 0.

4. In addition, the partial correlation of economic background with college major, holding constant college selectivity, was just -.059, while the contrasting partial relationship, between college selectivity and major with socioeconomic background constant, was -.246.

5. Seventy-five percent of all graduates entered directly, compared with 62.5 percent of nongraduates.

6. The actual share of editorial manpower in daily newspapers was estimated in the preliminary survey of news organizations to be 55.8 percent (see Table 2.1), which is somewhat lower than the share of raw recruits reported here. The ratio scores reported in Table 4.4 are calculated from manpower shares which turned up in the sample of individual journalists, which because of differential completion rates in different media sectors, vary somewhat from the estimates in the first survey. The proportion of respondents working for dailies was .603, and the ratio of current manpower to raw recruits was therefore estimated as .603/.582 = 1.04.

7. It might be added that treating job histories sequentially rather than in reverse order results in similar ambiguities: for some persons "first" jobs would be current jobs still in process of completion, while for others they would be the first in a series of employments.

8. The method of calculating these ratios was as follows: since .5026 of all departures were from daily newspapers, and .5181 of all recruitment was into dailies, the expected proportion of total moves within dailies would be .5026 × .5181 = .2604. The actual proportion of moves of this type, however, is indicated in Table 4.8 to be .3879. Internal moves within dailies thus occur more frequently than would be expected by chance, and the value .3879/.2604 expresses the degree of overrepresentation, 49 percent.

9. The table actually covers just 96.7 percent of the previous media jobs members of the sample had held since information was preserved only for a respondent's current employment and a maximum of four previous employments.

5
The Division of Labor within Journalism

There are three main activities in journalism: (a) news gathering, reporting, and other types of news writing or production; (b) editing and news processing; and (c) the supervision and management of editorial operations. These three classes of activity, in varying mixes, encompass most of the things newsmen do, and also serve to differentiate the primary environs within which journalists work. Although most actual news writing may be done within the confines of an office, journalists who do news gathering spend a large amount of time on their news beats covering events or contacting news sources. Editing, news processing, supervision, and management, on the other hand, are all functions which are performed inside the organization. This distinction is of more than passing significance for it also differentiates the nature of a journalist's social contacts, the sources of day-to-day demands which impinge upon his work, and the degree of his first-hand familiarity with the events, topics, and personages in the news. Moreover, a journalist's status and recognition in the professional community as well as in society at large are determined largely by the news writing he does, while his income and status in the organizational hierarchy are more a function of whether he manages editorial operations or directs the work of other journalists.

Just as individual newsmen differ greatly in reputation and influence, so too do news organizations. Some have national and even international visibility, others are regional in impact, and many have local influence only. Where a few gain the attention of decision makers in government and industry, most reach the rank-and-file citizenry only. And while some have major influence on the day-to-day work of practicing newsmen, most have little or no impact on the professional community.

This chapter focuses on the job activities newsmen perform and on the organizational settings in which they perform them. The first section describes the variety of job functions in news-media journalism, and discusses how these functions shift over the course of careers in the media. The effect of organization size on the division of labor in journalism is then discussed, and following this, the news organizations which newsmen themselves regard as most reliable and as most useful in their own work are identified. The chapter then concludes by comparing the characteristics of those in supervisory and nonsupervisory positions in both prominent and less prominent news organizations.

Journalistic Functions

Most journalists would consider news writing at the core of the journalistic enterprise. As A. J. Liebling (1961, p. 225) once noted, however, there are at least three types of news writers: the reporter, who writes what he sees; the interpretive reporter, who writes both what he sees and what he construes its meaning to be; and the "expert," who interprets things he has not seen at all. Despite Liebling's concern over the decline of eyewitness reporting in journalism, news writing of that type is still the most common job function performed by a journalist. More than three-quarters (78.8 percent) of the sample said they did reporting on a "regular" or "occasional" basis, and of these persons virtually all (94.2 percent) claimed they had done the primary news gathering on at least one story during the previous week. Moreover, 61.2 percent of all reporters classified their most typical assignments as "hard news," reports of actual events and occurrences, and only 12.0 percent labeled their most usual work as news analysis, interpretive news writing, or in-depth reporting.

Part A of Table 5.1 shows the numbers of print and broadcast newsmen engaged in various forms of news writing or production. First, it should be noted that about a third of all media journalists (34.7 percent) are assigned to specific newsbeats. This means that among those who do any reporting at all, about 44.0 percent report on just one particular area of news, while 56.0 percent cover a range of different topics. Table 5.1 also indicates that beat assignments are considerably more prevalent in print than in broadcast journalism: in fact, when the figures are recalculated just for reporters, they indicate that 47.4 percent in the print sector compared with just 29.2 percent in the broadcast sector are assigned to a specific newsbeat.

Aside from reporting, the most common type of writing activity that journalists engage in is the preparation of editorials. In the sample as a whole more than one in four (26.8 percent) said they wrote editorials at least occasionally; yet only 15.4 percent had written an editorial during the previous week, only 8.7 percent had written more than one the previous week, and only 11.3 percent claimed to be the chief editorial writer in their organization. Despite the fact that fairly large numbers of journalists share in the preparation of editorial statements for their organizations—and more in the broadcast media than might generally be thought—it would appear that the number who do so on a regular basis is quite limited.

Among print newsmen, as many as 29.4 percent said they wrote a column at least occasionally (21.9 percent had written at least one a week during the previous month), and another 11.9 percent reported they did feature writing from time to time; however, no other type of reporting or writing activity was mentioned by more than one print newsman in ten. In the broadcast sector, between 10 and 15 percent said they prepared news commentaries, or produced documentaries or news specials, and 8.2 percent produced or hosted public affairs discussion programs.

In overview, then, it is clear that while news-media journalists engage in a variety of different writing or reporting activities, the straight reporting of "hard news" is still the most prevalent journalistic activity by far.

Though a much less visible aspect of a journalist's work, sizable numbers are also involved in editing or processing the news. When asked, "How much editing or processing of other people's work do you do?," 34.1 percent responded "a great deal" and another 37.5 percent said "some." In addition to reporting news, a majority of journalists also perform behind-the-scenes editorial duties on work initiated by others—activities such as editing stories for content or grammar, doing rewrites, checking the factual accuracy of information, or editing news dispatches for length. Both the variety and the prevalence of these activities confirm that mass communicated news is more a product of collective than strictly individual effort. Moreover, while reporting and editing tend to be specialized functions, many newsmen perform both; 16.9 percent said they did reporting regularly *and* also did "a great deal" of editing, and over half (52.9 percent) said they were called upon to do both things at least part of the time.

It should also be noted here that 36.9 percent of print newsmen compared with just 20.6 percent in the broadcast sector said they did "a great deal" of editing or news processing. Even though comparable numbers of persons in the two sectors do at least some editing, the volume of this work is considerably greater in print journalism. This difference can also be observed in the other figures in Part B of Table 5.1, which indicate that more print than broadcast newsmen carry out each of the editorial duties listed. The largest difference (13.4 percent) is in editing for spelling and grammar, which is not surprising since broadcasters are mainly concerned with the spoken word.

The third major function in journalism is the supervision and management of news operations. Although news organizations must coordinate a variety of operations, our interest here is confined to persons in charge of editorial functions: media personnel whose responsibilities lie exclusively in areas such as production, technical direction, circulation, or advertising were explicitly omitted from the sampling universe. Even excluding these types of personnel, however, more than two journalists in five (41.9 percent) reported having supervisory or managerial responsibilities of one type or another. A total of 28.1 percent said they had influence on hiring or firing decisions, 27.9 percent supervised one or more reporters, 16.5 percent had charge of a news department, and 11.1 percent claimed executive responsibility for all news operations in their organization.

Although three types of activities have been identified here, the basic division of labor within journalism is between those activities which bring a journalist into contact with the external social environment—news gathering, news writing, and reporting—and those performed inside the organization—editing, news processing, supervision, and management. It is between these sets of activities that the distinction between "staffers" and "executives" (Breed, 1950) is most usually defined, and around which specialization of function tends to occur in news-media journalism. For example, the amount of editing or news processing a journalist does is positively related to the number of editorial employees he or she is responsible for ($r = .318$), while reporting frequency is negatively related both with the amount of editing one does (r = -.286) and the number of editorial employees supervised (r = -.380). Thus even though sizable numbers of reporters may have editing or supervisory responsibilities, and many "executives" keep a hand in at reporting, these two work roles tend to be differentiated from one another.

Job Functions and Career Stages

As in most occupations, the specific tasks a journalist performs are determined by experience and longevity in the field. To begin, Figure 5.1 charts for the sample as a whole the number of newsmen involved in reporting, editing, and supervision or management at various career points. From this chart it is evident immediately that participation in all three of these journalistic activities is affected by one's experience. Close to 80 percent of all journalists start out their careers as full-time reporters, but this proportion declines almost continuously with increasing tenure in the field. By contrast, the numbers who do editing, news processing, supervision, and management all increase over time. Even among veteran newsmen, however, it should be noted that a majority continue to do reporting on a regular basis, though it is also evident that among those with more than twenty-five years of experience more have administrative responsibilities than do regular reporting. More generally, then, it is evident that as newsmen accumulate experience they come to devote less and less time to news gathering and reporting, and more and more time to internal organizational activities. These shifts are to be expected, of course, and it is no secret that formal line authority within an organization is a perquisite which one is likely to acquire only with experience.

One way to identify career stages within an occupation is to chart the ages of persons who perform specific job activities, and Table 5.2 therefore orders a variety of news-media functions by the median ages of the persons who perform them. Although use of the median statistic here has the effect of compressing career stages into a brief time span, the table identifies the chronological sequence of job responsibilities within both print and broadcast journalism. From these data, shifts are evident in the general functions newsmen perform, in the scope of their administrative responsibilities, and in the types of news writing they do.

Turning first to print-media functions, the data once again illustrate a transition over time from news gathering and reporting to internal organizational functions. Those who do regular reporting and cover specific news beats are younger on the average than those who do editing, news processing, supervision, and management. The scope of a newsman's managerial responsibilities is also seen to broaden progressively after the age of forty: those in charge of news desks are younger than those who manage departments, who in turn are younger than those who oversee general editorial operations. Finally, the data reveal a chronological sequence in the types of news writing journalists do. In the print media, the news writing "career line" would appear to begin with "hard news" reporting and with assignment to a news beat, then progress to feature writing and interpretive reporting, then to writing a column or doing reviews, and finally, to writing editorials.

In the broadcast media, some of these same patterns are evident while others are not. Persons with managerial responsibilities are certainly older than those involved in reporting and news gathering, but with the exception of editorial writing, there is no evidence of a transition from straight news reporting to other more personalized reportorial forms. In fact, those who prepare news commentaries, do news analysis or interpretive reporting, or host discussion programs are *younger* than those who cover news beats, report "hard news," or do regular reporting.

These results are perplexing, but can perhaps be interpreted in terms of three related facts concerning broadcast journalism— the lopsided distribution of stations of different sizes; the ages of newsmen employed in small and large enterprises; and the nature of news operations in organizations of differing size. In 1971, there were some 7,868 broadcast stations on the air in the United States,[1] most of which employed at least one full-time newsman. Apart from the networks and a limited number of stations in the larger urban markets, however, news staffs in broadcast organizations tend to be very small. In total 57.3 percent of broadcast journalists, compared with just 24.2 percent in the print media, work in organizations with ten or fewer full-time newsmen, and among radio newsmen, over a third (36.3 percent) work in news departments of just one, two, or three persons. A second piece of pertinent information is that newsmen in small stations are younger than their counterparts in the networks and larger stations: the median age of those in news departments with more than ten employees is 33.3 years and with ten or fewer, 29.0 years. Third, and more important, news operations in small and large broadcasting organizations differ markedly. In small stations, a newsman's primary responsibility—and often his sole responsibility—is to compose and deliver news reports taken directly from the wires. In very small stations, of course, these same persons would also be responsible for any other news or public affairs features programmed by the station. In these kinds of settings, then, broadcast newsmen are virtually studio-bound, and do not cover news beats or do reporting in the more usual sense of these terms. Career mobility in broadcast journalism, moreover, does not usually imply a shift from outside to inside assignments, but rather a shift from omnibus news responsibilities in a small station to more limited duties in larger ones. Many broadcast journalists begin their careers in small stations, move on to reporting jobs in larger stations, and then eventually move into production or managerial responsibilities in these larger organizations. The heavy mobility from radio to television noted in the previous chapter is consistent with this interpretation, since news staffs in television generally are larger than in radio. In summary, the apparently reversed career patterns of broadcast journalists may be explained by the fact that most broadcast newsmen work in small news departments, that newsmen in small stations are studio-bound yet have omnibus responsibilities for news and public affairs programming, and that upward mobility in broadcast journalism means moving from smaller to larger markets.

In general, broadcast newsmen are younger than their colleagues in the print sector. As indicated by Table 5.2, the median age of radio and television newsmen is 30.8 years, compared with 36.5 years for the industry as a whole, and 38.1 years for print journalists. Several factors probably contribute to this overall difference. For one thing, the difference may well reflect the relative maturity of the two sectors of the industry, since it is typical for the labor force to be younger in developing than in established industries. As an illustration, Bogue (1969, p. 263) reports that in 1960 the median age of the experienced male labor force in the railroad and railway express industry was 47.3 years, while for males in the air transportation industry it was 35.6 years. For women, the comparable figures were 45.3 and 27.3 years.[2] Part of this discrepancy between the media, therefore, may be a temporary phenomenon related to the current stages of development of print and broadcast journalism in the United States. Another contributing factor is that newsmen's roles in the broadcast sector often call for show-business skills and personal attractiveness in addition to journalistic competence, and it is possible, therefore, that there is a premium on youthfulness throughout broadcast journalism. This may be particularly true of radio, since many radio stations program primarily for young audiences. Finally, other differences between the two sectors of the industry may also affect the course of a journalist's career. Informational broadcasts are by no means the programming staple in American broadcasting: indeed, in terms of budgets and revenues, news and public affairs programming is very much a secondary production activity. As a result, one does not typically advance to the top managerial levels of broadcast organizations and at the same time continue to carry out functions as a journalist. In the print media, on the other hand, it is possible to move to the very top of the organizational ladder and still retain one's identification as a journalist. Even though daily newspapers serve wide functions for their readers, the dissemination of news, information, and opinion—rather than entertainment—is still the *raison d'etre* of the contemporary newspaper. The paucity of older newsmen in the broadcast sector may also be related to the fact that when broadcast newsmen are organizationally mobile, they no longer identify or function as journalists.

Whatever the primary explanation, it is evident that basic journalistic activities in the broadcast media are performed by personnel who are an average of five to ten years younger than their print media counterparts.

More generally, these results suggest that there are two dimensions of career mobility in news-media journalism, one operating along the organizational status hierarchy, and the other along the news-writing dimension. Although most newsmen start out as reporters, it would appear that by the mid-thirties a print journalist must orient himself to one of two career paths—advancement through the administrative echelons, or advancement to more specialized and presumably more prestigious and economically rewarding forms of news writing. Successful mobility along the organizational track results in the acquisition of line authority over the functioning of a news organization and over the work activities of other newsmen.

Advancement up the news-writing hierarchy, on the other hand, is marked by shifts from anonymous to personalized news writing, from straight reporting to news analysis and interpretation, and from a focus on the events of the day to a focus on policy advocacy. These transitions, it might be added, are also consistent with Liebling's (1961, p. 225) estimates of the "worldly consideration" accorded different types of news writers.

The results thus suggest a bifurcation of career lines into what might be termed "professional" and "administrative" tracks. This is not to say that veteran newsmen participate in just one of these two sets of activities. It has already been noted that many experienced newsmen do reporting or other news writing and that newcomers to the field take on supervisory or administrative duties quite early in their careers. From the evidence presented thus far, however, it is not clear whether journalists tend to move along just one of these career routes, or whether upward mobility in the news media implies advancement along both tracks simultaneously.

Some clarification on this point emerges from Table 5.3, which shows the relationships between pairs of work activities performed by newsmen in the two media sectors. The job activities represented in this table include three measures of administrative responsibility (having managerial duties of one type or another, the number of editorial employees who report to a person, and the amount of editing or news processing one does); two "professional" job functions common within both media sectors (reporting and editorial writing); three news-writing activities unique to print journalism (writing a column, features, or reviews); and three "professional" activities unique to broadcast journalism (producing documentaries or news specials, preparing news commentaries, and producing or hosting discussion programs). Positive values in this table indicate that activities tend to be performed by the same persons, negative values indicate differentiation of the two functions, and values which approximate zero imply that there is no functional relationship at all between performance of the two activities.

(1). *Administrative functions.* In both sectors of the media the three measures of administrative activities (variables 1 to 3) all correlate positively with one another, though it is evident that the association between news editing and other types of managerial duties is more substantial within print than broadcast journalism. In general, however, having managerial responsibility in the news media implies control both over news content and over the work activities of editorial employees, and these responsibilities tend to be shared by the same people.

(2). *"Professional" activities.* Only modest relationships are evident among the various "professional" activities newsmen perform. Employing linkage analysis (McQuitty, 1964), two very loose clusters were identified among print journalists, the first consisting of writing editorials and columns, which are correlated at .165, and the second linking reporting, feature writing, and doing reviews, which show weak though positive interrelationships. Among broadcast newsmen, the linkage analysis yielded a single cluster containing all five "professional" activities, with the strongest links between writing editorials and preparing news commentaries ($r = .162$), and between doing commentaries and reporting ($r = .154$). Comparing the two sectors, then, there would appear to be a somewhat sharper division of labor in print than in broadcast journalism between personnel who do straight reporting and those who do news analysis or communicate opinions. More generally, however, the low correlations suggest that the various journalistic activities represented here are fairly independent, and certainly do not make up a *set* of job tasks that most newsmen perform from time to time.

(3). *The connection between "administrative" and "professional" tasks.* The most interesting figures in the two matrixes are those which relate "administrative" with "professional" activities. In both the print and broadcast sectors, all three indicators of administrative responsibility correlate *negatively* with the frequency of reporting a journalist does, and *positively* with whether or not he writes editorials. Throughout the news industry, reporting and editorial writing are linked with positions on the hierarchy of a news organization—reporting being done by persons who are fairly low on the status ladder, and editorial writing by those fairly high up. Other professional functions, on the other hand, appear to be more independent of the administrative hierarchy. Among print journalists there is very little association between having managerial responsibilities and writing a column, features, or reviews—the strongest association being just .073, between having managerial duties of one type or another and writing a column. Among broadcast newsmen, the relationships are slightly stronger, and also appear to be more complex since two of the "professional" activities, producing documentaries or news specials and doing news commentaries, are positively associated with indicators of managerial status, while the third, producing or hosting a talk show, is negatively related. In broadcast journalism, specialized "professional" functions are not quite as independent of positions on the administrative hierarchy as they are in print journalism.

From these results it can be concluded that some types of "professional" activities are well integrated within the administrative structure of news media while others are not. This is suggestive of the distinction between "line" and "staff" activities in an organization, line activities constituting basic organizational functions, and staff activities those which provide specialized services to line functions or line functionaries. Reporters and editorial writers clearly occupy positions on the line authority hierarchy, while columnists, reviewers, feature writers, commentators, documentary producers, and talk show hosts tend to be staff roles in American news organizations. From this same perspective, reporting and editorial writing might also be identified as the *core* journalistic functions of a news organization.

To sum up, "administrative" and "professional" career lines in news-media journalism do appear to be fairly distinct. As one moves beyond reporter status, the main alternatives are between mobility through the administrative hierarchy, in which case one may come to exercise professional skills primarily by writing editorials, or mobility into specialized journalistic roles, in which case one does not accrue line authority within the organization. Breed's (1950) distinction between "staffers" and "executives" might well be extended to include a third status category, the "staff specialist."

Organization Size and Journalistic Practice

Apart from career stage, the most important factor influencing the work a journalist does is the size of the news organization for which he works. Just as in other industrial settings so too in news-media journalism the division of labor becomes more elaborate and specialization of function begins to appear when news organizations expand their size. As the number of editorial employees in an organization increases, a newsman's job functions become much more clearly delimited, perhaps by full-time beat assignments at the news-gathering end, or by full-time managerial responsibilities among those at the other end of the status hierarchy. While in small organizations executives may do some reporting, and staffers may have editing or managerial duties in addition to reporting, these combinations of duties are much less likely to be done in large news organizations. Moreover, even though the absolute number of employees who carry out specific job tasks increases, specialization of function has the effect of lowering the proportion of total employees who engage in specific job tasks. Two ways in which organizational growth affects the division of labor in journalism are (a) that the number of newsmen who carry out specific types of duties will become proportionately fewer; and (b) that the range of journalistic functions performed by individual newsmen will become narrower.

Table 5.4 illustrates the first of these processes by relating the size of the organization a journalist works for with whether or not he carries out various tasks. The table includes journalistic functions common to executives and staffers in both sectors of the news industry, and demonstrates that in larger organizations all types of functions—news gathering, editing, and management—come to be concentrated in proportionately fewer hands. Although organization size does not have much of an impact on the proportion of journalists who do reporting, it is clear that reporters in larger news operations are likely to cover more circumscribed areas of news. It is executive functions, however, which become most centralized in large organizations. Of the three strongest values in the table, two are administrative tasks—recruiting or terminating employees and managing money—while the third, editorial writing, is, as has been seen, a role performed by newsmen who are fairly well integrated into the administrative hierarchy. The main effect of increasing organization size, in other words, is to reduce the number of professional personnel who participate in decisions which bear on the overall functioning of the organization—decisions such as who will work for the enterprise, what editorial stands the organization will take, or how budgets will be structured and allocated.

The effects of organizational growth on specialization of function may also be observed in the degree to which key functions are differentiated in news organizations of differing size. Earlier in the chapter, for example, it was noted that the amount of reporting a journalist does is negatively associated (r = -.286) with the amount of editing or news processing he does—which is to say that in general these functions tend to be performed by different people. The extent to which these activities are differentiated, however, varies markedly with organization size: in news organizations which employ fewer than twenty-five newsmen, the correlation is just -.063, but it increases to -.402 in media with between twenty-five and 100 employees, and is -.463 in organizations which employ more than 100 newsmen. Since similar patterns were found for other pairs of job tasks, it is clear that individual responsibilities become more specialized in larger news organizations.

From these data, there would appear to be two major consequences of organizational growth in journalistic practice: first, the control of editorial operations becomes more hierarchical, and proportionately fewer newsmen participate in key decisions; and second, newsmen become more specialized in the work they perform, and as a result become further and further removed from the final products of their labor. Just as in other spheres of the industrial order, growth in news operations is accompanied by increasing bureaucratization and by increasing specialization. Drawing from the literature on professionals in bureaucracies (for example, Hall, 1968), these conditions in turn should make it more difficult for a journalist to maintain professional autonomy over his work.

Formal control over a journalist's work may occur at several points: at the assignment stage when decisions are made whether or not to cover a story; at the news-writing stage when different elements of information have to be selected and different aspects highlighted; and in the editing stage, when material is processed before being communicated to the public. Autonomy for a journalist thus involves having control over assignments, freedom in deciding how a story should be handled, and freedom from editorial interference from final gatekeepers.

Indicators of the autonomy newsmen feel they have are presented in Table 5.5 for the 78.8 percent of the sample who do reporting on a regular or occasional basis. The measures reported here are as follows: (a) the percentage who indicated they had "almost complete freedom" in deciding which aspects of a news story should be emphasized; (b) the number who said they had "almost complete freedom" in selecting the stories they worked on; (c) the percentage who claimed that they themselves and no one else controlled the assignments they got; and (d) the number who claimed that their material was not subjected to editing by other persons in their organization.[3] Examination of the values in the right-hand column of the table reveals that levels of perceived autonomy vary considerably on these measures. While three-quarters said they had a free hand at the news-writing stage and six in ten in choosing what they worked on, slightly fewer than half said they actually had control over their work assignments, and fewer than a third claimed they were able to pass their work through the organization without editorial scrutiny. From these data, levels of perceived autonomy among newsmen would appear to be fairly high, although a majority do recognize that control over the initiation and final acceptance of their work lies with others.

Table 5.5 also compares these measures among those working in organizations of different sizes, and reveals that on all four criteria newsmen in larger organizations are more likely to perceive their autonomy as circumscribed. The effect of organization size on autonomy would appear to be strongest at the news-processing stage (where the percentages shift downward by 30.2 percent), second strongest at the assignment stage, and least pronounced at the news-writing stage—where the effects are not linear, and the widest discrepancy (19.3 percent) is found between small- and middle-sized news organizations. In addition to these measures, there was evidence that other journalistic functions are also more tightly controlled in larger news organizations. For example, organization size was found to be negatively correlated with the amount of influence editorial writers said they had both in deciding topics for editorials ($r = -.305$), and in deciding what should be said in an editorial ($r = -.230$). In overview, there seems little doubt that newsmen in larger news operations perceive more constraints over their professional autonomy.

For purposes of further analysis, the four measures presented in Table 5.5 were combined to form an index of perceived autonomy, the index being constructed simply by summing the number of areas out of four on which journalists claimed freedom of action. Scores on this measure were fairly evenly distributed: 19.1 percent indicated they had autonomy on all four measures, 25.1 percent on three out of the four, 21.6 percent on two, 19.8 percent on just one, and 14.3 percent on none at all. Scores on this index ranged from zero to four, with a mean of 2.15 and a standard deviation of 1.33. While the main

use to be made of this index will be in the analysis of journalists' job satisfaction in a later chapter, it should be noted here
that in addition to being correlated negatively with organization
size (r = −.349), scores on this index were, as one might expect,
positively correlated with the scope of one's managerial responsibilities[4] (r = .488), and with the number of years one had
been employed in the news media (r = .223). Neither of these
other correlates erases the relationship of organization size to
autonomy, however, since the partial correlation between size
and autonomy, controlling for experience in the field, was
−.394, while the partial relationship controlling for scope of
managerial duties was −.265. Professional autonomy can therefore be interpreted as a perquisite which journalists acquire with
longevity in the field and with increasing status on the organizational ladder, but it is also something which one is much more
likely to realize in a small news organization. To sum up, organization size has an influence both on the nature of the tasks a
newsman performs, and on the amount of professional freedom
he has in carrying out his work.

Newsmen's Ratings of News Organizations

Before identifying the news organizations regarded most
highly by practicing newsmen, it should be noted that on the
whole journalists feel that the American news media do a
creditable job of informing the public. As indicated by Table
5.6, more than half of the sample rated the performance of
their own organization and of the news media in general as
either "outstanding" or "very good," while fewer than 15 percent assigned evaluations of "fair" or "poor" in answer to either
question. The response distributions on these two questions also
appear to be virtually identical, and it might be added that a
cross tabulation of the answers confirmed that a majority, 51.1
percent, answered the two questions in the same way. Most
journalists thus feel that the organizations they work for do no
better or worse a job than most other news organizations. On
the whole there are many more advocates than critics of media
performance among contemporary practitioners in the field,
and newsmen appear satisfied that their industry does its job
well.

At the same time, however, journalists are able to identify
the organizations which they regard as exemplars of journalistic
excellence. Their opinions in this regard were obtained from the

two following questions: (A) Which three newspapers or other news organizations do you consider to be the fairest and most reliable?; and (b) Which three newspapers or other news organizations do you rely on most often in your own work? Although many organizations were nominated in answer to one or the other of these questions, only a small number were cited with any meaningful frequency. For example, on the question of fairness and reliability a total of 624 different organizations received at least one vote, but only 101 received more than one vote, and only thirty-four were named by ten or more different persons.

Table 5.7 lists the twenty-five news organizations which received the most mentions in answer to these two questions, and also shows the top-ranked organizations on the combined measures, which we will argue indicates the overall prominence of a news organization in the eyes of members of the professional community. The news media identified in these lists, it should be re-emphasized, are the ones cited most often for their fairness and reliability and for their day-to-day utility by a representative national sample of 1,313 newsmen and by an additional thirty-six Washington correspondents selected at random from the 1971 Congressional Directory. The figures in this table are unweighted, and thus represent the actual numbers of journalists who named each organization.

Although interpretation of these results should be straightforward, the following points should be noted: First, it is clear that only a very small number of news organizations have what might be regarded as nationwide visibility among journalists. Although the New York *Times* topped both lists, and the *Associated Press* was second on both criteria, only six other news organizations—the Washington *Post*, the *Wall Street Journal, UPI*, the *Christian Science Monitor*, the Los Angeles *Times*, and *Newsweek*—received more than 100 votes on either dimension. No single organization was therefore identified by an actual majority of the respondents.

Second, it is evident that organizations named in answer to one question also tended to be named in answer to the other: nine of the top ten organizations on the first list reappear in the top ten on the second, as do nineteen of the top twenty-five.

Third, although organizations cited for their fairness and reliability were also cited for their usefulness to journalists in their own work, there are some notable exceptions. The

Christian Science Monitor and the St. Louis *Post-Dispatch* were named much more often as fair and reliable news organizations than as newspapers journalists relied on in their own work, while the reverse was true of the San Francisco *Chronicle* and the New York *Daily News*. Both major press services also received more citations as useful than as fair and reliable news organizations, although it should be acknowledged that both the *AP* and *UPI* were regarded highly on the reputational criterion as well. Most daily newspapers, on the other hand, received more votes for their professional standards than for their instrumental utility.

Fourth, all branches of the media except weekly papers and individual radio or television stations are represented in the top-rated media. Of the top twenty-six in overall prominence, eighteen are dailies, three are broadcast networks, three are national news magazines, and two are wire services.

Fifth, and last, it is noteworthy that nine of the ten most prominent organizations in the country, and seventeen of the top twenty-six, are based either in the Northeast or in the Washington-Baltimore area. The hegemony of the eastern seaboard in American journalism is in no way illustrated better than by the fact that a majority of the news organizations newsmen regard as leaders in the field are located within that geographic area.

After these votes were tallied, the number of mentions each news organization received was transferred to the records of individual newsmen employed in those organizations. In this way, then, it is possible to classify individual journalists in terms of the prestige of the news organizations for which they work. When these operations were carried out, the distribution of the sample as a whole on the three measures turned out as shown in Table 5.8. In terms of overall prominence, 7.9 percent of newsmen work for organizations cited more than 100 times by other journalists, about one in seven (13.8 percent) work for media named more than twenty-five times, and just under a third are employed by organizations which were not named by anyone. These distributions thus reflect the pyramidal shape of the prestige hierarchy within the industry.

Characteristics of Journalists in Prominent News Organizations

For purposes of this analysis, news organizations are arbitrarily defined as nationally prominent if they were cited by more than ten journalists in the sample either as one of the fairest and most reliable news organizations in the country, or as one of the three organizations they relied on most often in their own work. On the basis of this criterion, 23.3 percent of the sample are regarded as working for prominent news organizations. In the discussion which follows, newsmen are also subdivided into supervisory and nonsupervisory categories ("executives" and "staffers") according to whether they reported managerial or supervisory responsibilities of any type. As noted earlier, 41.9 percent of the sample is categorized as supervisory by this criterion. When these dimensions are combined, comparisons can be made in terms both of organizational and individual statuses, and this subdivision results in the following distribution of the sample: 7.6 percent have supervisory status in an organization rated as prominent by other journalists, 15.7 percent occupy nonsupervisory positions in prominent organizations, 34.3 percent are supervisory personnel in nonprominent media, and the largest proportion, 42.4 percent, have "rank-and-file" status in nonprominent organizations.

Table 5.9 presents summary measures for a variety of characteristics of executives and staffers employed within these two categories of media. First, from Part A of the table, it is evident that there are marked differences in the social origins of those in the "elite" and "nonelite" strata of the news industry. Journalists in prominent organizations are much more likely than others to have had fathers who were college graduates, and who were employed in professional or managerial occupations. Moreover, it should be noted that these differences are found among those at both status levels within the organizations, which means that the differences stem from recruitment rather than promotion practices.

In terms of religious background, the data reveal that there are somewhat fewer Protestants and Catholics—and considerably more Jews—in the more prominent media. Here again the differences are a function only of the prominence of an organization and do not reflect an individual's position inside it. Although Jews are overrepresented in the prominent media, the representation of other minority groups is quite different. Perhaps the most noteworthy figures here are those which indicate that the sample failed to locate a single black American in a supervisory position within a prominent organization, and that only 3.6 percent of staffers in these organizations are black.

Some 6.3 percent of executives in less prominent media were black Americans, although here it has to be noted that most of these would be functionaries in the black press. As concluded much earlier, there are very few black Americans in the main-line news media, and the results here suggest further that there are virtually none among the journalistic elite. With regard to sex, the results indicate that women are underrepresented on both status dimensions—and in fact more so in terms of their intra-organizational status than in their presence within prominent media. The participation of women ranges from 9.0 to 26.9 percent across the four groupings, a difference of 17.9 percent. Of this difference, about 5 percent can be accounted for by their relative absence in prominent media, but about 13 percent stems from their underrepresentation at supervisory levels. On the basis of these findings, one could conclude that women do have a more difficult time than men in gaining employment in more prestigious media, but they face even greater difficulties when it comes to being promoted to managerial positions in any news organization.

In overview, one American minority group, Jews, would appear to be overrepresented in prominent media, while at least two others, blacks and women, are underrepresented.

In terms of regional origins, the results indicate that many more staffers than executives hail from western states, but this outcome is to be expected since staffers are also younger than executives. The differences, in other words, may only reflect the fact that because of relatively greater population expansion the West has been able to produce more newsmen in recent years than it did previously. There are no marked differences between prominent and nonprominent news organizations in terms of the regional origins of their employees, although slightly more in the prominent stratum were born in the South, and slightly fewer come from the West. More pronounced differences are evident, however, in the regions in which journalists were trained. Supervisory personnel in elite news organizations are considerably more likely than others to have graduated from schools in the Northeast, slightly more were educated in the South, and considerably fewer graduated from colleges and universities in the West.

Part B of Table 5.9 clearly indicates that educational levels are markedly higher in the nationally prominent media, and once again, the differences here are related more to organizational prominence than to job level. Over three-quarters of both executives and staffers in the more prestigious media are college graduates, compared with just about half in the remainder of the industry. One interesting result here is that in terms of degree holders, staffers in prominent media have more schooling than executives, while in nonprominent organizations the reverse is true. This pattern suggests *either* that educational levels are rising faster in prominent organizations than they are in the rest of the industry, *or* that newsmen with college training advance more quickly to administrative positions when they take employment outside of the elite sector of the field.

In addition to differences in amount of schooling, Table 5.9 also reveals differences in the "quality" of schools attended by persons in the two media categories. About twice as many executives—and three times as many staffers—in prominent than in nonprominent organizations graduated from colleges and universities rated by Cass and Birnbaum (1970) as among the most selective in the country. Since slightly more supervisory than nonsupervisory personnel also went to elite schools, it is evident that recruitment and promotion advantages accrue from having been trained in more selective schools. More generally, however, there is little doubt that the news organizations regarded most highly by members of the working press do in fact recruit manpower with more substantial educational qualifications.

This overview concludes by considering a new topic, which has been a central theme in the recent conflict between the news media and the government, namely: the party affiliations and political dispositions of American newsmen. When asked to identify their party affiliation near the end of the interview, 35.5 percent of newsmen said they were Democrats, 25.7 percent identified themselves as Republicans, 32.5 percent said they were independents, and 5.8 percent chose other answers. American journalists are therefore predominantly Democrats or independents, although compared with the adult population as a whole, there are fewer newsmen who identify as Democrats, slightly more who say they are independents, and just about the same number who are Republicans.[5] These distributions vary substantially between personnel in the two media strata, however: there are many more Democrats and independents in the elite press than there are in the rest of the industry, and many more Republicans in news organizations not noted among journalists for their prominence. Moreover, in the prominent stratum, shown in Part C of Table 5.9, virtually all executives identify either as Democrats or independents, and only 8.5 percent call themselves Republicans. In nonprominent organizations, on the other hand, the party affiliations of executives are almost evenly balanced. Staffers in nonprominent media are somewhat less likely to be Republicans than their bosses are, but at the same time their affiliations are more similar to those of the persons they report to than they are to either group in the more prominent stratum. All in all, there are marked differences in the political affiliations of journalists who work in organizations of differing prominence.

Similar discrepancies are found on another indicator of political dispositions. The final question in the interview asked newsmen to describe their "general political leanings" along the liberal-conservative dimension, the question being phrased in terms of their left-right leanings.[6] In answer to this question, 7.5 percent described their leanings as pretty far to the left, 30.5 percent said they were a little to the left, 38.5 percent saw themselves as middle of the road, 15.6 percent said they were a little to the right, and 3.4 percent said they were pretty far to the right. Another 3.7 percent either could not place themselves on this continuum, or did not care to do so. Journalists as an aggregate therefore are somewhat to the liberal side of center, though there are few who would qualify as outright radicals on the basis of this measure.

These distributions vary considerably between those in the two media sectors, journalists in the elite stratum being much further to the left than those in the rest of the industry. In the prominent media, 62.9 percent of executives and 52.8 percent of staffers see themselves to the left of center, while in the remainder of the industry, just 28.5 percent of executives and 40.5 percent of nonsupervisory personnel do so. Perhaps the most striking feature about these results is that in the prominent media the "managers" are further to the left than the "workers," while the opposite and more usual situation prevails in the rest of the industry. Executives in nonprominent news media are the most conservative of the four groups, though it should be pointed out that even within that group liberals outnumber conservatives 28.5 to 24.8 percent. From these data, it is obvious that newsmen who work for the top news organizations in the country have quite different political and social orientations than their colleagues situated elsewhere.

Summary

From an analysis of the work tasks performed by journalists of different ages, it is concluded that there are two major career tracks in news-media journalism. For some, careers in the media lead to supervisory and managerial roles, organizational functions necessitated by the fact that news media must sift through hundreds or even thousands of items of information each day in order to define the limited number which will be communicated as the news of the day. Newsmen who are successful on this career path, labeled the "administrative" path, acquire considerable power and status within their organizations, but have little visibility as individual journalists. These persons occupy key positions in the news system, however, since they control both the information which will be gathered and the information which will survive to be printed or broadcast. Some also become editorial writers, and as such, anonymous spokesmen for the policies advocated by their organization. The "administrative" career track thus cements a close integration of the individual journalist and the organization.

By contrast, the second career route loosens rather than strengthens integration into an organizational structure. Successful mobility along what is termed the "professional" path leads to more individualized and personalized journalistic roles, in which one becomes an "expert" or a "personality" in one's own right. In the print sector the syndicated columnist is perhaps the epitome of success on this dimension, while in broadcasting the network anchorman or commentator represents comparable levels of professional achievement. The results also suggest, however, that the two career tracks may be less differentiated in the broadcast sector than in the print, and that career mobility in broadcast journalism may be governed more by the size of the market in which one works than by the specific functions one performs.

Though large news organizations are more powerful and prestigious than small ones, and though, as shall be confirmed later, they also pay better, there are nonetheless costs for the journalist who works in them. Large news organizations exert more formal controls over the work a newsman does, and they also narrow the range of functions he performs, thus removing him to some extent from the final product of his work. There are therefore at least two major career dilemmas a journalist must face: in choosing between an "administrative" or a "professional" career; and in choosing between an organizational milieu which maximizes chances of influence and financial rewards or one which maximizes chances of professional autonomy.

A pyramidal status hierarchy pervades the news industry, and a very small number of predominantly eastern-based organizations dominate the field. Journalists in "elite" organizations differ in important ways from their counterparts in the rest of the industry: they start out from more advantaged positions economically, they obtain more and better schooling, and perhaps as a result of these influences, they end up thinking quite differently about political and social issues. Whether or not they are also better journalists is a question not answered in this study; how they act and think as professionals, however, is a topic covered in the next two chapters.

Notes

1. Source: *1971 Broadcasting Yearbook*, p. 11.

2. Bogue also reports the 1960 medians for the communication industry at 35.5 years for men and 31.9 years for women. This suggests that personnel in the news media are slightly older than those working in other sectors of the communications field.

3. The actual question wordings and response distributions for these measures were as follows: (A) How much freedom do you usually have in deciding which aspects of a story should be emphasized? Almost complete freedom, 75.9 percent; a great deal, 21.8 percent; not too much, 2.4 percent. (b) How much freedom do you usually have in selecting the stories you work on? Almost complete freedom, 60.1 percent; a great deal, 26.3 percent; some, 10.7 percent; none at all, 2.9 percent. (C) Who has responsibility for assigning the stories you work on? Respondent indicated no one else did, 46.2 percent; someone else identified, 53.8 percent. (D) How much editing do your stories get from others in your organization? A great deal, 7.6 percent; some, 60.1 percent; none at all, 32.3 percent.

4. Scope of managerial responsibility is measured with values from zero to three, as follows: 3 = supervisory or managerial responsibility at the level of the organization as a whole; 2 = departmental level responsibility; 1 = responsibility for a news desk or a news program; and 0 = no supervisory or managerial duties at all. For the sample as a whole, this measure had a mean of .834 and a standard deviation of 1.10.

5. Erskine (1971, pp. 491-493) reports the party affiliations of adults in three age groups from information obtained in a sample survey conducted by the Gallup organization during the summer of 1970. Although the population totals are not reported there, calculations from the figures presented indicate that as of August, 1970, approximately 45 percent of American adults twenty-one and over identified as Democrats, approximately 28 percent were Republicans, and approximately 27 percent called themselves independents.

6. The specific phrasing of the question was as follows: "And finally, how would you describe your general political leanings—would you say you are pretty far to the left, a little to the left, middle of the road, a little to the right, or pretty far to the right?"

6

The Journalist
as a Professional

Recent developments in the long-standing battle between the press, both electronic and print, and the government have raised once again questions about the security and stability of the professional role of American journalists. In addition to, or perhaps as a result of, these renewed political conflicts, the credibility of newsmen in the public mind is disturbingly low. The increased frequency of contempt citations of newsmen by grand juries for not revealing their sources of information, and increased concern about "shield" laws for newsmen call into question a fundamental claim of all professions—the right to control their work free from outside interference. There are those who argue that once journalistic lips become unsealed not only will journalists lose what remains of their professional status but also a press operating without fear or favor will be doomed.

This chapter will deal only indirectly with these issues since the broader course of social and political events will determine what will be the final outcome of these trends. The following pages will briefly outline the history of the process of professionalization in journalism and then present a discussion of the actions and values of American journalists which are relevant to their claim that they are, in fact, professionals.

Journalism as a Profession

It is not simply idle sociological speculation which prompts the inclusion of a chapter on the professional aspects of journalism since this concern is rooted solidly in the journalistic community itself. Journalism educators have addressed the problem by specifying the characteristics which journalism must display to be accepted as a profession, and Kimball (1965) explicitly asks if journalism is an "art, craft or profession." Others in the field, such as Bleyer (1918), Desmond (1949), Hohenberg (1968), and Stone (1970) simply assume professional status for their occupation. Fewer are the iconoclasts who call journalism a trade (Alsop and Alsop, 1958) or who, more neutrally, refer to the "job of the reporter" (Reston, 1945). Perhaps a fair summary of the nature of these concerns is presented by MacDougall (1963, p. 5): "The immediate question is not whether . . . journalism *should be* a profession but whether it *is* one to any appreciable extent" (italics in the original).

Unfortunately for journalism, MacDougall's question is not easily answered. First, in order to make an informed judgment of the extent to which journalism meets the criteria of a profession, a set of analytic characteristics sufficient to qualify an occupational group as a profession must be agreed upon. What is clear from even a cursory review of the literature on professions is that there is no generally accepted definition of a profession, since nearly every author on the subject offers a slightly different set of appropriate criteria. This problem can be dealt with more easily than the second area of difficulty, however, and the following paragraphs will address in more detail the extent to which journalism has met some of the criteria. But, second and more problematical, serious question has been raised about the very meaning of the word "profession." Becker (1962), for example, has argued that in addition to its analytic meaning, the term implies a positive moral evaluation. In terms of MacDougall's admonition, whenever we talk about whether or not journalism *is* a profession, we are also talking about whether it *should be*.

Perhaps the more fundamental problem, as Hughes (1970, p. 350) suggests, is to identify the circumstances in which people attempt to turn an occupation into a profession, or the stages which characterize such transformations. After examining several historical professions, Wilensky (1964, pp. 486-490) concluded that an occupational group moves through the following sequence of stages in becoming established and accepted as a profession: (1) it begins to pursue an area of work as a full-time occupation; (2) it establishes a training school; (3) a professional association is formed; (4) representatives of the occupation agitate politically to win legal support for the right to control their work; and (5) the professional association promulgates a formal code of ethics.

Journalism, in one way or another, has passed through all five of these stages, some more successfully than others. Although newspaper work in this country did not begin as an independent full-time occupation, by the 1830s the population increases in metropolitan centers such as New York, Philadelphia, and Baltimore, and the increased literacy rate among these populations, provided the economic base necessary to support news-gathering activities on a full-time basis. When in 1833, Benjamin Day hired George Wisner, a veteran of London police courts, to cover police and crime news in New York City, journalism had emerged as a full-time occupation.

Formal professional education for journalists began soon after the Civil War. By 1878, the University of Missouri offered two courses in journalism, and in 1893, the Wharton School of Business at the University of Pennsylvania began offering five courses which, according to Sutton (1945, pp. 10-11), compared favorably with later instructional offerings. The first recognized school of journalism was opened at the University of Missouri in 1908, and it was not long before many other colleges and universities offered an expanded curriculum. By 1940 there were some 542 separate schools where some degree of training in journalism was available.

For an occupation to be considered a profession, however, recruits to the field must also be exposed to a body of abstract knowledge which is the particular province of the profession. It is here that formal recognition of journalism as a profession is often challenged, since as a recent critic of journalism education has remarked, "there is no system of abstract propositions to which new recruits are exposed and without which they cannot practice" (Boyd-Barrett, 1970, p. 181). Whether or not his assessment is entirely accurate, the issue of what fledgling journalists should be taught is almost as old as journalism itself, and as noted in Chapter 3, there is little consensus on this question even today. Historically, there have been two main schools of thought about the nature of education for journalism: "practical" versus "background" instruction. In the contemporary period the "background" view would appear to be the more prevalent, and a study of syllabi of schools of journalism in 1958 (UNESCO, 1958, p. 32) found that three-quarters of all courses consisted of general background instruction. While it does seem to be the case that newsmen do not require specialized training to practice journalism, there is now and has been for some time a very great awareness of the importance of some kind of training for journalists. Given the fact that only about three journalists in five have even finished college, however, the main problem confronting the field today may be in requiring practitioners to complete *any* college or university program rather than in insisting upon their exposure to a specialized curriculum.

Journalism has a long history of professional organizations. A national professional association was begun in 1885 when the International Editorial Association was founded, and in 1887, the American Newspaper Publishers Association (ANPA) was established. By late in the nineteenth century at least some segments of the occupation were represented by national organizations.

In addition to these somewhat specialized national organizations, there were several state press associations in existence before 1900. Although these state associations were not unconcerned with professional issues and were in some cases influential in starting professional schools of journalism, it was not until 1912 that a national association, the American Association of Teachers of Journalism (AATJ), was formed to deal explicitly with professional education in journalism. More recently, the Association for Education in Journalism (AEJ) has assumed primary responsibility for evaluating and accrediting professional education in the field.

Other professional groups were also concerned with the quality of professional practice in American journalism. In 1922, Casper S. Yost of the St. Louis *Globe-Democrat* led in the formation of the American Society of Newspaper Editors (ASNE), a reaction to the increasingly heavy business focus of ANPA. Membership in ASNE was not open to all professionals in the field, however, and was limited in the main to editors-in-chief, managing editors, and editorial page editors of dailies in cities with populations greater than 50,000. In 1923, the ASNE began publishing *Problems of Journalism*, an annual volume devoted to issues important to the journalism profession.

In addition to these professional associations, honorary societies of journalists reward professional achievement and sponsor improvement in the field. *Sigma Delta Chi*, founded at DePauw University in 1910, has both undergraduate and professional chapters, but is much more a professional than a college organization, and is also known today as *The Society of Professional Journalists.* A second honorary society, *Kappa Tau*

Alpha, was established at the University of Missouri also in 1910, and sponsors research in journalism. Finally, *Theta Sigma Phi*, known today as *Women in Communication*, was founded at the University of Washington in 1909 as an honorary sorority for women in journalism.

Despite the apparent wealth of journalism organizations, the fact remains that because of First Amendment protections there is no single qualifying association in journalism, and the functional diversity which characterizes the news media in general is thus paralleled in professional associations. At the most inclusive level, the honorary societies offer membership to most practicing newsmen, and identification as a journalist is usually a sufficient criterion for membership in these associations. The specialized professional organizations tend to be more restrictive in their admissions policies, however, and in addition they tend to exert more influence on the professional conduct of their members. The picture of journalism that emerges from this pattern is one of a collection of diverse segments only loosely united under the label of journalist. Each segment attempts to exercise some control over its members, but there is little if any attempt to influence the entire occupational group.

In rating journalism with respect to Wilensky's fourth stage of emergent professions, political agitation, a long-standing debate is encountered involving the relationship of a free press to its government. The history of this relationship has been a particularly stormy one, marked by periodic attempts by the government to limit what journalists consider the constitutional protection afforded the press. There is as yet no final constitutional or legal settlement of this dispute. In general, the journalistic community seems reluctant to depend on legal protections to its rights, preferring instead to rely on constitutional guarantees which are less subject to the political whim of particular administrations.

Finally, journalism associations have articulated formal codes of ethics. In 1923, ASNE offered the *Canons of Journalism*; the AEJ and AASDJ (American Association of Schools and Departments of Journalism) have presented codes for the accreditation of programs in journalism education; the Radio and Television News Directors Association (RTNDA) developed a code of ethics for broadcast journalists in 1966; and *Sigma Delta Chi* adopted a new code in 1973. All of these would suggest that journalism has passed through the final stage on its way to becoming accepted as a profession. It should also be noted, however, that the codes adopted by associations of professional newsmen in the print sector tend to be quite different from those of their counterparts in broadcasting. Reflecting protections afforded by the First Amendment, print-media codes tend to be lofty expressions of journalistic ideals, while broadcasters' codes reflect their fear of government regulation, or of regulation to a greater degree than is now experienced. Finally, it should also be noted that the codes adopted by broadcast newsmen tend to be more stringent than those set by the *National Association of Broadcasters* (NAB) for the broadcasting industry at large. Skornia, for example, has charged (1968, p. 201) that the terminology of the NAB code for radio and television "clearly illustrates unenforceably weak, ambiguous, evasive and permissive language."

Given the above discussion, there seems little doubt that at least in the abstract formal sense, journalism can be considered a profession: it is clearly a full-time occupation; there are established training facilities for its practitioners; several professional associations for working news people are in existence; there is legal sanction, of a kind, for its work territory; and formal codes of ethics have been developed. The extent to which practicing newsmen *identify* as professionals is quite another question, however, and there is some disagreement among observers on this point. Thus, while Lyons (1965) feels that journalists do in fact act as if they were professionals, Cater (1959) and Kimball (1965) suggest that newsmen often are ambivalent to accept this identification. Evidence from the study will be used in trying to assess the extent to which newsmen act and think as professionals.

Integration into the Professional Community

Participation in the professional culture of an occupational group may be measured in several ways. As Greenwood (1957, p. 12) and others have noted, however, all professions operate through networks of formal and informal groups, and one clear indicator of a journalist's identification with his profession is the extent of his formal and informal social ties with other journalists. In this section newsmen's participation in voluntary organizations and associations of journalists and their informal social contacts with other members of the professional community are examined.

(1). *Formal organizations and associations.* In addition to information on membership in unions and in general community organizations, members of the sample were asked whether they belonged to any organizations or associations primarily for people in journalism or the communications field. Names were recorded for up to five specific organizations named, and the responses to this question were tabulated for the sample as a whole in Table 6.1. From these data, it is evident that fewer than half of all journalists (45.3 percent) belong to professional organizations of any kind, and that there is no single organization which embraces more than a small minority of the practitioners in the field.

Several categories of organizations are differentiated in this table. First are the clearly professional associations, those organizations whose primary concerns are with the working journalist as a professional. Examples of organizations of this type are the American Society of Newspaper Editors or the Radio and Television News Directors Association, and in total some 33.4 percent of the sample identified themselves as members of one or more organizations of this type. It is also evident that only about a third of these memberships are in organizations which are national in scope: in fact, only about one newsman in eight (12.8 percent) belongs to any type of national professional organization. Even more striking, however, is the fact that there are no national professional organizations in journalism which attract as members even as many as 2 percent of the total manpower in the field. A similar diversity characterizes the local organizations, which were so numerous and the percentages of members so small that they could not be listed separately.

The second group of organizations, though hard to characterize, consists of the honorary societies in journalism. That these organizations are important in the community of journalists is reflected by the fact that as many as 15.7 percent belong to such societies. Moreover, one of these societies, *Sigma Delta Chi*, has the largest single membership of any voluntary organization in the field, with as many as 15.1 percent of all journalists reporting membership in one or another of its chapters. Although these organizations often represent the voice of journalism in response to external threats to the field, they differ from purely professional associations in that an element of prestige is attached to membership in them, and they are not typically concerned with the internal regulation of their members.

The third category identified in Table 6.1 is made up of social organizations and clubs whose main purpose is to provide facilities for journalists to gather socially. The many local press clubs mentioned by the respondents were grouped together in this category, but as is evident from the figures, fewer than one in ten (8.2 percent) reported membership in associations or press clubs of this type. This is not to say that only this many newsmen make use of press clubs, of course, since many are open to all members of the working press and do not require formal membership in order to be utilized. Nonetheless, only a small minority of newsmen actually belong to organizations of this type.

What, then, can be concluded from these data regarding the professional participation of journalists? Compared with other professions, it would appear that the involvement of journalists in professional associations is fairly weak. From other data, for example, it can be estimated that well over half of all physicians in the United States belong to the American Medical Association (AMA), and that slightly over a third of all lawyers are members of the American Bar Association (ABA).[1] Although information on the other organizational affiliations of these groups is not available, there is little reason to doubt that their overall involvement in professional associations is considerably greater than it is among journalists.[2] Quite clearly there is no umbrella organization within journalism even remotely comparable to the reach of the AMA or the ABA. The closest approximation to a blanket organization within journalism is *Sigma Delta Chi*, which until recently at least has been primarily an honorary society. The data in Table 6.1 thus describe an occupational field with a multitude of special interest organizations, most of which are local or regional in scope and relatively small in total membership.

At this point, it is necessary to add that voluntary associations are not the only work-related organizations to which journalists belong, and that a substantial number of newsmen also reported membership in a union or guild. In total, 28.8 percent of the sample indicated such an affiliation, the primary organizations being the American Newspaper Guild, to which 21.5 percent belonged, and the American Federation of Television and Radio Artists (AFTRA), in which 4.9 percent reported membership. A variety of other trade unions were also mentioned, principally by broadcast newsmen, but there were none in which membership was claimed by more than one-half of 1 percent of the sample.

In overview, a majority of newsmen, 62.2 percent, do belong to some type of work-related organization, whether a union or guild, a professional association, a press club, or a Greek-letter honorary society. This diversity makes it extremely difficult to characterize journalism in occupational terms, and there would appear to be little of a unifying nature to an occupation in which sizable numbers belong to trade unions, many are members of professional associations, some belong to both types of organizations (a total of 11.7 percent is estimated), while the largest number of all are not affiliated with any type of work-related organization. Kimball's (1965) quandary over the terms "art," "craft," or "profession" for journalism can be readily understood in view of the heterogeneity represented in this pattern of organizational affiliations.

In addition, there would appear to be very little difference in the organizational participation of print and broadcast newsmen. Restricting the focus to membership in professional associations, Table 6.2 reveals that although newsmen in television are somewhat more likely than their colleagues in dailies to belong to at least one professional association (36.1 percent compared with 31.7 percent), the overall rates of participation in the two broad sectors are virtually identical, 33.4 percent for print newsmen and 33.6 percent among broadcasters. Despite these similarities, sizable differences were found among different categories of media *within* the two broad sectors. For example, within the print sector, the mean number of memberships among journalists in weeklies was considerably higher (.590), while for those in both news magazines and wire services, they were lower (.294 and .283, respectively). Within the broadcast sector, the mean for radio newsmen was lower than for those in television, .422 compared with .503. These variations suggest that membership in professional associations may be related to characteristics of the news organization a journalist works for, and at least in the print sector it would appear that levels of participation are higher among those who work in smaller news organizations, news media located in smaller communities, or those less likely to be noted for their prominence. The precise relationship of these factors to levels of participation will be explored later.

(2). *Informal social contacts.* Another indicator of identification with journalism is the amount of nonwork activity which newsmen share with other people in their field. As a measure of informal social contacts among newsmen, members of the sample were asked to estimate the percentage of people they saw socially who were connected in some way with journalism or the communications field. Responses to this question are interpreted as a measure of informal involvement with professional colleagues. Table 6.3 reports the levels at which newsmen in the two sectors of the media are integrated into informal networks of colleague relationships. From these data it is evident, first of all, that about a third of all journalists concentrate the majority of their informal social relationships within the professional community. Although comparable statistics for other occupational groups are not available, it can be concluded that the often-noted tendency of journalists to associate among themselves is true at least for a substantial minority. Only about one journalist in ten indicated being completely isolated from informal social contacts with colleagues.

Informal contacts are also seen to be more prevalent among broadcast than print journalists: the rates are an average of 5.8 percent higher among television than daily newspaper personnel, and they are 7.8 percent higher in the broadcast sector compared with the print sector as a whole. Once again, substantial variations were found within the print sector, and since these are not reported in the table, they should be noted in passing: just 16.6 percent of the contacts of newsmen in weeklies were with other journalists, while the rates for magazine journalists and those in the wire services were substantially higher, 37.7 and 44.5 percent, respectively. These differences again suggest the importance of an organization's size, prominence, and environment in explaining the social affiliations of journalists. For the present, however, it can be concluded that broadcast journalists, though no more likely than print journalists to belong to professional associations, do have more informal contacts with their professional colleagues.

Factors Influencing Patterns of Participation

Thus far two measures of professional identification have been presented and the similarities and differences between print and broadcast newsmen on these measures have been discussed. In addition to the sector of the media in which an individual works, several other factors contribute to the extent to which one identifies with his professional field. These factors include such things as the individual's age, both chronological and professional, his educational background, characteristics of the organization which employs him, and his position within that organization. At this point the relative influence of these factors on patterns of formal and informal participation in the professional community will be explored through multiple regression analysis. No assumptions are made here about the causal ordering among these factors other than that they are all assumed to be temporally prior to, and to have an influence on, professional identification.

Table 6.4 reports the results of this analysis,[3] and indicates that quite different factors affect the two types of professional participation. Looking first at formal participation, the results indicate that two factors, the number of years a journalist has been employed in the news media and the scope of his administrative responsibility within his organization, have by far the strongest influence on the number of professional associations to which he belongs. None of the other seven factors appears to make much difference in this regard.[4] For informal social contacts, on the other hand, five factors yield regression coefficients of .100 or larger, and in order of magnitude these are as follows: (1) chronological age—informal professional contacts are more characteristic of younger than older journalists; (2) media sector—newsmen in the broadcast media interact socially more often than print journalists do; (3) organization size— journalists in larger news organizations are more likely than those in smaller ones to associate among themselves; (4) organization prominence—rates of contact are higher among those who work for nationally prominent news organizations; and (5) city size—informal contacts are more prevalent in large than in small urban places.

On the basis of these results it is concluded that formal and informal professional participation serve quite different functions within American journalism. Membership in professional organizations is a characteristic of those who are established in the field—though not necessarily of those who have gained prominence within it. Formal participation is best predicted by knowing a person's professional age and his position within the hierarchy of a news organization, but little is gained from having information about the type of news organization for which he works.

Levels of informal professional contact, on the other hand, can be interpreted, first, as a characteristic of journalists who are moving up in the field; second, as a characteristic of broadcast journalism; and third, as a phenomenon related to the demographic environment within which newsmen work. Levels of informal contact are best predicted by knowing that a journalist is young, that he works in radio or television, and that he is employed in a large and prominent news organization located in a large city.

It is significant that organizational prominence affects the two types of professional integration in different ways. After the effects of city size and organization size have been controlled, it turns out that organization prominence has a slightly negative effect on formal participation (beta = -.023) but a moderate and positive effect on informal participation (beta = .101). This would suggest that journalists who work for nationally prestigious news media are integrated more within informal colleague networks than they are within the formal organizational structure of the profession, a fact which may explain in part why the political and social predispositions of those in the "elite" stratum differ so markedly from those of journalists in the rest of the industry.

In overview, these results are interpreted as indicating two distinctive modes of professional integration serving quite distinctive functions. Professional associations serve primarily to reinforce the professional identification of experienced newsmen who have advanced successfully along the "administrative" mobility track. An informal network of colleague relationships, on the other hand, provides a mechanism for integrating younger journalists into the profession, and quite independent of this also functions as a milieu for professional contact among broadcast journalists, journalists in large urban areas and large news organizations, and those working within what their colleagues regard as the elite stratum of the news industry.

Journalists' Values Regarding Work

Professional identification is also characterized by distinctive attitudes and values regarding work, and this chapter concludes by discussing briefly the prevalence of such attitudes among American journalists.

As a result of extended training, the professional comes to feel that his special abilities entitle him to carry out his work free from interference or pressure from persons either outside or inside the profession. Professional autonomy and freedom from supervision are considered to be of great importance to the professional, and the solo lawyer and the physician in private practice are prime examples of professionals who achieve a high degree of autonomy and self-regulation in their work. As observed in the previous chapter, some journalists are also able to work without these kinds of constraints, although many, and particularly those in large organizations, are subject to a range of controls in this regard. To the extent that journalists are oriented as professionals, however, they are expected to regard these matters as especially important.

Another attitude which traditionally has been defined as part of the professional work ethic is a commitment to public service, a value which for many is interpreted as providing services to clients. Given the nature of mass communication it can be argued that journalists do not have clients, since the ultimate recipients of the products of their skills are audiences rather than individuals. The transmission and interpretation of information is clearly an activity which can be interpreted as a public service, however, and to the extent that journalists are motivated in these terms, they can be considered to be professionally oriented.

A final element in the professional work attitude is what might be termed a sense of "calling" to a field of endeavor, a commitment to one's work which Kornhauser (1962, pp. 1-2) identified as the "belief that the development and exercise of expertise is worthy of a lifetime and carries its own reward." Most professionals, in other words, view their work as more than a "job." As Freidson (1970, p. 70) put it, work for a professional becomes part of his "identity." This type of commitment, when present, should be manifested in an individual's reluctance to leave his profession for increased monetary reward.

To determine the aspects of work journalists valued most highly, members of the sample were read a list of job characteristics and asked to judge how important they thought each one was. The actual phrasing of this question was as follows: "I'd like to find out how important a number of things are to you in judging jobs in your field—not just your own job but any job.

For instance, how much difference does the pay make in how you rate a job in your field—is pay very important, fairly important, or not too important?" Several other aspects of jobs were covered in a similar fashion, including the following which are pertinent to the present discussion: "the amount of autonomy you have," "freedom from supervision," "the chance to help people," "job security," and "fringe benefits."

Table 6.5 summarizes the answers to these questions by showing the average ratings journalists assigned to different job aspects on a scale where two is the highest possible score, and zero the lowest. Comparisons can also be made here between newsmen in the print and broadcast sectors, as well as between those working in daily newspapers and television. Turning first to the results for the sample as a whole, it is clear that journalists regard those aspects of work which are part of the professional work ethic much more highly than they do financial rewards or other tangible benefits which accrue from one's employment. Public service ("the chance to help people") is rated first, and this can be interpreted as clear evidence of a prominent public service orientation among newsmen. Autonomy and freedom from supervision are rated second and third, respectively, and these results thus confirm that even though journalists may not be able to control their work, the ability to do so is not unimportant to them. All three of the top-rated characteristics, then, are aspects which are integral to a professional orientation to work, and those aspects which are not part of the professional work ethic are of lesser importance: job security is rated fourth, pay, fifth, and fringe benefits, sixth.

Table 6.5 also reveals that even though scores on specific questions do vary somewhat among those in different sectors of the industry, there are no reversals in the rank order of the six characteristics within any of the subgroups. Newsmen in dailies, in television, and in the print and broadcast sectors more generally assign the same relative importance to the six job aspects identified here. Moreover, the differences in scores which do appear between the groups do not follow any consistent pattern, and it is not possible therefore to conclude that newsmen in one or the other sector are the more "professionalized" in their thinking. Broadcast newsmen put more importance on how much a job pays than print journalists do, but they also rate public service higher, and this, as we have argued, is an important element in the professional work attitude.

Broadcast journalists also assign less importance to fringe benefits and freedom from supervision, while the ratings of the two groups on the importance of autonomy and of job security are identical.

From these patterns it is clear that journalists in both sectors of the news industry espouse professional work values. Newsmen clearly are concerned with the service aspects of their work, they place a great deal of importance on being able to work independently, and the fact that they de-emphasize monetary rewards and other tangible benefits can be interpreted as indicating a high level of commitment to the type of work they do. From this attitudinal profile, in other words, it is concluded that American journalists in the main approach their work from a frame of reference similar to that found among traditional professional groups.

Summary

Although there is no compelling need either sociologically or practically to categorize journalism in occupational terms, this chapter attempted to fit journalism to the model of a traditional profession. In so doing general structural characteristics of the field and relevant aspects of the behavior and attitudes of its practitioners have been discussed. The results of this analysis are uneven. In terms of formal structural criteria, journalism easily qualifies as a profession since the field has passed through all of the historical stages which mark the emergence of a profession. Moreover, in terms of their values regarding work, journalists seem to be oriented as professionals: they value public service, autonomy and freedom from supervision, and tend to de-emphasize the importance of economic and other tangible rewards. It is in their organizational behavior, however, that journalists are not like other professionals, since their rates of participation in professional associations are comparatively low. It is significant that there is no single professional association in journalism which is influential enough to speak for more than a small minority of the practitioners in the field. This fact makes it difficult to define journalism in occupational terms, and it is this characteristic perhaps more than any other that reinforces the heterogeneity, segmentation, and lack of unity found within the field as a whole.

Notes

1. The 1970 census revealed that there were 334,000 doctors of medicine and 355,242 lawyers in the United States. Source: U.S. Bureau of the Census, *Statistical Abstract of the United States*, Ninety-third edition. U.S. Government Printing Office, Washington, D.C., 1972, Table 95, p. 68, and Table 258, p. 158. (Hereafter cited as U.S. Bureau of the Census, 1972a.) There were 219,000 members of the AMA and 136,451 members of the ABA in 1972, according to M. Fisk, ed., *Encyclopedia of Associations*, Vol. I (Detroit, Mich.: Gale Research Co., 1972). From these figures, rates of membership in the AMA would be estimated at 65.6 percent, and in the ABA at 38.4 percent.

2. Both medicine and law offer their practitioners an array of specific occupational associations for specialized subgroups. A count of these associations yields an estimate of 245 associations for physicians and eighty for lawyers. Source: M. Fisk, *Encyclopedia of Associations*, pp. 330-345, 705-803.

3. The table reports the standardized regression coefficients for nine predictor variables on formal and informal participation, and also shows the zero-order relationships (Pearson correlations) of each independent variable with the two measures. Standardized regression coefficients permit us to assess the relative impact of each of the independent variables on participation while holding constant the influence of all other factors. The multiple correlation coefficients were .281 for formal memberships, and .360 for informal social contacts. Since these values are low, no claim can be made that patterns of participation have been *explained* by this analysis, and the emphasis in interpretation must therefore be phrased in terms of the relative influence of the various factors.

4. Interpreting beta values of .100 or higher as meaningful.

7
Definitions of Journalistic Responsibility

Many occupations and professions within American society today are experiencing internal dissent over the definition of responsible professional practice. Splits between "conservative" and "progressive" or "establishment" and "radical" wings are visible within science, education, sociology, city planning, law, medicine, and social work, to cite just a few fields. These cleavages, which reflect what Rein (1970) identified as a search for relevance to problems of contemporary society, have been interpreted by Flacks (1971, p. 116) as an outgrowth of the student movement of the sixties: "In a sense, the spirit of the student movement and the campus revolt is being carried into the medical complex, the law office, the government bureau, the newspaper office, the research center, the professional convention, and the faculty meeting." Within journalism, however, debate over responsible professional practice has had a relatively long-standing history. Although the focus of this debate has shifted from decade to decade in response to the changing social and political climate, the essence of the controversy can be identified in competing views of the functions of the news media in American society, in conflicting assessments of the public's need for and right to information, and in divergent images of the nature of news itself.

This chapter focuses on newsmen's conceptions of the functions of the news media in American life, and on their beliefs regarding the proper role of the journalist in gathering news. The first part of the chapter discusses several themes which have characterized debate on these matters in recent decades, and reports the views of contemporary newsmen on a number of issues central to this debate. Efforts are next made to differentiate value positions into more or less coherent sets of professional orientations, and the chapter then concludes by investigating the personal, social, and institutional factors related to these value-sets.

"Neutral" and "Participant" Journalism

At the turn of the century, criticism within American journalism was focused on the excesses of an unrestrained market-oriented journalism guided by what Siebert (1956) labeled a "libertarian" philosophy of the press. In response, the principal direction of American journalism during the first half of the twentieth century was toward establishing itself as a profession, and it was this era, as has been noted, which saw the proliferation of professional associations and journalism schools, the articulation of codes of professional ethics, and the maturation of the ideology of "objective" reporting. By the end of World War II, however, debate within the professional community had shifted, and critical attention came to be focused on the shortcomings of an obsessively objective and socially complacent style of journalism. Today debate within the field would appear to pit proponents of a professionalized, objective, restrained, and technically efficient journalism against those advocating a socially responsible journalism inspired by some of the same norms which had been the objects of earlier reform.

To borrow Cohen's (1963) terms, the current adversaries are perhaps most accurately identified as proponents of a "neutral" as opposed to a "participant" press. In the former perspective, the news media constitute an impartial transmission link dispensing information to the public: news is seen to emerge naturally from the events and occurrences of the real world, and it is sufficient for the journalist to be a spectator to the ongoing social process and to transmit faithfully accurate communications about it. Responsible journalism is therefore achieved by adherence to norms of objectivity, factual accuracy, and the verification of information. Indeed, as Tuchman (1972) has noted, objectivity and factual accuracy may become ritualized as justifications for the truth-value of the information the reporter transmits. The newsman's relationship to information is thus one of detachment and neutrality, and his relationship to news sources is straightforward—sources merely provide the reporter with news to be reported. In this image, the primary journalistic sins are sensationalism—overstatements of the natural reality of events; and bias—a violation of the observer's neutrality vis-à-vis information.

In the image of a "participant" press, on the other hand, the news media are accorded a more challenging role. Although the nature of news once again resides in ongoing social process, the journalist must play a more active, and, to some extent, a more creative role in the development of the newsworthy. In this image there is not so clear an expectation that newsworthy information will reveal itself naturally, as there is an assumption that the most significant news of the day will come to light only as the result of the journalist's imposition of his point of view. Here the newsman has personal responsibility for the information he seeks to transmit, and his relationship to news sources is more circumscribed: sources provide leads but the reporter must sift through them for the real story. Whether one assumes that information is purposely withheld by sources or is merely buried in the complexities of modern life, that which is most worthwhile journalistically is believed to emerge from the active involvement of the journalist in the news-gathering process. Furthermore, to be newsworthy, information must be reported in context, and it is the journalist's task to provide the background and interpretation necessary to give events meaning. In this sense, the primary journalistic value is relevance, and the cardinal sins, news suppression and superficiality.

To further differentiate the active-passive dimension of the two styles, the neutral journalist allows the control of content to be vested in the events observed, while the participant sees control as vested in the journalist himself. This distinction has been noted by Carey (1969, p. 32) in contrasting the role of the "professional communicator" of contemporary times with the classical role of the journalist:

> With the rise of "objective reporting" . . . the journalist became a reporter, a broker in symbols, who mediated between audiences and institutions, particularly but not exclusively government. In this role he loses his independence and becomes part of the process of news transmission. In this role he does not principally utilize an intellectual skill as critic, interpreter and contemporary historian but a technical skill at writing, a capacity to translate the specialized languages and purposes of government, science, art, medicine, finance into an idiom that can be understood by broader, more amorphous, less educated audiences.

Several works have appeared in recent years to suggest that the contemporary journalist may often be caught between these competing expectations. Cohen (1963), for example, argued that the public affairs reporter holds two conceptions of the role of the press, one guiding him as a neutral reporter and another defining his active participation in the policy-making process. Moreover, Cohen emphasized that this duality pervades every aspect of the public affairs reporter's existence, which he characterized as a "bifurcated professional existence." Nimmo (1964), Dunn (1969), and Chittick (1970) also discuss the multiple roles of the public affairs reporter, and point to the delicate balance between objective detachment and subjective involvement. And Kimball (1965, p. 249), in an almost Parsonian formulation of role dilemma, discussed the newsman's role in terms of competing expectations of personal involvement and affective neutrality: "In a sense the reporter must learn to master two opposite psychological states. One is the capacity to immerse himself in the stories he is sent to cover so completely that he actually relives them. The other is to be able to detach himself from these same intense involvements, to stand outside the experience and place it in perspective for the reader." In Kimball's view, the key professional attribute of the journalist is the capacity to remove himself from intense experience and still be able to write about it.

Conceptions of Press Functions

At this point the prevalence of "neutral" and "participant" perspectives among contemporary American newsmen will be explored. The primary data to be considered in this regard are the assessments newsmen made regarding the importance of several different activities performed by the news media in our society. Toward the middle of the interview, members of the sample were presented with eight different activities performed by the news media, and were asked to rate the importance of each one along a continuum ranging from "extremely important" to "not important at all." The evaluations newsmen made of these functions, which were selected to represent activities consistent with images both of a neutral and participant press, are reported in Table 7.1, which lists the eight functions by the level of positive endorsement each received.

In this list, the first, second, fourth, and seventh activities were intended to represent press functions consistent with the definition of a socially responsible participant press. Investigative, analytic, and interpretive reporting all describe journalistic

activities in which the shape and character of the news are structured more by the efforts of the newsman rather than by those
of news sources. As such they are consistent with the spirit of
participant values as we have defined them here. Moreover, to
accord the news media a role in the development of national
policy is by definition to endorse participant journalism, and to
stress an educative function for the media is to accord the journalist professional responsibility and judgment in the selection
of news content.

By contrast, the third, fifth, sixth, and eighth items listed in
Table 7.1 represent press functions much more in keeping with
a neutralized modern-day libertarian press. Getting information
to the public as quickly as possible precludes the possibility of
providing much background and context, and in addition, is to
emphasize a journalist's technical prowess rather than his
familiarity with substance. Emphasis on verified information
lies perhaps at the heart of so-called "objective" journalism, and
to disseminate news which is of interest to the widest possible
public is central to the classical libertarian view of the functions
of the press in a democracy. Finally, to emphasize the entertainment function of the news media is to locate standards of news
judgment within the audience rather than with the journalistic
practitioner; as such, endorsement of this function suggests
more a passive than an active journalistic role.

Inspection of the results in Table 7.1 indicates more widespread support among newsmen for participant than for neutral
press functions. That government is always news is confirmed
by the fact that more than three-quarters (76.3 percent) of the
sample strongly endorsed the media's watchdog role in investigating governmental activities. In addition, more than six in ten
(61.3 percent) felt it was extremely important for the media to
provide analysis and interpretation of complex problems. In
interpreting these responses, it should be noted that the interviewing in this study was conducted just a few weeks following
the publication of the Pentagon papers. It is not unlikely, therefore, that the questions on investigative reporting were linked
by many respondents with that series of events. If this is in fact
the case, it indicates widespread support for those actions
among American newsmen. More generally, the fact that
investigative efforts of the press were endorsed even more
strongly than factual veracity represents strong testimony as to
the salience of aggressive approaches to journalism within the

professional community. At the same time, of course, a majority of newsmen did feel it is extremely important for the media to transmit information quickly and to communicate only verified factual information. Moreover, the fact that assessments of the importance of factual veracity were measured negatively— as the importance of *staying away* from stories where accuracy could not be verified—would yield somewhat less positive overall endorsement than would the same dimension described positively. In other words, it is hard to imagine that many newsmen would defend the value of unverified information over that which had been checked out, and it is usual for newsmen to check information with more than one source when developing news stories.[1]

While the response distributions described in Table 7.1 are informative, they provide no basis for arguing that the measures represented there are in fact linked to broader frames of reference regarding journalism. Indeed, the fact that a majority of newsmen strongly endorsed functions which at face value represent "neutral" and "participant" values would suggest that the most typical value orientation among journalists may be one which combines elements of both perspectives. Two questions must therefore be addressed at this point: whether newsmen's beliefs regarding media functions are in fact patterned; and if so, whether the belief-sets meaningfully can be labeled as "participant" and "neutral."

To deal with these questions, responses to the eight media activities were subjected to factor analysis.[2] Although the first two factors identified in this analysis explained only 41.8 percent of the common variance, the loadings on these factors were consistent with expectations. The first, second, and fourth items in Table 7.1 all revealed positive relationships with the first factor, with the highest loading (.375) found for the fourth item, discussion by the media of national policies in process of formulation. Together, then, attitudes favorable to investigative reporting, to the analysis and interpretation of complex problems, and to the media taking an active role in the development of national policy form the nucleus of what can be interpreted as an orientation toward participant journalism. Responses to these three questions showed no relationship to the second factor.

The third, fifth, sixth, and eighth items, by comparison, all showed positive loadings on the second factor and zero or slightly negative loadings on the first. The strongest loading on the second factor (.417) was revealed by the sixth item, the importance of concentrating on news of interest to the widest possible public. On this basis, the meaning of the second factor can be interpreted as a contemporary version of a libertarian philosophy of the news media.

Finally, the seventh item, development by the media of intellectual and cultural interests of the public, turned out to be related positively to both factors, and, contrary to expectations, was related somewhat more closely to the libertarian than to the participant factor (.185 compared with .132). Endorsement of this function of the news media, therefore, would not appear to have clear-cut meaning in terms of the principal dimensions revealed by the other responses. Because of this, responses to this question were not used further in the analysis.

These results provide empirical confirmation of the existence of alternative belief systems regarding press functions. At this point in the analysis other issues were also examined for possible connections with the two groups of values, and from these efforts two additional sets of responses were located which were clearly differentiated along the neutral-participant dimension. The first of these measured opinions regarding crusading and social reform functions of the press, and the second, opinions on the usefulness of underground media. From Table 7.2 it is clear that more newsmen support than reject crusading and social reform efforts by the news media, since over a third of the sample (34.9 percent) thought there were too few crusaders in the media while just 22.3 percent felt there were too many. The reactions of mainstream journalists to the underground press movement could similarly be described as moderately positive, since a majority (58.8 percent) felt these media served some useful purpose on the national scene. At the same time, however, only a small proportion (11.3 percent) were willing to endorse these activities with unqualified support.

In the context of the present discussion, the most relevant fact is that favorable opinions regarding crusading and social reform efforts by the media showed average Pearson correlations of .197 and –.075, respectively, with the core items of the participant and neutral dimensions, while the comparable figures for favorable assessments of the usefulness of the underground media were .143 and –.118.

On the basis of these findings and the logical connection of advocacy journalism to participant values, responses which supported crusading journalism and underground-media activities were added to the three items identified in the first factor to form a Likert-type scale of dispositions favorable to participant news-media functions. The five component items were weighted equally in this scale, and the resulting scores ranged between five and twenty points, with a mean of 15.30 and a standard deviation of 2.82.[3] In similar fashion, the four core items of the second factor were combined to produce a scale measuring favorable orientations to neutral journalistic functions.[4] Values on this second scale ranged from four to sixteen, with a mean of 11.94 and a standard deviation of 2.46. The correlation between the two resulting scales was −.187, indicating that a journalist endorsing one set of media functions was likely to eschew values on the other dimension. Neutral and participant conceptions of the news media would appear to represent alternative and on the whole incompatible definitions of journalistic responsibility.

While the full range of these scores will be used later in this chapter, the joint distribution of the sample on a more limited number of categories will be examined first. In Table 7.3 the sample is divided into nine subgroups, with divisions made approximately at the upper and lower quartiles on each value scale. From these figures it is possible to estimate the number of newsmen who view the role of the media as predominantly participant or neutral, as well as the number who hold more balanced outlooks. Adding the percentages across the diagonals, for example, indicates that 8.5 percent of the sample were predominantly participant in outlook, 21.4 percent were moderately participant, 35.4 percent held balanced views, 25.1 percent were moderately neutral, and 9.7 percent were predominantly neutral. By combining the two value scales in this fashion, conceptions of journalistic responsibility form roughly a normal distribution, which means that it is more common for newsmen to hold balanced than extreme viewpoints regarding their professional role. Despite the fact that neutral and participant values tend to be antithetical, in other words, it can be concluded that most newsmen do in fact hold patterns of beliefs which combine elements from each perspective. This outcome reinforces Cohen's (1963) observation regarding the contradictory role of the professional journalist.

"Whole-Truthers" and "Nothing-but-the-Truthers"

Further insight into the nature of these competing belief systems emerges from an analysis of the criticisms journalists made of the American news media. Since these data are of interest in their own right, we will first review the types of shortcomings newsmen most often level at the media, and then relate the criticisms they make to their beliefs regarding appropriate media functions.

From the right-hand column of Table 7.4 it is evident that two themes dominated journalists' criticisms of the media: in answer to the question, "What is the most valid criticism that can be made of the news media today?," over a quarter (28.4 percent) cited some aspect of *what* the media cover, while well over half (57.4 percent) focused on shortcomings pertaining to *how* information is handled in the media. Within these general categories, however, a second and more interesting dimensionality was also evident. In criticizing the media for content coverage, for example, some newsmen (11.4 percent) spoke of topics they felt were covered too much, such as crime, "bad news," or "sensational news," while another somewhat larger group (17.0 percent) was more concerned with news topics the media do not cover. Within this latter group, some charged the media with overt censorship ("They don't report everything–if it's against the policies of the paper, it just doesn't get reported"), others scored the paucity of certain types of news, such as international news or news of minority group affairs, while still others felt that space or time limitations severely restricted the overall scope of news coverage possible. Those who criticized the media on grounds of their substantive coverage could be clearly divided into those critical of the media for what they *do*, and those critical of the media for what they *fail to do*.

In similar fashion, criticisms of how the media handle information could also be differentiated into faults of overstatement and understatement. For example, a quarter of all newsmen (25.7 percent) scored the media for biased coverage, for lack of objectivity, or for what one respondent termed the media's "inherent tendency to manipulate and color news." This charge, in fact, was the most prevalent single theme leveled by newsmen against the American media. On the other hand, just about the same number (23.3 percent) talked of the superficiality of news coverage, or of the failure of the media to present information in sufficient depth or context. In the words of one newsman, the media "emphasize only the obvious and fail to grapple with more important and complex issues." Within both general categories, media criticism was split between citations for errors of commission and errors of omission. These two themes were either explicitly or implicitly present in over three-quarters of all criticisms mentioned by newsmen, and interestingly, the distribution was relatively even between the two types of citations: 40.3 percent of the criticisms could be interpreted as errors of omission; 37.1 percent as errors of commission.

Finally, another 8.2 percent of the answers focused on other performance faults, such as sloppy reporting or the dependency of print and broadcast organizations on the wire services, while another 14.2 percent covered a wide variety of topics and could be lumped together only as a residual category. Within the latter grouping, for example, were criticisms of the media for their insensitivity to new ideas, for their disregard (or over-regard) for audience preferences or interests, or for their imperviousness to constructive criticism.

Table 7.4 also reveals that the criticisms journalists make of the news media are strongly related to the types of professional values they hold. Those who endorse participant values are much more likely to emphasize things the media do not do—areas of content they do not cover, or stories they fail to cover in sufficient depth—while those with neutral value orientations are much more concerned with faults of commission—content which is given too much coverage, or information which is biased or lacking in objectivity. These differences are clearly evident in the responses of the two extreme groups: among the group with predominantly participant values, citations for neglected content outnumbered mentions of superfluous content by 20.3 percent, while criticisms for superficiality were mentioned 18.4 percent more often than criticisms of bias or overstatement. Among those with predominantly neutral values, on the other hand, mentions of overcoverage were slightly more numerous than criticisms for neglected content (by .5 percent), while there were many more citations for bias than for superficiality (by 22.9 percent).

These results add significantly to our understanding of the principal axis of value segmentation within journalism. The participant image of professional responsibility is one which defines the primary role of the journalist as revealing the *whole-truth*: it is the obligation of the news media to seek out all relevant news, and to prepare the news with sufficient care and in sufficient depth that all relevant information is presented. Professional responsibility from the neutral perspective, on the other hand, defines the journalist's primary obligation more in terms of presenting *nothing-but-the-truth*. In this image, the media should transmit only news which can be factually verified, and only that which is presented in a manner which does not reflect the personal values of the newswriter.

Correlates and Determinants of Professional Values

At this point we will explore the relationship between scores on the two value scales and a variety of social and professional characteristics of journalists. Our primary concern in this analysis is to identify the factors and processes which produce or reinforce different value orientations among professional journalists. The general frame of reference guiding this analysis is drawn from the sociology of occupations and professions, and more specifically from the study of occupational socialization. Models of professional socialization such as developed by Sherlock and Morris (1967) or Moore (1969) explain the evolution of the professional in terms of a chain of prior influences which include early background factors leading to recruitment into a field, the type of professional training received, and the nature of post-training career influences emanating from the work setting. As Bucher and Strauss (1961) have noted, however, most studies of the professions too readily assume a unity of interest and perspective among incumbents of occupational groups, and as a result tend to ignore those forces which produce heterogeneity. Our principal concern at this point in the analysis is to identify factors which account for the divergent definitions of professional responsibility found among American journalists.

To approach this problem, a wide variety of personal, social, and job characteristics was correlated with scores on the two value scales. Table 7.5 summarizes the results of this analysis by reporting two sets of results, the zero-order correlation coefficients between thirteen background factors and scores on the participant and neutral scales, and the beta coefficients resulting from a regression analysis in which these same factors were combined to predict scores on the two scales. The independent variables used in this analysis are clustered into four groups in Table 7.5. The first group consists of years of formal schooling, sex (measured as a "dummy variable" with males scored as 1 and females as 0), chronological age, and professional age (the number of years the person had been employed in the news media). The second group contains three measures of job status: income; the number of editorial employees who report to a person; and the scope of a newsman's managerial responsibility— whether he has responsibilities for an entire news organization, for a department, for a news desk or news program, or no such duties at all. The third group is made up of three measures of the work milieu: the size of city where one is employed; organization size (measured by the number of editorial employees in an organization); and the prominence of the organization within the professional community (the number of times it was named by other members of the sample for its fairness and reliability or as an organization which newsmen rely on in their own work). Finally, the last group consists of three indicators of a journalist's professional and social integration: the number of professional associations belonged to, the percentage of informal social contacts which are with persons connected with journalism or the communications field, and the number of non-work-related organizations belonged to in the community at large.

Preliminary inspection of the results indicates that the relationships are in general quite low, and that even in combination the thirteen factors do not explain much of the variance in value orientations: the multiple correlation coefficients for the participant and neutral scales are just .347 and .340, respectively. At the same time, however, the table indicates several factors which differentiate positions on the two scales, since the regression and correlation coefficients, though modest in size, have opposite signs. The main implications of these results will now be reviewed.

(1). *Professional values in journalism are shaped by one's educational experiences.* From the first group of factors, it is clear that conceptions of participant press functions are associated with higher levels of formal schooling while neutral orientations are associated with lower. Formal schooling, in fact, turns out to be the strongest single predictor of participant values (beta = .180), and though negative in its influence, is the third strongest predictor of scores on the neutral scale (beta = -.170). This outcome suggests immediately that the great diversity in formal schooling currently found within journalism may be the primary source of segmentation within the field. Participant views of journalistic responsibility would appear to emerge out of one's experience in higher education, while neutral values are a product of apprentice-type experiences, of career lines in which one learns to be a journalist in the context of practical skills, and of concrete routines rather than abstract principles and theories.

At this point it should be noted that the characteristics included in the regression analysis are restricted to those on which observations could be made for all journalists in the sample. In addition, however, professional values were also associated with the "quality" of college a newsman had attended. Among newsmen with college degrees, college selectivity was positively associated with holding participant values (r = .116), and negatively related to holding neutral values (r = -.154). The most highly educated and possibly the best trained journalistic practitioners thus tend to embrace participant ideologies of the press and to eschew neutral-libertarian conceptions. At the same time, little relationship was found between professional orientations and what journalists had studied in college: majoring in journalism was positively but weakly correlated with positions on the neutral scale (r = .082), and showed virtually no relationship at all to holding participant values (r = .010).

(2). *Newsmen appear to become more neutral in outlook as they grow older.* Chronological age is a second characteristic which clearly differentiates newsmen's positions on the two-value dimensions, and is the strongest single predictor of scores on the neutral scale (beta = .194). Despite the fact that levels of schooling vary sharply within different age groups, age has independent effects on the values newsmen profess. Moreover, the regression coefficients on both value dimensions are larger for chronological age than for professional age, which is to say that professional outlook is more a product of stage of life than stage of career. This result would also suggest that it is persons who enter the news media relatively late in their careers who endorse neutral press functions most strongly, and that newsmen who come to the media after working first in other occupational fields view the field quite differently from those who enter directly out of college.

While the effects of age seem straightforward in Table 7.5, the impact of career longevity is less clear-cut. Examined by itself, tenure in the field is positively related with neutral values (r = .098); yet the net impact of experience on neutral values turns out to be negative (beta = -.070). Once the relationship of experience to age, income, and other factors is taken into account, in other words, the positive effect of professional age on neutral orientations becomes reversed. This is not to say that longevity in the field heightens the salience of part:. ipant values among newsmen: on the contrary, Table 7.5 shows that the net effect of experience on participant values is also negative (beta = -.019), albeit only slightly so. Together, these results se᷈ n to suggest that as newsmen gain experience they devᴜiᴜ, ᴏre balanced or integrated views of how the press should cᵪ ᴊrate, and are more reluctant to stress one function of the media to the exclusion of others. The net effect of increased tenure in the field, in short, is to dampen a newsman's commitment both to participant and neutral values, at least as pure ideological stances.

In general, then, participant images of journalistic responsibility are characteristic of younger and better educated newsmen, while neutral orientations are more characteristic of those who are older and less well educated. Being older and being better educated have opposite effects on value orientations. While it remains to be seen whether the increased levels of education which can be expected in the field will alter the prevalence of participant role conceptions among journalists, it can be concluded at least for the present that younger college-educated newsmen think very differently about their profession than do older non-college-trained journalists.

(3). *Men score lower than women on both value dimensions.* Although sex is not a strong correlate of professional values, the results in Table 7.5 do indicate that women had somewhat higher scores than men did on *both* the neutral and the participant scales. This is evidenced by the slightly negative values both in the correlation coefficients and in the standardized regression coefficients: "being male," in short, has the effect of lowering scores on both the neutral and participant dimensions. This outcome is both surprising and difficult to interpret. Intuitively, at least, one might have expected the aggressive participant orientation to represent more a male- than a female-centered approach to journalism. Yet this is clearly not the case. At face value the results indicate that men endorsed fewer media functions as important than women did, and while this might in turn suggest that men in journalism are more skeptical or critical of media operations, no supporting evidence could be found to bolster this interpretation. Men and women were about equally critical of overall media performance,[5] had about the same levels of professional respect for their editors,[6] and were equally positive in assessing the competence of reporters in their own branch of the media.[7] About the only consistent difference between men and women in their evaluation of the media, in fact, was in the types of criticisms they leveled at the media: in this regard, more men than women scored the media for news suppression or superficiality of coverage (41.1 compared with 34.0 percent of their total criticisms), while more women than men criticized the media for bias, sensationalism, or news content covered too much (44.7 compared with 34.9 percent of total criticisms). While this fact is consistent with the differences between men and women on the neutral scale, it does not clarify why women also endorsed participant values more often, and we are left with no satisfactory explanation for the latter discrepancy. Whatever the real explanation, it can at least be concluded that the more aggressive participant stance regarding news media functions is not primarily a male-focused definition of professional responsibility.

(4). *The types of career paths journalists follow have an influence on their professional values.* Conflicting results emerge when different measures of organizational status are related to scores on the two value scales. While income level is associated positively with participant values and negatively with neutral, the reverse is true of a second measure or organizational position, the number of editorial employees for which a journalist is responsible. Moreover, to add to the complexity, the scope of a journalist's managerial responsibilities, while correlated negatively with participant values at the zero-order ($r = -.086$), turns out to have a slightly positive effect on participant values (beta = .029) when considered in combination with the other variables in the analysis. The main dilemma here, however, is to explain why scores on the participant scale should be affected positively by income but negatively by the span of supervisory control a newsman has.

Our interpretation of these results is that participant values are consistent with and functional to professional advancement as a journalist, while neutral values, because of their compatibility with organizational goals, are conducive to career mobility along the administrative path. As was argued in Chapter 5, the number of editorial employees a journalist is responsible for is a fairly direct and unambiguous measure of administrative power within the news media, and Table 7.5 demonstrates that this variable is associated positively with neutral value orientations, and negatively with participant. Advancement up the organizational hierarchy, in other words, reinforces neutral values and dampens a newsman's commitment to participant journalism.

Although newsmen with more administrative responsibilities would also realize higher incomes, the *net* effect of income in this analysis can be interpreted as an indicator of professional rather than administrative status, since the standardized regression coefficients represent the effects of income on professional values *after* the relationship of income to position in the organizational hierarchy has been taken into account. Journalists who make more money but do not have a heavier load of managerial duties, in other words, would be paid more because of their experience and value as "star" reporters, commentators, or columnists. The net effect of income, in short, reflects advancement along the professional career track, and as the results indicate, professional advancement strengthens participant rather than neutral values, those orientations more related to news writing than to media management.

To reiterate, our interpretation of these results is that definitions of professional responsibility within journalism articulate with the career paths newsmen follow. Those who are most successful as reporters continue to endorse participant functions of the press because it is these journalistic norms and standards which are more likely to inspire the type of work for which a journalist gains professional recognition. Pulitzer prizes and other awards in journalism are typically given for excellence in investigative or analytic reporting, not for the size of audience a newsman appeals to, or for efficiency in meeting deadlines. Neutral values, on the other hand, are much more directly related to organizational goals. Reaching large audiences and reaching them quickly enhances the economic interests of news organizations, and a rigid adherence to the canons of "objective" reporting serves to protect a news organization from potential libel suits. Neutral professional values are thus more functional to career advancement through the organizational hierarchy.

(5). *Professional values reflect the demographic and organizational environments within which newsmen work, but are related most directly to city size.* Participant values were endorsed most often by journalists working in large cities and in large and prestigious news organizations, and all three of these contextual factors correlate negatively with neutral values. When the influence of these factors is considered simultaneously, it turns out that the value scales are discriminated best by city size: in the regression analysis the net effect of organization size on neutral values becomes positive (beta = .136), while the net effect of organization prominence on participant values is negative (beta = -.083). In view of this, we would interpret the impact of the work environment primarily as the effects of population density, and only secondarily as the effects of characteristics of news organizations. In other words, even though larger and more prestigious media may provide the type of work setting in which it is possible for a journalist to engage in the more aggressive participant style of journalism, this would be explained in large part by the fact that chief and prominent news organizations are located in the major urban centers. We would conclude, in short, that professional orientations are reinforced more by the external environment in which newsmen work than by the characteristics of the media for which they work.

(6). *Professional orientations among journalists are related to their patterns of social relationships.* Finally, Table 7.5 shows that the types of social relationships journalists engage in are associated with the professional values they hold. These connections are clearly visible in the correlation coefficients reported in part (d) of the table, although it is equally clear that when analyzed in conjunction with other variables in the regression analysis, patterns of social interaction do not have much strength as predictors of value orientations. From the correlation values, however, it is evident that scores on the participant value scale are higher among journalists who are more integrated into informal networks of colleague relationships (r = .155), while neutral values are positively associated with the number of non-work-related organizations and associations journalists belong to in the wider community (r = .104).[8] Moreover, negative relationships turn up in the cross comparisons—participant values with membership in voluntary associations (r = -.157), and neutral values with frequency of colleague contacts (r = -.100). Interestingly, membership in professional organizations and associations fails to discriminate in any consistent fashion between the two types of values.

These patterns suggest that participant images of journalistic responsibility are reinforced by informal ties within the professional community, while neutral values are sustained by one's formal attachments within the community at large. Paradoxically, then, it is participant rather than neutral journalism which calls for the independence of the journalist from community ties, since it is the capacity to investigate, analyze, or crusade which would be compromised by formal allegiances with news sources. Indeed, to support investigative reporting and crusading is to endorse an approach to journalism in which conflict relations are to be expected between the journalist and vested interests in the external environment. The participant journalist thus values detachment from external social ties in order to preserve editorial freedom, and for him associations with professional peers provide the sequestration necessary to reinforce a commitment to conflict-based news values.

Those oriented to neutral-libertarian journalism, on the other hand, value editorial neutrality to news content in order to sustain relationships with news sources. The implications suggested by this are similar to what Janowitz (1952) and Breed (1958) concluded from their studies of the community press: neutral journalism is oriented to news which binds the social order together rather than to that which generates conflict and dissent. Just as the participant journalist holds conflict-based news values, the neutral journalist is consensus-oriented. The latent function of news which is of interest to the widest possible public or which provides entertainment and relaxation is to solidify rather than to exacerbate the status quo. Formal social ties within the external community do not represent cross-pressures for the neutral journalist: on the contrary, these contacts strengthen rather than undercut his sense of journalistic responsibility.

To conclude this discussion, it should be noted that a negative relationship ($r = -.218$) was found between the number of voluntary associations a journalist belonged to and the extent of his involvement in informal social relations with professional peers. These two types of social interaction thus seem on the whole to be incompatible. Belonging to voluntary associations and to professional organizations were positively related ($r = .186$), on the other hand, while there was virtually no relationship at all between the extent of one's formal and informal professional connections ($r = .029$). Patterns of social integration among journalists thus appear to be split along a formal-informal continuum, and as has been seen, this split is helpful in identifying the themes a newsman is likely to emphasize in defining his role as a journalist.

Summary

Recent struggles between the government and the news media have tended to obscure a new wave of self-criticism within the American journalistic community. The past decade has witnessed the growth of a lively alternative press, the appearance of several new journalism reviews and of scores of professional media watchers, heated debate over a so-called "new journalism," a rising consciousness of minority status among women in the field, and "counter conventions" of newsmen disaffected from the established associational structures of professional journalism.

This chapter has focused on value cleavage within contemporary journalism, and it has been argued that the principal axis of this cleavage revolves around familiar themes—objectivity versus subjectivity, detachment versus advocacy, observer versus watchdog, and libertarian neutrality versus social responsibility. These issues differentiate proponents of "neutral" and "participant" styles of journalism, belief systems which form the basis of occupational "segments" within journalism—subgroups organized around alternative professional identities and ideologies. While most practicing newsmen subscribe to elements of both viewpoints, these two segments are visible as pure ideological types among practicing newsmen.

As in other occupations, the segments within contemporary journalism are differentiated clearly along lines of education and training, and would suggest, therefore, that the great diversity of educational background found within the field today may well be the primary source of the current segmentation. Proponents of the opposing styles are also identifiable by the career paths they follow, participant values describing those more successful in pursuing news-writing careers, and neutral values those who have advanced through the positional hierarchies of news organizations. Participant images of journalistic responsibility thus seem more consistent with the role of the journalist as a "solo professional," while neutral values fit closely with the role of a professional in an organizational setting. Participant values are also more characteristic of younger journalists, and neutral values of older.

Finally, professional orientations reflect the type of environment in which journalists work and the kinds of social integration they manifest. Participant values are more characteristic of those who work in large cities and of those whose primary social ties are with professional colleagues rather than in the community at large. Neutral definitions of professional responsibility, by comparison, are more prevalent among newsmen employed in smaller population centers and among those with more extensive formal ties within the wider society.

Notes

1. In response to the question, "How often do your stories involve news gathering from more than one source?," 56.6 percent said "most of the time," 35.1 percent said "sometimes," 7.9 percent answered "rarely," and just .4 percent said "never."

2. A principal component solution was employed, using a varimax rotation, with 1.00 in the diagonals of the correlation matrix.

3. Responses to the three questions on the importance of media functions were given the following scale values: extremely important, 4; quite important, 3; somewhat important, 2; not important at all, 1. Responses to the question on crusaders and social reformers were scored as follows: too few, 4; about the right number, 2; too many, 1. For the question on the underground media, the scale scores were: very useful, 4; somewhat useful, 3; not useful at all, 1.

4. The four items were weighted equally and scored in the same fashion as the media functions in the first scale.

5. When asked how good a job of informing the public they thought the news media were doing, 54.3 percent of men and 54.4 percent of women answered "outstanding" or "very good."

6. Some 75.2 percent of men and 74.0 percent of women said they had "a great deal" of professional respect for the person they reported to in their organization.

7. Virtually the same numbers of men and women (68.0 and 68.2 percent, respectively) rated a majority of news reporters in their branch of the media as "competent professionals."

8. Some 54.8 percent of journalists in the sample said they belonged to one or more voluntary associations in the wider community, and a total of 72.3 percent reported membership either in a professional or a community organization. Contrary to folklore, then, journalists are no more likely than other American adults to shy away from connections with voluntary organizations in the society at large: recent figures reported by Almond and Verba (1968, p. 108) reveal that 57.4 percent of American adults belong to secondary associations or organizations of one type or another.

8

Rewards and Satisfactions in News-Media Journalism

At this point attention shifts to consider financial rewards and sources of job satisfaction and dissatisfaction within news-media journalism. The first part of the chapter examines levels of financial remuneration within the field, and discusses how incomes vary within different sectors of the industry, different regions of the country, and among persons with different background characteristics and job functions. The relative impact of these factors on earnings is then assessed by means of regression analysis. The second part of the chapter deals directly with the question of morale. After identifying the characteristics of newsmen likely both to remain in and to leave the news media, the chapter concludes by assessing the salience of a variety of concrete and intangible factors on the extent to which journalists say they are satisfied with their employment.

Income Levels

Table 8.1 shows the amounts newsmen reported as their total personal incomes, before taxes, from work in the communications field during 1970.[1] Persons who were not employed in the news media during 1970 are omitted. The average (median) income for a journalist in 1970 was $11,133; a quarter (24.9 percent) earned less than $8,000, and close to one in five (18.4 percent) made more than $16,000. Although not shown in the table, incomes ranged from under $2,000 to $75,000, with approximately 3.0 percent earning more than $30,000.

Fortunately, 1970 census data are available against which to evaluate these figures. In a report issued in 1973 (U.S. Bureau of the Census, 1973b, p. 49), the median income of male editors and reporters between the ages of twenty-five and sixty-four is listed as $12,210 for 1969. Although this figure is substantially higher than the $11,133 estimated in Table 8.1, the discrepancy is not unexpected since the persons omitted from the census estimate—women, men under twenty-five, and men sixty-five and over—are in the main found in the lower income echelons of the news media. When these persons (who in combination constitute 30.9 percent of all full-time news-media personnel) are omitted from our own estimates, the median rises to $12,507, some $297 higher than the census estimate. This latter discrepancy can be accounted for, in turn, by several additional differences between the census data and our own. In the first place, the present study is restricted to news-media personnel while the census estimates are not; second, our working definition of a journalist includes some news people (such as announcers) who would not be included in the census category "editors and reporters"; and third, the estimates from our study are for 1970 rather than 1969. A fourth source of variation would be sampling error.[2] In view of these additional sources of discrepancy, the two estimates can be interpreted as surprisingly close.

Although journalism has never been noted as a highly lucrative field, other figures from the census report show that journalists' incomes in 1969 were at about the mid-point of occupations classified in the professional and technical category by the census. For example, the median income in 1969 for men twenty-five to sixty-four in all professional, technical, and kindred occupations was $12,237,[3] just $27 higher than the figure estimated for editors and reporters. Average earnings among editors and reporters in 1969 were considerably higher than those of secondary school teachers ($9,886), were slightly higher than those of accountants ($11,969) or sociologists ($11,797), and were considerably lower than those of lawyers and judges ($20,139) or physicians, dentists, and related practitioners ($20,190). On the average, editors' and reporters' incomes in 1969 came closest to those of computer specialists, who earned $12,222. In general, income levels within journalism seem comparable to those of other fields which require similar amounts of education and training.

Sources of Variation

The most striking feature about incomes in news-media journalism is the extent to which they vary along different dimensions. Tables 8.2 and 8.3 illustrate the main sources of this variation, Table 8.2 focusing on geographic and industrial characteristics, and Table 8.3 on the personal characteristics of rewsmen and the job functions they perform.

(1). *Media sector.* Journalists' incomes are highest by a considerable margin in the national news magazines, and are much lower in radio and in weeklies than in other sectors of the media. Although not shown in the table, average earnings were somewhat higher in the broadcast than print media—$11,281 in television and radio combined compared with $11,033 in dailies, weeklies, and news magazines combined. Yet more variance is found *within* media sectors than *between* them: earnings were $2,624 higher in dailies than weeklies and were $2,292 greater in television than in radio. Levels of compensation in the wire services were comparatively high, roughly equivalent to those in television. In overview, these differentials are perfectly consistent with the patterns of interorganizational job mobility noted in Chapter 4, where manpower was seen to flow from weeklies and radio into dailies, from radio into television, and from daily newspapers into the wire services and news magazines.

(2). *Region.* As in most other occupations, average earnings in journalism vary sharply in different parts of the country. They are highest in the Pacific states, second highest in the East North Central region (Ohio, Michigan, Indiana, Illinois, and Wisconsin), and third highest in the Middle Atlantic states—the heart of the news industry. The lowest levels of compensation are found in the South Central subregions, with the East South Central states (Alabama, Mississippi, Tennessee, and Kentucky) at the very bottom. Average earnings are as much as 73 percent higher in the Pacific coast states than in the deep South. When the subregions are grouped, earnings are found to be highest in the West and lowest in the South. Due to a sizable income differential between the Mountain and Pacific states, however, the net advantage of the Northeast is reduced to just $129 a year, and in similar fashion, comparatively low incomes in the West North Central states lower the overall median for the North Central region below that for the Northeast.

While these differences are striking, they are a fair reflection of the regional discrepancies in earnings found within the labor force as a whole. When journalists' earnings in the nine subregions are ranked against average family incomes in 1969 (U.S.

Bureau of the Census, 1973b, p. 5), for example, the rank-order correlation (rho) turns out to be .733, indicating a fairly high consistency between journalism and the labor force as a whole. Three discrepancies in these rankings should be noted, however: first, the New England states, where median family incomes in 1969 were highest in the country while journalists' earnings were just fifth highest; second, the South Atlantic states, seventh of nine subregions in average family income but fourth highest among journalists (perhaps reflecting the influence of the Washington press corps); and third, the Mountain states, fifth highest in family income, but seventh within journalism. Other than for these reversals, however, the two sets of rankings are identical.

At this point it should also be noted that a positive but somewhat weaker relationship (rho = .515) was found between newsmen's average earnings and the net migration ratios for journalists in the nine subregions. In Chapter 4 it was noted that the subregions with the most favorable migration ratios within journalism were the Middle Atlantic states, the Pacific region, and the Mountain states, areas which, respectively, ranked third, first, and seventh in median earnings. While in general newsmen do migrate to regions where income levels are higher, there are some significant departures, particularly in their movement into the Mountain region. And while ecological correlations can sometimes be misleading when interpreting individual behavior, the results suggest, nonetheless, that factors other than strictly economic ones may motivate the migratory decisions of some newsmen.

(3). *City size.* Another important source of variation is market size. Table 8.2 reveals that incomes rise from a median of $8,314 in communities under 10,000 in population to $14,787 in places with over a million inhabitants. Earnings among journalists are therefore 78 percent higher in the largest urban settings than in the smallest.

(4). *Organization size.* Earnings are also related strongly to organization size, and are as much as $4,918 higher in media which employ 100 or more editorial personnel than in those which employ ten or fewer. At this point, however, it should be noted that since large news organizations tend to be located in the larger cities, it is not at all clear whether income levels are affected more by organization size or by community size. For that matter, all four factors considered thus far are closely interrelated: virtually all national news magazines are edited in large cities (many in New York); weekly papers are both small in staff and, as noted in Chapter 2, are most typically published in small communities; and population density is much greater in some regions of the country than in others. Thus, while earnings in journalism do vary substantially by region, city size, media sector, and organization size—and, it might be added, with organization prominence[4]—the net impact of these factors on levels of remuneration can only be determined if the data are subjected to multivariate analysis. Before presenting this analysis, however, the relationship of background characteristics and job functions with income levels will be reviewed.

(5). *Sex.* From Table 8.3 it is obvious that a significant gap exists in the earnings of men and women in the news media. While this differential ($4,221) is not as great as that found between the sexes in the broader category of professional and technical occupations,[5] it is substantial nonetheless. It should also be noted that while at first glance this gap might be attributed to differences in the educational qualifications[6] or professional experience[7] of men and women in the news media, the results of the regression analysis which will be presented later in the chapter clearly demonstrate that sex itself is one of the main sources of variation in journalists' incomes. And while the status of women in the media will not be discussed at length here, evidence both from this and other studies makes it clear that career opportunities for men and women in the news media differ markedly: men have better chances of being recruited into the media to begin with; they are more likely to be assigned "important" news beats early in their careers; and they have much better chances of eventual promotion into positions of organizational responsibility.[8]

(6). *Age.* As in the labor force at large, earnings in journalism peak during the middle working years, and decline thereafter. The highest average incomes are found among those in their late thirties and early forties. There is an important qualification to this pattern, however, and it is illustrated in Table 8.4. Here it can be seen that the general pattern obtains only for women in the field, not for men. Incomes among men rise continuously in each successively older age group, while among women they peak in the twenty-five to thirty-four age group, and decline steadily thereafter. These data thus describe a continually widening income gap between the sexes. Up to the age of thirty-five, the differentials are fairly modest: men's earnings are 36 percent higher than women's among persons under twenty-five, and are just 17 percent higher in the twenty-five to thirty-four age group. In the thirty-five to forty-four grouping, however, the differential jumps to 64 percent, widens further to 76 percent among those forty-five to fifty-four, and is as much as 86 percent higher for men among those aged fifty-five or older. The economic costs of being a woman in journalism thus become much more real as careers progress.

(7). *Years of schooling.* Returning to Table 8.3, it can be seen that earnings in journalism do not increase as a simple linear function of years of formal schooling. Newsmen with graduate degrees do command the highest salaries on the average, but earnings are higher among those who never went to college at all than among those with some college, while college graduates made more in 1970 than those with some graduate training. These inversions reflect the rising educational levels in the field, and the fact that younger newsmen on the average have had more formal schooling than veterans. The net impact of education on earnings can be assessed only after these changes have been taken into account. It should be noted, nonetheless, that among current practitioners in the field the range in earnings between those with the most and the least schooling is just $1,831 a year.

(8). *College selectivity.* Despite these ambiguities, definite economic advantages accrue to newsmen who graduate from highly rated colleges and universities. When the colleges newsmen attended are divided into three groups on the basis of national selectivity ratings (Cass and Birnbaum, 1970), a differential of $2,727 a year emerges between the top and bottom thirds of the continuum. It would appear that graduates from top-rated schools either place themselves better in the field to begin with, or are able to advance more rapidly into higher paying positions wherever they happen to locate.

(9). *Managerial functions.* Table 8.3 confirms that journalists who have managerial responsibilities earn more than those who do not. Somewhat surprisingly, however, average earnings are higher among heads of news departments than among those with more far-reaching responsibilities. Since in the sample a good number of those in top managerial posts worked for weekly papers, radio stations, or other small news organizations, however, this inversion can probably be attributed to salary differences between large and small news organizations. In the aggregate the differential between those in top managerial positions and those with no managerial duties at all is just $2,924.

(10). *Number of employees supervised.* A much wider income spread emerges when newsmen are classified by the number of editorial employees they are responsible for—a measure of administrative responsibility which automatically takes organization size into account. Incomes range as much as $7,720 along this continuum, and persons in charge of twenty-five or more editorial employees have the highest earnings found in any single category in the table ($17,793). Though earnings may well increase as newsmen move out of news gathering and take on managerial functions, the critical factor would appear to be the size of the organization within which one assumes a position of administrative responsibility.

Multivariate Analysis of Income Levels

At this point the relative effects on income levels of the various factors discussed in the preceding section will be assessed. The results from two multiple regression analyses are displayed in Table 8.5, the first dealing with the sample as a whole, and the second with college graduates only.

To carry out these analyses, it was first necessary to convert three factors from nominal into ratio measurement. First, sex is here measured as a "dummy" variable, with men assigned scores of one and women scores of zero. Positive coefficients in the results thus measure the impact of being male on one's earning capacity. Second, to take geographic variation into account, individuals were given regional scores equivalent to the median family income in 1969 within their subregion.[9] The effects of region in the results can therefore be interpreted as the impact of general regional prosperity on journalists' earnings. Finally, to account for variation due to salary scales within different sectors of the news industry, individual newsmen were assigned sector scores equal to the median income of all editorial employees within a given branch of the media. The impact of media sector in the results can similarly be interpreted as the effects of rates of remuneration within the six branches of the news industry. The predictor variables included in the two analyses are identical save for one exception: in the sample as a whole the effects of education are measured by years of formal schooling, while in the college graduate subsample, college selectivity scores are substituted for years of formal schooling.

From Table 8.5 it is evident that the eleven predictors explain 46.7 percent of the total income variance in the sample at large, and 45.2 percent of the variance among journalists with college degrees. The predictors are ordered in the table according to their relative impact on earnings—as reflected by the values of the standardized regression coefficients (beta values). Because of the large sample size, virtually all of these beta values are statistically significant, but in keeping with the reporting style adopted throughout this volume the results will be commented upon from the perspective of their practical rather than statistical significance.

Turning first to the results in Part A of the table, it is evident that the best single predictor of income is the length of time one has worked in the news media. Professional age is a much stronger determinant of earnings than is chronological age, and even though a positive relationship exists between age and income in the sample at large (r = .324), the effects of age per se are negligible after professional experience is taken into account. It is more experienced rather than simply older newsmen who earn the higher incomes.

Since city size emerges as the second strongest predictor, it can be concluded that earnings are affected more by market size than by other geographic or contextual influences. Although regional prosperity does have a visible independent effect on income levels (beta = .123), the direct effects of community size are much stronger (beta = .259). The effects of city size would also appear to explain away much of the impact of organization size and media sector on income levels.

The most startling finding to emerge from this analysis is the importance of sex as a determinant of earnings in news-media journalism. Sex is the third strongest predictor of income levels among journalists in general, and is the second strongest predictor among those who hold college degrees. One is further ahead in predicting earnings by knowing simply that a journalist is a man than by knowing what his job functions are, what region of the country or sector of the industry he works in, how much formal schooling he has had, or the size or prominence of the news organization he works for.

At the same time, however, a journalist's income is affected independently by the job functions he performs. Even after controlling for experience in the field and for organization size, those who perform managerial duties or are responsible for the work of other newsmen do end up with the higher incomes. Generally, then, organizational rather than professional career lines would appear to be the more lucrative.

It should also be noted that when the influence of other variables in the analysis is taken into account, the media sector a journalist works in and the prominence of the organization he works for have relatively minor effects on economic rewards. It is years of schooling, however, which turn out to be the weakest predictor of all: education has virtually no direct effect on earnings. This is not to say that there are not indirect effects of schooling, however: indeed, having more education can help a journalist place himself better in the industry to begin with, and may also hasten his advancement into more responsible positions. What the results indicate is that after these and other processes have occurred, if they do, there is no additional effect of education on earnings.

While much the same pattern is found for journalists who hold college degrees, there are three differences which should be noted. The first is that among college graduates earnings are predicted better by sex than by city size, thus suggesting that the economic advantages which accrue from being male are even more pronounced among journalists with college degrees than is generally the case. The second difference is that for college graduates the relative impact of the two measures of administrative responsibility is reversed, a shift which eludes easy explanation. And the third difference is that educational background, when measured by the selectivity of the college one attended, does make a visible difference on earnings (beta = .106). Apparently *quality* but not *quantity* of schooling does have a direct impact on one's economic chances in news-media journalism.

In overview, these results are neither unanticipated nor peculiar to journalism. Professional experience is the prime determinant of income levels in journalism, but this would also be true in most other occupations, and is a fundamental regulating principle of the wage structure throughout our economy. The fact that persons who work in large cities and in more prosperous regions earn more is also not idiosyncratic to journalism: these sources of variation are quite consistent with wider economic regularities. Moreover, the fact that journalists in managerial and supervisory positions have higher incomes can likewise be interpreted as expected. The most revealing finding to emerge from the analysis is the critical role that sex plays in the determination of newsmen's income—though even this situation is by no means unique to journalism. Nonetheless, the results of the regression analysis show that the income differential between men and women *cannot* be explained away as a function of differences in training, job functions, industry location, region, age, or experience. It is quite evident, rather, that men and women in the news media do not receive equal pay for equal work. It can only be concluded, therefore, that a systematic wage discrimination favoring men pervades the American news industry.

Career Commitment

In view of the high rates of job mobility within news-media journalism, it is something of a surprise to discover that levels of organizational commitment and job satisfaction within the field are also quite high. In the sample as a whole, 62.9 percent of those who expected to be working at all in five years hoped they would still be employed in the same news organizations, and almost seven in eight (87.1 percent) gave positive rather than negative responses to a direct question on job satisfaction.[10] Despite high labor turnover and folklore to the contrary, journalists as a group are not particularly dissatisfied with their lot. Compared with the labor force as a whole, in fact, their level of job satisfaction can be described as relatively high: Table 8.6 shows that 48.5 percent of newsmen compared with 45.2 percent of the (1962) labor force said they were "very satisfied" with their jobs, while just 12.9 percent of the former compared with 17.0 percent of the latter indicated some degree of overall dissatisfaction.

It should be noted at this point that the two measures of employment satisfaction to be discussed in this section—dispositions about remaining with current employers and estimates of overall job satisfaction—are closely interrelated: responses to the two questions show a high overlap (gamma = .747), and the percentages who said they hoped to remain with current employers ranged from 87.4 percent among those who were "very satisfied" to just 20.2 percent among those who were either "somewhat" or "very" dissatisfied. Journalists' ratings of their job satisfaction, in other words, would appear to be a fairly good indicator of their intentions to seek new employment.

While in the aggregate newsmen cannot be characterized as an unusually disgruntled lot, the estimates for the sample as a whole tend to mask wide discrepancies in organizational commitment and job satisfaction among newsmen of different ages. To illustrate this variation, Figure 8.1 charts the two measures for newsmen in different age groups, and demonstrates conclusively that both commitment to employers and claims to high job satisfaction are far more prevalent among older than younger newsmen. Intentions to remain with current employers go up from 26.3 percent in the youngest age group to 88.4 percent in the oldest, while the numbers who judge themselves as very satisfied rises from 33.5 to 86.8 percent. Job satisfaction is therefore fairly low among those just starting out in the news media, and increases only as newsmen become established. Both trend lines rise steadily from the twenties through the late forties, show a downward shift during the fifties, and then a renewed upswing after the age of sixty. Although most dissatisfied newsmen are young, it is not uncommon for journalists well along in their careers to become disenchanted with their jobs, their employers, or both. The timing of this downward shift would also suggest that disenchantment may occur at the point when newsmen come to realize they have advanced as far in the field or in their organization as they are going to be able to.

Figure 8.1 also indicates that journalists under twenty-five were more likely to be satisfied with their jobs than committed to their employers. In all other age groups, on the other hand, levels of organizational commitment are higher than is the incidence of strong feelings of job satisfaction. Many young journalists thus expect to change their employers even though they may have little fault to find with their jobs. The more general pattern illustrated in these data, however, is for organizational commitments to develop earlier than a strong sense of job satisfaction. By about the age of thirty a majority of newsmen are working for organizations they want to stay with for at least a five-year period, but it is not until nearly forty that a majority can say they are very satisfied with their jobs. It would appear, then, that most newsmen spend their twenties shopping for an organization to work for, and then devote their thirties to working themselves up through positional hierarchies. By the age of forty, more than 80 percent seem content to stay put, and the curve for organizational commitment then flattens out—though it does not reach its highest point (92.4 percent) until later, during the early sixties. The curve for job satisfaction, on the other hand, does not level off in this fashion: apart from the sharp dip in the late fifties, job satisfaction increases continuously throughout newsmen's careers.

It is often claimed that journalism is a field which suffers a heavy attrition of its experienced manpower—some would say of its most promising and talented personnel. The fact that journalists as a group are considerably younger than the labor force as a whole would tend to support at least the first part of this claim. In order to assess the flow of manpower out of journalism, newsmen's employment aspirations will be examined in greater detail. To begin, Table 8.7 estimates the numbers in different age groups who hoped to be employed in various locations in five years. In the sample as a whole, 62.0 percent were committed to their current employers,[11] 21.8 percent were oriented to finding jobs elsewhere in the news media, 6.6 percent hoped they would be employed outside of the news media, 1.4 percent expected to retire, and 8.2 percent were undecided about their employment plans.

Two groups are of particular interest here: those with aspirations to leave the news media and those still undecided about their career plans. Together, these groups make up 14.8 percent of the total sample, about one journalist in seven. Table 8.7 shows that most of these persons come from the younger age groups, though not from the youngest: newsmen with intentions to leave the media are most numerous in the twenty-five to twenty-nine cohort, where they represent 12.9 percent of the age group, while those undecided about their futures are most numerous in the thirty to thirty-four group, where they represent 15.4 percent of the cohort. Together, persons in these categories make up 23.8 percent of newsmen in their late twenties and 21.2 percent of those in their early thirties. Mobility aspirations are highest of all in the under twenty-five group, but only 15.7 percent of journalists that age have questions about remaining in the news media while an actual majority (58.0 percent) hope to change employers within the media. After the early thirties the percentages of potential media dropouts fall—to 14.1 percent in the thirty-five to thirty-nine group and then to 8.2 percent among those in their early forties—and it would appear, therefore, that after the age of thirty-five most newsmen who plan to enter other fields of employment have already done so. It can be concluded that rates of attrition from the media reach their height during the years between twenty-five and thirty-four: between a fifth and a quarter of all journalists this age either decide definitely to leave or question their commitment to remain. This period, then, is clearly the most critical in accounting for manpower loss from the news media: in fact, of all journalists in the uncommitted group, an actual majority (51.2 percent) are found in this age group.

In what ways do these newsmen differ from those committed to remain in the news media? To address this question, Table 8.8 describes four categories of newsmen in the twenty-five to thirty-four age group: "stayers," those who hope to remain with their current employers; "shifters," those who hope to change employers but remain within the news media; media "defectors," those with definite aspirations to seek employment outside the media; and finally, "undecideds," those unsure of where they want to be working in five years. As is evident in the table, these four groups differ in many ways. Rather than discuss these characteristics one at a time, the results will be summarized by presenting a descriptive portait of each group.

(1). *Stayers.* Not surprisingly, this group is overrepresented with women, which perhaps more than anything else reflects the more restricted mobility opportunities of women compared with men in our society. It is somewhat more revealing, however, to discover that stayers are also less likely to be college graduates, less likely to hold graduate degrees, and considerably less likely than other groups to have attended highly selective colleges and universities. Journalism graduates, on the other hand, are relatively numerous among stayers, although not as numerous as they are among shifters. The group also includes a proportionate representation from the broadcast sector and from more prominent news organizations.

Perhaps the main clue to the relative contentment of this group lies in the fact that though their educational credentials tend to be low, their average earnings are above the median for the age group. Stayers are therefore moderately successful journalists, and their commitment to their employers as well as to the field in general can probably be attributed to this fact.

The most striking characteristic of this group, however, is that relatively few hold participant professional values. While 38.4 percent of all newsmen twenty-five to thirty-four are predominantly "participant" in outlook, these values are shared by only 24.4 percent of the stayers. One might wonder whether the relatively favorable economic position of persons in this category may not be a consequence of the fact that the journalistic values they advocate are by and large compatible with the economic goals of news organizations. Newsmen in this category are also the ones most likely to feel they have a great deal of autonomy in their work.

(2). *Shifters.* This group is overrepresented with journalists from the broadcast sector, where rates of job mobility are relatively high, and with journalism majors. The central character of this group, however, seems related more to the fact that while their educational credentials are competitive with the age group in general, their earnings are on the average $559 a year below the median for the age group. Shifters do not seem to be placed well within the industry, since they have the lowest representation of any of the four groups in the nationally prominent news organizations. Shifters, then, are less successful than stayers, a situation which fits perfectly with their orientation to seek different employment within the field.

(3). *Defectors.* Journalists oriented to leaving the news media are most distinguishable by their low incomes. Compared with the age group as a whole, defectors are less likely to have graduated from college, but interestingly, those who do have college degrees were more likely to have obtained them from elite schools. Compared with stayers and shifters, fewer defectors were journalism graduates, more are oriented to participant professional values, and fewer score high on perceived autonomy. Most important, however, defectors are journalists who are not particularly well placed within the industry and whose earnings are low: their disaffection from the news media can probably be understood primarily in these terms.

It should also be noted at this point that only a minority of these newsmen were oriented to leaving the communications field altogether since 56.6 percent identified some branch of the industry other than the news media in which they hoped to be situated in five years. Some 25.6 percent hoped to work either as freelance writers or as writers in other types of organizations, 15.7 percent aspired to nonjournalistic careers in the broadcasting or film industries, and another 7.8 percent hoped to work in public relations or advertising. Among those oriented to other fields were 20.4 percent who mentioned one of the professions, most frequently teaching, 12.2 percent who wanted to enter business, and 2.8 percent who aspired to careers in government or politics. On the whole, most defectors from news-media journalism do not leave the communications field altogether, but move either to editorial or noneditorial positions in other branches of the industry.

(4). *Undecideds.* This group constitutes an enigma, for it contains newsmen who clearly are among the most highly trained and the most successful within the cohort. Undecideds are heavily overrepresented with college graduates, with advanced degree holders, and with graduates from elite colleges and universities. Moreover, average earnings in this group are high— almost $2,000 above the median for the age group—and more than a quarter (25.7 percent) work for nationally recognized news organizations. By all objective criteria, this group represents an elite among younger newsmen. Why, then, should these persons be so indecisive about remaining in the field? While a definitive answer to this question cannot be offered, the figures in the two bottom rows of the table suggest one explanation: namely, that these newsmen experience a considerable gap between their professional ideals and their opportunities to pursue these ideals in their work. Of the four groups, undecideds are by far the most strongly committed to participant professional values, yet they are also the group least likely to report a high level of editorial autonomy. Since in the sample as a whole participant values and perceived autonomy were found to be negatively related ($r = -.137$), it is not unlikely that newsmen oriented to this style of doing journalism either do experience more editorial constraints or at least feel that they do. In any event, the reluctance of these newsmen to commit themselves to long-term careers in the news media may very well result from frustration over their inability to pursue the canons of journalistic excellence to which they are so strongly committed. Newsmen in this group are also highly trained, of course, and may therefore have more real career alternatives open to them. This in turn would enable them to remain uncommitted for a longer time. Whether these journalists eventually become stayers or shifters rather than defectors is impossible to say, but the results do confirm that many of the best trained, best situated, and perhaps most skilled young newsmen in the field today are at least potential dropouts from the news media.

These results indicate that concerns regarding the flow of talented manpower out of the news media are not unfounded. Moreover, while a good share of the job mobility journalists manifest can probably be attributed directly to economic opportunities, the data suggest that it may be other sources of dissatisfaction which lead some of the more qualified young newsmen to leave the field. It is quite clear that those who commit themselves early to long-term careers in the news media think very differently about journalism than do those who do not. While ultimately it may be economic considerations which catalyze final decisions to defect, strains between professional ideals and organizational expectations do seem to weaken the commitment of some of the best young newsmen.

It is also clear from these results that graduates from journalism schools are more likely to develop a long-term career commitment to the news media than are college graduates from other backgrounds. When the percentages are calculated in the opposite direction, for example, it is found that 80.3 percent of all journalism school graduates compared with just 68.0 percent of graduates from other fields fall into the committed group (stayers plus shifters). While this may imply only that persons who decide early on careers are more likely to remain committed to them, it is also possible that formal training in journalism better socializes newsmen to the kinds of work norms which will be expected of them in the news media. It is also possible, of course, that because of their more specialized training, journalism school graduates have fewer career alternatives open to them by the time they reach mid-career stages.

This part of the discussion concludes on an anomalous note: when rates of commitment to the news media are calculated for twenty-five- to thirty-four-year-old newsmen with different amounts of formal schooling, it became clearly evident that levels of commitment decrease steadily as educational credentials increase. These results are reported separately in Table 8.9, where the proportions of stayers and shifters within the groups are seen to vary from 59.5 percent among advanced degree holders to 89.2 percent among those with no college experience at all. To the extent that formal educational credentials can be considered a valid indicator of the quality of manpower in a field, then, one can conclude only that journalism is an occupation in which the most talented personnel are the ones most likely to leave.

Sources of Job Satisfaction and Dissatisfaction

This chapter concludes with an assessment of the sources of job satisfaction and dissatisfaction among newsmen. To begin, Table 8.10 relates job satisfaction with a variety of personal and job characteristics of newsmen in two age groups. Five sets of factors are differentiated here: background and personal characteristics, community and organizational characteristics, job functions and status positions, characteristics of the work milieu, and finally, professional values. Although none of the figures reported here represent particularly strong relationships, the results do illustrate the types of factors which are both related and unrelated to newsmen's morale.

(1). *It is evident that standards of professional practice within the work setting are of considerable importance to newsmen.* Within both age groups the strongest correlates of job satisfaction are the feelings newsmen have regarding professional standards within the work milieu. Among those under forty, job satisfaction is related most strongly to opinions regarding how good a job one's news organization does in informing the public, while for those forty and older the strongest correlate is the amount of professional respect newsmen have for the person they report to within their organization.[12] Standards of journalistic excellence are therefore of considerable salience to the morale of working newsmen, and would seem to be more important even than concrete rewards and benefits. Newsmen who respect the organizations they work for and the editors they report to are the ones who are happiest with their employment situation.

(2). *Job satisfaction is also related to the editorial constraints under which newsmen work.* Section D of Table 8.10 includes several measures of the freedom reporters and editorial writers feel they have over their work, items 14 and 19 focusing on control over the selection of assignments, and items 15 and 18 on editorial freedom in the preparation of news stories and editorials. In all of these cases positive relationships are evident between autonomy and morale.[13] From a comparison of the sizes of these relationships in the two age groups, however, we would conclude that control over assignments is of greater

significance to older than to younger newsmen. This is particularly true for reporters, where the correlations are .162 and
.256, respectively, for the two age groups. Other realities of the
newsroom, on the other hand, appear to have stronger effects
on the morale of younger journalists. For example, the quality
of the editing reporters feel their work is subjected to is the
second strongest correlate of job satisfaction—in this case of
dissatisfaction—among younger newsmen (r = −.305), but is of
much lesser salience to those over the age of forty (r = −.085).
Deadline pressures show a similar pattern of effects.

These results suggest that with the passage of time newsmen
become more accepting of deadline pressures and of the news-
processing realities of media journalism, but at the same time
become less tolerant of constraints over the selection of assignments. Deadlines, improper editing, and lack of control over the
selection of work are displeasing to virtually all newsmen, but
veterans in the field seem more accepting of the former constraints while younger newsmen are more tolerant of the latter.

(3). *Concrete rewards and benefits are by no means irrelevant
to morale, but seem to be more salient to younger newsmen
than to older.* Part C of Table 8.10 indicates a moderate positive
relationship between income and job satisfaction among
younger newsmen (r = .171), but virtually no association at all
among those over forty (r = .041). Low earnings are therefore a
definite source of dissatisfaction to younger journalists. By
about the age of forty, however, it would appear that most of
those who are unhappy because of their economic prospects
have already departed the news media for other spheres of
employment.

Positive relationships are also evident between job satisfaction and the level of managerial or administrative status one has,
though it is clear that these relationships are weak. Nonetheless,
while earnings are more salient than positional status to the
morale of younger newsmen, the reverse is the case among veterans in the field. More generally, then, these data provide little
support for claims that newsmen lose interest in their jobs when
they take on administrative duties and move out of news gathering. Although a slightly negative relationship between job satisfaction and the amount of editing or news processing one does
is found among older newsmen, job satisfaction is completely
unrelated to the amount of reporting newsmen do.

(4). *Newsmen oriented to neutral professional values tend to be more satisfied than those committed to participant journalism.* Although the relationships are not particularly strong, part E of Table 8.10 indicates that levels of job satisfaction are related positively with holding neutral values, and negatively with holding participant values. This suggests that newsmen oriented to investigative, analytic, and advocacy reporting may find it more difficult to put their professional ideals into practice than do newsmen who define their role in more neutral terms. As such, these relationships can be interpreted as a reflection of antagonism between organizational and professional definitions of journalistic responsibility. From a bureaucratic perspective, for example, it could be argued that the interests of a news organization are served best by a defensive posture toward news—by strict adherence to the canons of objective reporting and caution in treating topics of potential controversy. This approach to journalism conflicts head-on with the self-images of newsmen oriented to participant professionalism, of course, and it is this arena of tension which accounts for their generally lower morale.

(5). *Job satisfaction is somewhat higher among women than among men.* Given the discrepancy in earnings between the sexes and the generally inferior status position of women in the news media, one might well expect levels of morale to be lower among women. Such is not the case, however, and the correlations in part A of the table indicate slightly higher levels of job satisfaction among women in both age groups. Although only the relationship in the older age group can be interpreted as significant statistically ($r = -.094; P < .001$), these results are of substantive interest, and as such merit further discussion.

It has been postulated by Lerner (1963) and others that levels of satisfaction in a population are a function of the relationship between achievements and aspirations—the ratio of rewards to wants. Persons who realize minimal achievements may nonetheless be satisfied with their situation if their wants are also low, and likewise, those who obtain greater rewards may still be dissatisfied if their aspirations exceed their accomplishments. This frame of reference suggests that the lower job satisfaction found among men, an advantaged group in the news media, may be due to higher expectations regarding concrete rewards, and some evidence is available from the study to support this interpretation. For example, when asked to define various elements of a good job in their field, 52.4 percent of men compared with just 38.7 percent of women stressed the importance of opportunities for advancement within an organization, while 28.7 percent of men and 15.3 percent of women said pay was very important. Expectations regarding positional status and monetary rewards are in fact higher among men than women, and the observed sex differences in job satisfaction can probably be explained by this fact.[14]

(6). *Newsmen with the strongest educational credentials tend to be the most dissatisfied.* Although the relationships are again modest,[15] the presence in both age groups of negative relationships between job satisfaction and years of schooling and between job satisfaction and college selectivity indicates that it is newsmen who come to the media with the strongest educational backgrounds who are the ones most likely to become disenchanted with what they find there.

(7). *Finally, levels of job satisfaction do not vary much within news organizations of different types, but older newsmen in the broadcast media clearly are more dissatisfied than their counterparts elsewhere in the industry.* An interesting reversal may be noted in part B of Table 8.10: whereas younger newsmen in the broadcast media seem somewhat more satisfied with their lot than their counterparts located elsewhere, levels of job satisfaction among persons over forty can definitely be said to be higher among print journalists. Why this reversal should occur is not altogether clear. One possibility is that while younger broadcast newsmen may enjoy relatively high incomes for their age, there may actually be fewer avenues for late career advancement open to broadcast journalists than to those in the print sector. One cannot typically advance into the higher administrative echelons of broadcast organizations and at the same time retain journalistic responsibilities, and older broadcast newsmen may thus feel more blocked in their chances for professional advancement. If so, this would account for their comparatively low morale.

Other characteristics of news organizations appear to have little bearing on job satisfaction—at least when examined singly. There is a hint that newsmen who work in smaller communities, for smaller news organizations, and for more prominent news organizations may be somewhat more satisfied with their circumstances, but all of these relationships are marginal. At the same time, however, these organizational characteristics are closely interrelated with one another, and this may obscure their independent effects on job satisfaction. For example, the influence of organizational prominence on morale may not be represented accurately by the zero-order relationships since virtually all prominent news organizations are also large and are located in large cities.

Multivariate Analysis of Job Satisfaction

Since other correlates of job satisfaction reported in Table 8.10 may also be confounded by the presence of secondary relationships—such as between autonomy and organization size, or between sex and positional status or income—it is important to try to estimate the net effects on job satisfaction of each of the factors reviewed in the previous discussion. Table 8.11 therefore combines seventeen variables to predict levels of job satisfaction. In this regression analysis, individual measures of autonomy have been replaced by scores on the Index of Perceived Autonomy, college selectivity is omitted so as to include both college graduates and nongraduates in the estimates, and two additional controls—chronological age and professional age—have been added in order to account for age variation within the two subgroups. Table 8.11 orders the predictors according to the independent contribution each makes to levels of job satisfaction.

From these results it is clear that even in combination the factors under consideration here cannot be said to *determine* job satisfaction among news-media journalists. In total, the seventeen predictors explain just 24.6 percent of the variance in job satisfaction among younger newsmen, and just 33.9 percent among those forty and older. At the same time, however, it can be concluded that a sizable number of these factors do contribute either positively or negatively to newsmen's morale,[16] and that most of the interpretations made in the previous section are supported by the results of the regression analysis. The results confirm that feelings regarding professionalism within the job milieu are the strongest single predictors of job satisfaction; that professional autonomy has an important bearing on morale; that earnings, deadline pressures, and professional values all predict job satisfaction better among younger than older newsmen; and that men—and particularly older men—are more likely than women to be dissatisfied. The most important new information to emerge from the analysis has to do with the effects of organizational characteristics on job satisfaction. With all other factors controlled, organizational prominence emerges as the second strongest predictor of morale among older journalists, while organization size is the sixth strongest predictor within that age group. Both of these influences are of lesser salience to younger newsmen, although the same general pattern of effects is found within the under-forty group, too. It is clear that newsmen are happier when they work for organizations which command some degree of visibility and respect within the professional community, and that all other things considered, journalists much prefer to work in smaller more intimate settings. This latter finding supports results reported by Samuelson (1962).

Summary

News-media journalism is an occupational sphere marked by high rates both of interorganizational labor turnover and attrition out of the field. We would estimate that between a fifth and a quarter of experienced young editorial personnel in the news media today seriously question their commitment to remain in the field. More important, perhaps, it would appear to be the most qualified young journalists who most seriously entertain thoughts of leaving. Moreover, dissatisfaction within this group does not seem to stem from economic grievances alone: to be sure, those who actually do depart may well be attracted away by superior economic opportunities, but job dissatisfaction for many young newsmen has to do more with professional considerations—discrepancies between journalistic ideals and day-to-day practices. It is younger newsmen who are affected most strongly by the competing expectations of professional and organizational definitions of journalistic responsibility, and it is younger newsmen oriented to participant professionalism who find the field least satisfying. Perhaps the crux of the manpower dilemma within the news media today is that the most promising and well-trained young persons being attracted into the field are inspired by an image of professional practice which in large part is incompatible with organizational realities.

News-media journalism is also a field marked by tremendous variation in levels of economic remuneration, although the variance in earnings can be accounted for largely by conventional influences—experience on the job, regional prosperity, market size, and job functions. But there are also marked differences in earnings between the sexes which cannot be attributed to any of these factors, or to differences in objective qualifications. We did not explore whether other minorities also experience differential economic treatment in the news media, and the reason we did not is that groups such as blacks or Latinos are represented so sparsely to begin with. There can be little question, however, but that the American news media levy a substantial surtax against their distaff professionals.

This discussion concludes the review of the personal characteristics and working world of news-media journalists, and completes the presentation of results from the survey of editorial personnel in the mainline news media. Before presenting conclusions of the study, however, the nature of journalistic manpower within a different media sector, that realm known popularly as the underground press, will be considered.

Notes

1. Before asking for financial data, respondents were reminded that all information collected in the survey would be confidential, and that neither persons nor organizations would be identified by name in the study reports. This reassurance was repeated since during the pretest interviews several newsmen were reluctant to divulge their incomes, some saying it was against the policy of their organization to make such information public. Just how widespread a practice this is within the field is not altogether clear, but in the survey itself 12.6 percent did decline to share this information with the interviewers—the highest refusal rate for any question in the interview. The distribution of incomes reported in Table 8.1, then, covers only seven out of eight of the newsmen who were interviewed, and coupled with the overall noncompletion rate of 15.3 percent in the survey means that incomes can be estimated only for about three-quarters of the persons originally selected in the sample (1 - .126 X 1 - .153 = .740),

2. The census figures are estimated from a 5 percent sample of "editors and reporters," while our own are based on a 6.45 percent representation of media "elites" and a 2.56 percent sample of rank-and-file journalists.

3. The median for women twenty-five to sixty-four in this category was just $7,172.

4. Average earnings were $14,095 among those employed in news organizations cited most often for their prominence by other journalists, and were just $9,699 among those in organizations not cited at all.

5. The difference in earnings between men and women twenty-five to sixty-four in professional and technical occupations in 1969 was $5,065. Source: U.S. Bureau of the Census, 1973b, pp. 2, 242.

6. Men in the media do have higher educational qualifications than women: 60.0 percent of men and 50.7 percent of women are college graduates; 8.4 percent of men and 6.6 percent of women hold graduate degrees; and just 12.6 percent of men compared with 19.7 percent of women have had no college training at all.

7. In Chapter 2 we noted that the median ages of men and women were 36.3 and 39.4 years, respectively. In spite of being younger, however, men have slightly more experience in the news media, an average (median) of 10.1 years compared with 8.2 years for women.

8. For documentation of these assertions as well as a full discussion of the status of women in the news media, see William W. Bowman, "Distaff Journalists: Women as a Minority Group in the News Media" (Ph.D. dissertation, Department of Sociology, University of Illinois at Chicago Circle, 1974).

9. Source: U.S. Bureau of the Census, 1971, Table 505, p. 318.

10. The precise phrasing of the two questions was as follows: (A) Do you hope to be working for the same organization five years from now, or would you prefer to be working somewhere else by then? (B) All things considered, how satisfied are you with your present job—would you say very satisfied, fairly satisfied, somewhat dissatisfied, or very dissatisfied?

11. When those who expect to retire are omitted from the calculations, the percentage who hope to remain with their current employers goes up to 62.9, as reported at the beginning of this section.

12. Samuelson (1962) also notes the significance of relations between newsmen and their editors. Four factors which differentiated a sample of newsmen employed in daily papers from a sample who had left were (a) prospects for the future, (b) estimates of the prestige derived from newspaper work, (c) attitudes regarding the quality of leadership in the organization, and (d) pay levels.

13. It can be added that scores on the Index of Perceived Autonomy were also related positively with job satisfaction. Among younger newsmen the correlation was .178, and among older, .156. While this indicates that professional autonomy is important to newsmen of all ages—and perhaps even more important to younger newsmen than to older—we will note in the text that the freedom to *select* assignments is more salient to older journalists.

14. For a fuller development of this argument, see Bowman (1974).

15. Three of the four values are statistically significant, however. Within both age groups the probability that the relationship between years of schooling and job satisfaction occurred by chance is less than .001. For college selectivity the relationship among older newsmen is significant at the .01 level, but among younger journalists it is not significant.

16. Among younger newsmen the first eleven variables listed—and among older newsmen the first fourteen—can be said with greater than .99 confidence to have independent effects on job satisfaction.

9
Journalists in the Alternative Media

Over the past decade what is generally referred to as the "underground press" has become a highly visible source of news and information for a portion of our population. If we live in metropolitan centers around the country, it is not an uncommon sight to see young vendors hawking the underground papers on the street corners of downtown areas. We also see these publications on newsstands next to our daily papers—and those not just from our own cities but from distant population centers as well. National distribution brought wide visibility to a number of these publications: *Rolling Stone*, the Berkeley *Barb*, the *L.A. Free Press*, and *The Great Speckled Bird* were all at one time readily available at our local newsstands.

This increased attention encouraged us to seek out and interview journalists working in this branch of the media. Other studies of the underground press—and there are many—have emphasized the relation of these media to social movements and have highlighted some of the more flamboyant personalities in the general underground movement. How the technology of the offset press made possible the proliferation of these media, the political and social climate which gave rise to them, and the role of the radical press in historical perspective are all common themes in recent works on the underground media.[1] Yet the same gap that existed in the literature on mainstream journalism is also found lacking in treatment of the underground, and little is known about the social characteristics or work activities of those who produce the content of these media. This section of the study tries to fill that gap.

Identifying Alternative Media and Their Personnel

"Underground" is a misnomer for the types of media of concern to us here. First of all, a truly underground medium would have an unknown source and the identities of its producers would not be readily ascertainable. Examples of these types of media do exist, of course, as there have been several instances in recent years in which large corporations have come under attack from "underground company newsletters" produced by employees who remain nameless for obvious reasons.[2] These are true underground media, but since they are ad hoc special interest publications and are typically short-lived, they do not really qualify as public communication media. The legendary "pirate" radio stations, operating beyond the United States territorial limits, would be near counterparts of underground media in the broadcast sector. All of these media fall beyond the scope of concern here, but their existence is noted in order to delimit bona fide "underground" media.

The media studied here are those popularly referred to as "underground" but whose locations and producers are readily identifiable from mastheads and other accessible information sources. These media are best termed "alternative," since in the eyes of both their producers and consumers they provide a content which is distinctly different in perspective and style from that offered in the mainstream media. For the most part, these media cater to "counterculture" tastes both in their symbolic and informational content. The running record of society they provide would be labeled radical, revolutionary, or antiestablishment by outsiders, and many would say that they reflect the discontent of some segment of our society, particularly the young. These media are alternative in another sense, too, in that they constitute a very different entry route into journalism. Although in the main study we did not interview any newsmen who had had extensive experience in the alternative media, examples of such career lines do exist—as in the case of one Chicago *Daily News* feature writer who had worked for *The Paper* in Lansing, Michigan, for *The Seed* in Chicago, and as the Chicago correspondent for *Rolling Stone* before joining the *Daily News.*

Data for this part of the study were collected by means of interviews and participant observation conducted by William Bowman in four metropolitan centers—San Francisco, Chicago, Detroit, and New York. This field work was carried out in two stages between March and August, 1971. In the first phase, contacts were established with a small group of alternative newspapers in these centers, and additional organizations and personnel were then added from the nominations of those already contacted. The basic plan for locating alternative media personnel was a snowball sampling strategy utilizing the networks of informal contacts extant among alternative news people. As we were to discover, informal networks of professional contacts are every bit as well developed among underground journalists as they are among those in the mainstream, and it was not difficult to compile a roster of eligible organizations and personnel in this manner. Ultimately the selection of organizations and personnel was based on reputational criteria: those media generally considered to be underground or alternative and whose representatives did not reject this labeling of their activities were the ones selected for study.

Representatives of the underground papers were also able to identify news people working in broadcast media considered to be underground or alternative. Most of these persons were employed at radio stations of the type known as "progressive rock" format stations, though we were interested only in news and public affairs personnel working in these stations. Other leads to alternative broadcast newsmen were provided by *Earth News Service*, a broadcast news service based in San Francisco which distributed a daily news packet to more than a hundred subscribers in the country at large. None of these broadcast organizations could be called underground by any stretch of the imagination: all are subject to external governmental controls, and many are owned by or affiliated with large broadcasting corporations, such as *Metromedia* or *ABC-FM*.

During the initial phase of the field work, our main goals were to establish contacts, list potential respondents, and neutralize any suspicions alternative news people might have based on previous experiences with snooping social scientists. As it turned out, our concerns in this latter regard were unfounded and we encountered no systematic reluctance to participate in the study. More than sixty organizations were contacted during this phase of the field work, and a roster of personnel of approximately the same number was drawn up for subsequent interviewing. During the short interval between the two field periods, however, substantial numbers of potential respondents were lost to us either because of personal moves or because of the demise of the paper for which they worked. In fact, between a quarter and a third of our original manpower pool had turned over within a three-month period—as valid an indicator as any of the high degree of instability within this sector of the media. These persons had dispersed widely in the interim: some had found their way into other media, both mainstream and alternative; some were rumored to be establishing new publication ventures in other cities; but the bulk had simply become missing persons on the underground scene. Thus while we encountered no significant personal antipathy to the study, the high level of manpower turnover in this sector proved to be genuinely problematic, and we were able to complete interviews with just thirty news people representing ten different organizations in the four locations.

This sparse yield caused us to reassess our goals for this part of the study. While our original plan had been to replicate the main survey on a small sample of news people from the alternative media, it quickly became clear that the persons we were interviewing were not strictly representative of the alternative sector. In the first place, our "sample" was overrepresented with those situated in the more stable sectors of the alternative media since the organizations they worked for had survived longer than most alternative media do. Moreover, it was also clear that the people we had reached were a kind of elite within the alternative stratum. Many were persons who had been singled out by others as leaders within the alternative press, and many were employed by the news services which supply written copy and other content to the rest of the alternative media. Rather than represent these persons as a sample in the strict sense of that term, we will refer to them as "spokespersons" for the alternative media. Our choice of neutral gender here is deliberate, in deference to the heightened consciousness to issues of sexism among alternative news people. There are "people" in the alternative media, but no "gals" or "dudes," and no consistent sex role differentiation as to editorial functions. Our respondents are spokespersons in another sense, too, since we discovered that they were virtually singular in purpose and perspective, and that most were personally committed to the same alternative life-style as their audiences. To be sure, these persons claimed to speak only for themselves, but we did not have to go far beyond them to find others with similar opinions and values: what these persons had to say could be heard in similar settings all over the country.

The Scope of Alternative Media

Though our inquiry is limited geographically, some effort will be made to estimate the number of persons involved in the production of these media in the country at large. Gathering data from which to make such estimates proved to be problematic from the outset. Although all of the broadcasting organizations defined here as alternative are listed in the FCC *Broadcasting Directory*, only the most prominent and long-standing underground papers, such as *The Village Voice*, appear in published directories such as *Ayer's Guide*. Private lists of underground papers are available,[3] however, and these together with subscription lists from underground news services gave us some basis for estimating the number of such organizations in existence. The Free Ranger Tribe at the *Underground Press Syndicate*, a clearinghouse of news, information, subscriptions, and advertising, listed fifty-two foreign and 130 domestic newspapers as members in the summer of 1971. Membership in this service spanned thirty-three states and the District of Columbia. *Liberation News Service*, sometimes described as the *UPI* of the underground, claimed a total of 537 domestic and 101 foreign subscribers as of April, 1971, though these numbers included several mainstream news media. When the *Liberation News Service* sold its 10,000-volume library of back issues to Amherst College in the fall of 1971, however, it contained over 650 different publications, living and dead. And as indicated earlier, *Earth News Service*, which was affiliated with *Earth Magazine*, now defunct, claimed over 100 subscriber stations on both the AM and FM bands as of March, 1971.[4] In addition to these sources, our spokespersons were able to identify additional publications appearing on no lists or in no directories. One general problem in undertaking a census of underground press organizations is that it is virtually impossible to pin down the exact number in existence at any single moment in time. The underground publishing scene changes almost on a daily basis, and the average life span of an underground newspaper is probably well under a year.

Other types of alternative media which have appeared in recent years include the new journalism reviews, exemplified by the *Chicago Journalism Review* and New York's (*More*). Although the content of these media is submitted in large part by newsmen employed in the mainstream media, these publications do maintain a small nucleus of full-time staff. During the early seventies there may have been as many as twenty of these publications in existence across the United States—from New England to Hawaii.

An often ignored yet increasingly persistent source of news and information, albeit for a highly specialized audience, is the high school underground press. These publications, which may number 1,000 at any one point in time, have their own alliances in the *High School Independent Press Service* (HIPS) and the *Cooperative High School Press Syndicate* (CHIPS). Though we have no more recent information, in 1968 HIPS claimed 400 paid subscribers nationally. John Birmingham (1970), the former editor-publisher of an alternative high school paper, notes that these publications are found not only in regular four-year high schools, but in junior highs and occasionally in elementary schools as well. Repression, lack of funds, and the constant graduation of editors make the half-lives of these publications very short indeed, and most ultimately disappear on graduation day, much to the relief of parents and school officials. We mention these media not to inflate our figures—they will not be included in the estimates—but to suggest what may represent an emergent training grounds for underground journalists. The existence of these publications means that the age when one can begin to gain experience in alternative journalism has been extended downward. One of our respondents, in fact, claimed to have started his own neighborhood paper at the age of nine.

Other sectors of the alternative media scene which are sometimes overlooked are the underground comics, which have become more oriented to social issues in recent years, the sex liberation press, best represented by *Screw* magazine, and documentary film and videotape media, possibly best represented by *Newsreel*, a national film organization, or *Top Value TV*, which produces documentaries for television. In 1972, there were at least six major underground comic book publishers in the United States, most located in the San Francisco Bay area or in the Midwest.

One further clue to the vitality of the alternative press in contemporary America is the appearance of its own version of a

Reader's Guide. By 1971, the *Alternative Press Index* compiled by the Radical Research Center at Carleton College in Minnesota, was indexing articles from more than seventy-five alternative publications. These services were offered on a quarterly basis to individuals, movement groups, libraries, educational institutions, and what they termed "military-corporate institutions," with higher subscription rates for the latter three.

In total we estimate that during the early seventies the alternative media sector in the United States consisted of between 600 and 1,000 newspapers and magazines (excluding high school papers), nearly 200 radio stations, and approximately 200 other enterprises, including comics, press services, syndicated columns, and journalism reviews. A conservative estimate of the national audience reached by these media would be ten million persons, the same figure estimated by *CBS News* in the 1970 documentary on the print sector of the alternative media.[5] Although the *CBS* figure does not take radio audiences into account, we would guess that these listeners for the most part are the same persons who read the underground papers.

Estimating the full-time manpower employed in the alternative sector also presents myriad difficulties, and our efforts at precision in this regard are admittedly presumptuous. Alternative media are structured much more loosely than mainstream news organizations: job titles are not universally employed, and responsibilities for the various tasks involved in putting together the final product are often shared equally by all concerned. Moreover, the content of many of these publications comes largely from contributors in the wider community. Nonetheless, there are many persons in the alternative media whose only employment and only source of income is that derived from their work in these organizations, and it is this pool of editorial manpower that we will attempt to delimit here.

Staff sizes varied markedly in the sixty-odd organizations we contacted. They ranged from lone persons in some radio stations to staffs of thirteen and fourteen, respectively, in an underground news service and a public-broadcasting television station. Virtually all radio news staffs consisted of either one or two full-time persons—which is not much different from non-network radio stations in the mainstream. The radio news service, too, was produced almost exclusively by the efforts of two full-time persons. Although one alternative newspaper consisted of just two full-time personnel—a paper described by its

editor as a "community newspaper" relying on editorial contributions from the community at large in a roughly participa-
tory journalism scheme—most underground papers employ
somewhat larger staffs. We would estimate the average size of
these papers to be six full-time editorial persons, while the average alternative radio station employs 1.5 persons. Estimating
staff sizes in other alternative media is even more hazardous
since this category includes various and sundry enterprises, but
a fair estimate would be that they employ four full-time persons
on the average. Applying these figures to the estimated number
of organizations in these categories results in a full-time labor
pool of approximately 5,900 persons in the alternative media as
of the early seventies (see Table 9.1). This would suggest, then,
that the alternative media currently employ fewer than a tenth
the number of personnel employed in the mainstream news
media. We should re-emphasize, however, that probably three to
four times this number of persons contribute editorially to
these media on a part-time, freelance, or occasional basis. We
can really go no further with these estimates, which are already
speculative, but we can conclude with some confidence that the
alternative media today provide employment for sizable numbers of persons who think of themselves as full-time journalists.

Organizational Contexts

Traditional hierarchical structures are rare in the alternative
media, and even where they exist the status differentiation
between executives and staffers is less marked than it is in the
mainstream media. Informality is the rule rather than the exception in the day-to-day world of alternative journalism, though
this relaxation of formal procedures can probably be attributed
as much to the size of the organizations in question as to the
values of their functionaries. Editorial control does operate
through decisions to include or exclude material, but there is
little editing in these media, and few of the articles, reports,
interviews, or broadcasts are ever processed by persons other
than their original producers. Decisions to include material are
often based on available space rather than on the merits of a
piece—though this is by no means dissimilar from the use of
filler in the mainstream media, nor as Gieber (1956) has noted,
from the day-to-day routines of wire editors in small-city
dailies. Nonetheless, news people in the alternative sector seem

to experience very few overt editorial constraints. There is little negotiation between reporters and editors over assignments. Deadlines are also more relaxed in the alternative media. Due perhaps to the periodicity of most print media in this sector, there seems a common assumption that "there's always next week" to get a piece into print, and few of the articles have the same built-in immediacy that journalists in daily papers experience in meeting the deadlines of the various editions. In fact, many journalists in the alternative media use the term "timeless" to describe the content of their work.

By far the most interesting and complex organizational schemes in the alternative media are the cooperatives and collectives. One observer at the Alternative Media Conference held at Goddard College in summer, 1970, noted that fully a quarter of the organizations represented there were run on the collective scheme or were an outgrowth of communal living.[6] Examples of alternative collectives include *The Great Speckled Bird* in Atlanta, *Liberation News Service* in New York, *The Berkeley Tribe*, and the *Fifth Estate* in Detroit. These are new structures in the media, unprecedented in the mainstream. Though *Time* and large daily newspapers often employ team reporting, the extent of their cooperative efforts does not extend to the limits found in the collectives. In these organizations all members have responsibility for major decisions, particularly on policy issues. Other alternative publications, though they may have positions called "editors," are in fact run so informally as to resemble the collective scheme. *Creem* in Detroit is a case in point.

Some of the collectives are extremely complex in organization. *Liberation News Service*, for example, is divided into three departments—editorial, printing, and graphics—with a rotating "troika" leadership, one member from each of the departments being responsible for two weeks at a time for the production of the twice-weekly news packets distributed to members. Decisions regarding the inclusion or exclusion of materials are made by these three members of the collective during their periodic service as managers. Collective meetings are also held at least once a week in spite of the existence of these elaborate administrative arrangements, and many other editorial decisions are made at these meetings. The members of the *Liberation News Service* collective admit that their organization structure is cumbersome at times, but they also feel that their sacrifice in time and energy is well worth the outcome: if the end product is good, all share the glory, and if they are less than satisfied, all share the blame.

Despite the absence of formal editorial controls, there is a high level of interdependence in the production of material throughout the alternative media. Rough drafts of copy are shared with fellow staff members, and are read for suggestions and comments as a matter of regular practice. Where supervisory relationships exist, they tend to be quite informal. If assignments are made by an editor, the directives are usually more on the order of suggestions, "Why don't you cover. . . ." More commonly, however, it is the responsibility of each staff person to develop his or her own material. In some cases areas of expertise are carved out informally over time, so that if one staff member comes upon an item of interest to someone else, the information is passed along.

It is clear that journalists in the alternative media have a great deal of freedom in selecting and writing their stories, and nearly all of our respondents presented this view of their activities. The only expressed constraints on journalistic freedoms were economic ones. There were many instances in which events could not be covered due to lack of resources, time, or staff, and we were frequently told anecdotes of stories which were missed because people could not hitch a ride to the places where the events occurred.

In general, economic constraints severely restrict the surveillance activities of these news organizations, and few are able to retain their own correspondents or news bureaus. On the other hand, there is much information sharing among alternative media, and it is not uncommon for friends in all parts of the country to send copy or information to these papers. News reports, stories, and reprints are widely shared among alternative news organizations in a manner reminiscent of the American colonial press (Weisberger, 1961, p. 18). Alternative radio personnel also depend on members of their audiences as sources of news and information, and through these informal networks are sometimes able to scoop the mainstream media. One of our spokespersons told of reporting the invasion of Alcatraz Island by federal authorities before it actually occurred and before any of the other San Francisco media had obtained the story: a Coast Guard enlisted man had phoned in a report of the preparations being made. A similar incident occurred preceding a wildcat strike by Bell Telephone workers when the radio journalist, who also happened to be a union steward for the International Brotherhood of Electrical Workers, was informed by the workers of the action they were about to take. These examples illustrate how being situated in the alternative sector makes one privy to information sources quite different from those available to journalists in the mainstream. The alternative media thus have alternative information nets as well, and these channels often furnish information that would be suppressed in official channels. Alternative news people are usually cut off from official news sources, of course: because they are frequently denied press cards by police departments, they cannot attend press conferences, and they find it difficult to gain access to public officials or their information officers. This is one of the reasons the content they produce may tell a different story than the mainstream's side: their sources of information differ.

In other respects, however, news gathering in the alternative media operates in much the same manner as in the mainstream. Even though their contacts differ, these journalists do establish regular information sources—usually their friends or friends of their friends—and they are very careful to protect these sources in order to maintain them for use in the future. In this regard, the contact system is pretty much a mirror image of the mainstream. The telephone is also an extremely important working tool in the alternative media just as it is in the mainstream, and its insulative qualities are often helpful in gaining access to official news sources: offering a formal title by way of introduction, or calling long distance, may yield much better results than visits in person. Telephone bills are consistently one of the major operating expenses throughout the alternative media.

Many alternative news people have the same "nose for news" and "street sense" that all good reporters are supposed to have, and many apply standard news-gathering conventions to their own work. For example, most feel it is important to check their facts and to try to utilize multiple sources. Telling both sides of a story is not always thought to be necessary, however: as one of our respondents put it, "the mainstream tells one side of the story, we give another."

Certainly one of the main differences between mainstream and alternative journalism is in level of specialization. Although journalists in the alternative media may claim certain topics as informal newsbeats, they are seldom limited to these content areas alone. In this respect they resemble general assignment reporters in the mainstream. Moreover, the job responsibilities of most alternative news people extend far beyond conventional editorial duties, and it is not atypical for them to be involved in the full range of tasks required in production and management. Their duties may involve any or all of the following: keeping books and managing budgets, correspondence, handling subscriptions and advertising, preparing copy and editing it when necessary, designing layout, setting type, and in some cases actual printing, photography and film processing, and transcribing interviews. In the alternative media "clean" and "dirty" work tends to be shared by all, and these duties are more frequently divided up equally than assigned regularly to specific persons. Because of the ever present financial pressures, staff members often work as fund raisers as well, soliciting donations or advertising from whatever sources may be available.

Alternative journalists are not the only ones who display this jack-of-all-trades quality, of course, as this kind of division of labor is often found in weekly papers and other small enterprises in the mainstream media as well. Specialization in journalism as in other fields of endeavor is very much related to size, and is seldom found in alternative journalism because few organizations in that sector are large enough to require or permit such specialization. There is one example of an organization which in its earlier years was popularly called an underground paper but which with growth and success has taken on all of the structural characteristics of large news organizations: that is, *Rolling Stone*. The staff at *Rolling Stone* now numbers close to 100 persons, including correspondents and those who write regular reviews of records, books, and other topics. *Rolling Stone*'s masthead lists advertising, circulation, subscription, traffic and marketing directors, and recent ads for personnel at these levels read much like those found in newspapers and trade magazines for account executives in advertising and marketing firms. Interestingly, the editor of *Rolling Stone*, when contacted, did not consider the publication to be an alternative or underground medium. Indeed, we were told that it had never been a paper of that type, but rather was a "straight" publication simply covering a different type of news than most others. With main offices in San Francisco and bureaus in London, New York, and Los Angeles, it is understandable why the organization might be viewed this way from the inside, even though it might be labeled differently by others. The parent company, Straight Arrow Publishers, Inc., has also branched out into the book-publishing business, and in addition markets a wide variety of youth paraphernalia. But *Rolling Stone* is very much the exception in its success, size, and mode of organization. The remainder of the alternative media may long for this type of expansion, but few are ever likely to achieve it.

Characteristics of Alternative Journalists

The presence of women is a highly noticeable differentiating feature of the alternative media. Although only eleven of the thirty persons we interviewed were women, our respondents confirmed our own observation that the sex ratio is virtually even throughout the alternative sector. In one of the news organizations studied, in fact, it was the policy to maintain a majority of women on the staff, and eight of thirteen staff members were female. Not only are women more prevalent in the alternative media, but also they occupy a status more or less equal to that of men. Women are not relegated to clerical roles or to women's pages in these media—there is no such thing as far as we know—while men become the managers and "star" reporters. One anecdote related to us about the *CBS 60 Minutes* program on the underground press reflects the heightened consciousness of these journalists to issues of sexism: when the CBS news team arrived at the offices of *The Great Speckled Bird*, the staff made sure that the film crew recorded only men at typewriters, thus emphasizing their views on societal norms regarding the place of women in the labor force.

In other respects, however, the characteristics of alternative news people are surprisingly similar to those of journalists in the mainstream. For example, although the people we interviewed were located in equal numbers in the East, the Midwest, and the West Coast, almost half—fourteen of thirty—had had their earliest roots in the Northeast. As in the mainstream, journalists in the alternative media come from the East more often than from anywhere else, and very few come from the South or the West. Moreover, a large majority of our respondents were from middle- and upper-middle-class origins. The occupations of their fathers ranged in status from a migrant laborer to the president of a large industrial firm, but eleven of thirty fathers were professionals, nine more were managers, officials, or proprietors, and a total of twenty-three of the thirty were from the white-collar rather than blue-collar sector of the labor force. Several of the women we interviewed wondered why we did not ask them what their mothers did—pointing to the sex bias in the social scientist's conceptualization and measurement of social class position. In spite of this omission, however, we can conclude that journalists in this sector, like their counterparts in the mainstream, are overrepresented with persons from middle-class beginnings. One difference between journalists in the two sectors, on the other hand, is in their religious backgrounds: eleven of our thirty respondents were from Jewish backgrounds, a considerably higher representation than the 6.4 percent found in the mainstream press.

Perhaps the most striking single characteristic of these journalists is their youthfulness. The median age of the persons we interviewed was twenty-three, and all but six were younger than thirty. Despite their youthfulness, thirteen of these persons were college graduates, and two held advanced degrees—one in education and one in theology, the latter having been pursued as a means of avoiding service in the armed forces. Among the college graduates, five had majored in English, three in social sciences, and one each in communications, philosophy, psychology, chemistry, and international relations. Only one of our respondents had completed a degree in media studies. An important fact about the formal schooling of these journalists was that fourteen were college dropouts, five of whom had begun to study for degrees in journalism or other media specialties but had become disgruntled and had dropped out after two or three years. These people made it clear that they felt the training they were receiving in media studies was less than adequate, and that they had *elected* to "learn by doing" in preference to completing their academic training. Our contention that these media provide an alternative point of entry into media careers would thus appear to have some validity—at least from the standpoint of the motives of the journalists themselves.

None of the preceding demographic variables give much insight as to how or why these journalists arrived in the alternative media rather than the mainstream, and it is not until we examine their politics that this point becomes clear. Only four of our respondents were affiliated with either of the conventional political parties—all four were Democrats—while the remainder described themselves either as unaffiliated, as independents, as "radicals," "revolutionaries," or "communists," or as members of other splinter groups of leftish stripe. When asked to describe their general political and social leanings, twenty of the thirty claimed to be "pretty far to the left," eight said "a little to the left," and only two chose other terms—one describing himself as a "conservative leftist," and the other as "both left and right, depending on the issue." Of the women interviewed, all but one located themselves on the far left. The oppositional stance of these journalists is illustrated well in the following answers to our question on party affiliation:

> I'm not registered. I don't believe in the electoral process.

> I'm a creative or reflective leftist; you are what you do, not what you say.

> I'm a communist in ideological terms, though I'm not a party member.

> I advocate communist revolution.

The degree of like-mindedness among these journalists suggests that political ideology was the primary force which attracted them into the alternative media. A good number spoke of activist involvements during their college years, of working in community organizations or as volunteers in day-care centers and the like. Moreover, for many, ideological commitments seemed to overshadow other identities, including those as professional journalists. From our observations, it was clearly evident that these persons were deadly serious about their work, with few smiles and little frivolity to be found in their often cramped quarters. Staff meetings in these organizations tend to be open and direct, and each point on an agenda is given exhaustive consideration. In spite of their informality, these journalists are very sensitive to the criticisms they receive, particularly those emanating from other alternative media or from audience members. In instances when the mainstream media cite their work, they are overjoyed and feel they have done their job well.

It is worth noting at this point that our respondents are highly reminiscent of the college radicals interviewed by Flacks (1967) at the University of Chicago. His group of antidraft protesters was also largely from upper-middle-class families, with highly educated fathers employed in professional and managerial occupations. Moreover, the protesters were better than average students, and were not social or academic "losers" in any sense. The comparison is remarkable when coupled with the ideological similarities between the two groups. Several of our own respondents could be accurately described as ex-student-protesters who had found in alternative journalism a continuing forum in which to express their discontent.

Political ideology, however labeled, is never hidden in the alternative media. In fact, "being up front" is a matter of principle to most alternative news people. One of our respondents, a radio newsman, had long made it clear to his audience that he adhered to a communist ideology, and argued that as long as people knew this beforehand, what he said in reporting the news would be understood to be from that perspective. This openness is one of the more consistent differences between mainstream and alternative journalism. In the mainstream media, ideological positions of news organizations may be well known, but the personal views of individual newsmen are typically hidden. Moreover, in mainstream news organizations, as noted in Chapter 5, the views of executives and staffers often differ quite markedly. In the alternative media, on the other hand, the ideologies of staffers tend to be consistent with those of management, though this is obviously more true for print than broadcast media since the latter tend to be owned by persons or interests in the straight world. This consistency is highly valued by alternative news people, and would explain why going against the politics of one's organization is felt by many to be a cardinal sin. Even in the broadcast sector, however, alternative news people feel they have a great deal of autonomy over the content of their broadcasts and commentaries. Few noted any disputes with owners, and in one incident reported to us, a journalist was supported by his station after he had reported news derogatory to one of the station's sponsors: when the sponsor objected, he was told by the station manager to take his business elsewhere.

A final indicator of the commitment of alternative news people is that few earn much by way of income. The median income of those interviewed was $35 a week, just a tiny fraction of the annual median of $11,133—$214 a week—in the mainstream media. Eight of those interviewed did earn more than $10,000 a year, and six of these eight were situated in the broadcast sector. The highest salary reported to us was in the $20,000 to $24,000 bracket, and the lowest, aside from that of an editor-publisher who drew no salary at all from his paper, was $22.75 a week plus room and board. Many of those work-ing in the collectives earned room and board in addition to their modest wage, though out of necessity many had to supplement their incomes with other employment. A few were supported by working spouses. It would be the rare person who would be attracted to alternative journalism by the money.

Given the youthfulness of these journalists, few have very extensive work histories to trace. Of the thirty interviewed, four had had no previous full-time jobs whatsoever, and only thir-teen had had prior media experience—seven in other alternative news organizations and six in the mainstream media. Moreover, few of those who had worked outside the media had been employed in jobs which would provide much preparation for doing newswork: the previous jobs they had held were as office or bookstore clerks, teachers, banktellers, a laborer, a longshore-man, a shoe salesman, a kibbutz farmer, a rock group manager, a community mental health worker, and a hospital chaplain. Only one person in the entire group had an employment history which could in any way be described as a "career": our oldest respondent, who was fifty-seven, described himself as a "retired management consultant turned newspaper editor." These results reflect the relatively loose entrance credentials demanded in this sector of the media.

While we have argued that the alternative media function as alternative entry routes for young people aspiring to careers in journalism, it is instructive that only eleven of our respondents, barely a third of the group, had definite aspirations to remain in the news media. Moreover, only three of these people—only one from the print sector—hoped to be working for the same organi-zation in five years. Ten others were undecided about their futures, while the remaining nine were oriented to working out-side of the news media. Within this latter grouping, four wanted to enter teaching, three mentioned community organization work, one hoped to establish a day-care center, and one wanted to raise animals. Just as few of these people had come to the alternative media with journalism backgrounds, only a few fashioned themselves pursuing long-term careers in the field. For many, journalism is seen as a temporary career line, work which is enjoyable for the present but not the focus of a life-time ambition.

Just as in the mainstream media, those journalists who were more established and whose earnings were higher tended to be the ones more committed to long-term careers in media journalism. In addition to their ideological commitment, journalists in the alternative sector are also realists: many seem aware that the organizations they work for may not survive long, and that in the not too distant future they will need to find employment which offers greater security and a more substantial standard of living. Change and mobility are very prominent features of the hopes and plans of these journalists, and this, of course, contributes to the constant labor turnover within this sector of the media. In most cases, alternative papers survive only as long as their founders remain wedded to working in them, and few become institutionalized to the extent of recruiting successive generations of functionaries. This constant turnover is both the strength and weakness of alternative journalism: it would account both for the high level of vitality so evident in these media, and for their lack of stability, development, and persistence.

Despite these orientations, news people in the alternative sector are a surprisingly contented occupational group. Almost two-thirds said that overall they were "very satisfied" with their current jobs, a rate considerably higher than the 48.5 percent found in the main sample. Autonomy, freedom from supervision, the opportunity to help people, and organizational editorial policies were the job aspects which were most important to these people, although interestingly, many also felt that opportunities for developing a reporting specialty were important. By comparison, tangible rewards and benefits—pay, fringe benefits, and job security—were rated less important, though several expressed a need to earn more money to support themselves and their dependents. As with journalists in the mainstream media, news people in the alternative sector are more likely to stress "intrinsic" than "extrinsic" rewards when considering the things about their jobs which are most important to them.

Orientations to Journalism

Alternative news people are prototypical participant journalists, and this theme dominates their perspectives on the professional responsibility of the journalist and on the functions of the news media in a democratic society. Our respondents were virtually unanimous in assigning high importance to investigative, analytic, interpretive, and advocacy functions of the press, and they eschewed journalistic priorities labeled as neutral in Chapter 7.

The salience of the issue of involvement versus detachment was clearly evident in the criticisms alternative news people made of the mainstream media. Two related criticisms were frequently expressed: first, that the news media evade their responsibility by failing to confront social problems in America; and second, that because of their preoccupation with "objectivity" and "detachment," the news media either consciously or unconsciously support the interests of established power groups in the society. The first of these themes is illustrated by the following remarks:

> My criticism amounts to what I call "yellow journalism," that is, emphasizing minor events to cover up real issues, which they ignore. [Respondent 9.]

> The news media are self-serving: all the stories are done in their own formula, answering their own questions, instead of the questions that might be of interest to the public. [Respondent 4.]

> Straight journalism is used to create and support mind-sets in the American public, which prevent coherent analysis of world situations. [Respondent 28.]

> The news media concentrate on "events" to the point of doing damage to "issues." [Respondent 3.]

Alternative news people thus score the mainstream media for their reluctance to explore the "whole truth" or to deal effectively with important social issues. In this regard, their views are similar to those of critics who charge that because of their commitment to objectivity the news media work to undercut any sustained public commitment to deal with social problems. Slater (1970, pp. 16-17), for example, has argued that the media reinforce evasion rather than confrontation: "the TV documentary presents a tidy package with opposing views and an implication of progress. . . . Thus, the ultimate effect of the media is to reinforce the avoiding response by providing an effigy of confrontation and experience." Where alternative news people depart most sharply from their ideological counterparts in the mainstream, however, is that they extend their radical analysis and argue that the mainstream media are not as detached as they claim.

The news media are centralized managers of public consciousness, basically devoted to the preservation of the present order. They collaborate with the interests of the ruling class by displaying only a timid curiosity about social issues, at the same time as our dissatisfaction with our lives skyrockets. [Respondent 18.]

The corporate aspects of the industry and its ties with big business lead to systematic bias and slanting of the news in their own economic interest. [Respondent 14.]

Generally, the media are too straight and uncritical of a number of sacred cows, including the government. [Respondent 5.]

Our respondents jumped at the opportunity to express their views on the concept of objectivity, calling it among other things, "a code word for protecting established interests," and a style of journalism which is "frequently apologetic of the status quo." Most alternative news people use the terms "fairness" and "accuracy" to define responsible journalistic practice, but the meanings of these terms are quite removed from the concept of objectivity in their minds. Most felt that objectivity is not really possible to attain. "We can't pretend to be objective, it's crazy! What we need to do is strive to tell the truth, which isn't necessarily objective [Respondent 15]." Part of being "fair" is being "up front" with one's biases—being honest with audiences, letting them know in advance where one stands, then presenting a point of view and letting them draw their own conclusions.

For the most part, alternative news people doubt that the mainstream press is either objective or truthful, although they feel that young persons entering the field today are more likely than established journalists to share their own definitions of journalistic responsibility: "(Younger journalists) are a lot more prone to question the goals and purposes of their employers; are more prone to question the established authority in the society at large, and are looking more for the chance to foster meaningful social change than for success in the classical American genre [Respondent 18]." These various perspectives highlight the definitions alternative news people make of their own role in society and in journalism. This self-definition includes two main ingredients: an opposition to the status quo, with a readiness to question the legitimacy of any social institution; and a commitment to involvement rather than detachment as journalists. "I think there is an 'old' and a 'new' professionalism. The 'old' try to pull themselves out of the culture to be observers. The 'new' journalist can't remove himself and withdraw his emotions, he can't observe without participating, and he does things because he wants to, not because he has to [Respondent 13]." In keeping with Slater, alternative news people share the view that detachment and objectivity are insulative mechanisms, designed and nurtured by those in power to protect themselves as well as the existing order which favors them. The proper role of the journalist is to become involved, active, critical, and questioning—positions which, of course, are entirely consistent with their own background and experiences as activists and protesters.

Some critics of the alternative media have emphasized the anti-intellectual quality of the underground movement, but from our own contacts with these news people we would reject this characterization. Indeed, a majority of our respondents looked forward to a time when they could continue their education, citing learning interests in terms both of technical competencies (such as photography or video technology) and academic disciplines (such as international relations, ecology, physical and biological sciences, and law). Most of these persons emphasized goals of personal growth and self-development over goals of formal certification, however, and a number voiced their distaste for professional training in journalism, objecting primarily to what they termed the "formula" approach taught in journalism schools. Those who had been employed in the mainstream media before entering the alternative sector felt their previous employers gave preference in recruiting to those with journalism degrees, a priority which they felt brought "technicians" rather than "journalists" into the media. Although not disavowing the importance of formal schooling, our respondents were quite ready to discredit professional training in journalism.

Alternative news people view themselves as the principal exponents of crusading journalism on the contemporary American scene. Many felt that the term "crusading" could no longer be legitimately applied to the mainstream media, and justified their claim by pointing to the numerous issues—protest against the war in Vietnam, concern with the environment, and sexism, to mention the most prominent—which gained visibility first in the alternative media and only subsequently were picked up by the mainstream. In response to charges of professional irresponsibility, alternative news people would reply that it is the mainstream news media which have evaded their social responsibilities, and that it has fallen to the alternative media to advocate needed social change. In this regard, some would define the alternative media as the conscience of the mainstream: "The underground has developed as a conscience for the straight media, bringing out issues and forcing the mainstream to cover them." Promoting necessary social change and putting pressure on the mainstream media to do so are viewed by alternative news people as their most significant contributions to American journalism. Journalists in the alternative sector differentiate themselves from their counterparts in the mainstream primarily on the basis of their greater commitment to social change and their more persistent vigilance in backing important but unpopular social causes.

Summary

Ideology is the cornerstone of alternative journalism. Among the persons interviewed, social, cultural, and political orientations were at the core of decisions both to enter the alternative media and to remain in them, and were a highly visible component of their work, work organizations, and personal lives.

Journalists in the alternative media are oppositional to American society and its culture, and are highly critical of the mainstream news media—which, they feel, ignore or suppress dissent, and serve primarily to protect established interests in the society. These journalists feel that the watchdog role of the press has been forgotten by the established media, and that it has fallen to them to assume this vital journalistic function. In addition to promoting perspectives not available in the mainstream press, they feel they have played an important role in putting pressure on the established media to cover previously ignored or tabooed issues.

Alternative journalists are change oriented, and are committed to active involvement in the pursuit of their ideals. For most, societal goals are more salient than professional ones. Unlike the bulk of their counterparts in the mainstream press, they believe it is proper—indeed essential—to meld their beliefs into their journalism, and as a result values are never far from the surface of their work. Our respondents were "participant" journalists in the extreme, emphasizing substance over technique, interpretation over speed of transmission, and advocacy over neutrality.

News people in the alternative sector are younger than their counterparts in the straight press, and are more likely to be women. Yet there are many other ways in which they resemble mainstream newsmen: they emerge out of the same social strata in American society; come from the same regions of the country; have comparable educational backgrounds; and place greater importance on "intrinsic" than "extrinsic" rewards from their labors. There are also parallels in day-to-day work routines in the two media sectors. Alternative news people are heavily dependent on the telephone in news gathering, and like all newsmen, develop and nourish their information networks. It is significant, however, that the news sources they rely on are not the same ones to which mainstream newsmen are connected. Alternative news people do not believe "objective" journalism is either possible or desirable, but feel they do apply professional standards of fairness and accuracy to their work.

Although the underground press movement in the United States experienced rapid growth during the sixties and early seventies, its future is uncertain. Employment opportunities in alternative journalism are still limited, few organizations survive longer than their first generation of producers, and many of the participants have little or no commitment to careers in journalism. For some, however, these media do represent alternative points of entry into the field, and it is likely that a small number will remain in the journalistic community. Levels of remuneration in these media are submarginal for most, though in the commercially more successful ventures, such as alternative radio, some kind of stable job market would appear to be emerging.

Alternative news media will probably flourish as long as their promoters feel there is a need for them, and currently there are few signs of a declining market for participant journalism in the United States. Yet if events such as the release of the Pentagon papers or those leading to the uncovering of the Watergate saga do in fact herald a shift to a more aggressive establishment press, then it is likely that the alternative media will lose some of their attractiveness for their largely youthful audiences. Perhaps, as their producers believe, the alternative media have already pricked the conscience of the straight media, and their vitality will subside along with the current decline of political radicalism within the youth culture.

Notes

1. For example, see Glessing (1970) or Leamer (1972).

2. Standard Oil and various branches of the Bell telephone system have been subjected to attack from these types of publications. See "Underground Papers Needle the Bosses," *Business Week*, October 9, 1971, p. 86, and "Corporate Life: The Dissenters," *Newsweek*, November 8, 1971, pp. 97-98.

3. For example, William D. Lutz, *Underground Press Directory*, 5th ed., 1970. This directory was available only from Mr. Lutz, P.O. Box 13603, University Station, Reno, Nevada, 89507.

4. The two young men who originally produced *Earth News*, both of whom were interviewed for this study, had, between the time of the interview and this writing, parted company. One of them maintains the *Earth News* operation, while the other has founded his own service for alternative outlets, known as *Zodiac News*.

5. Shown on *60 Minutes*, January 19, 1970.

6. From the field notes of Leonard P. Iaquinta, Communications Institute, Academy for Educational Development, New York.

10

Newsmen and Newswork
in America: Concluding Notes

This study has been concerned with the nature of manpower in the American news media, and with the situation of the individual journalist in an increasingly complex mass communication system. Though our attention here has been on the individual newsman, we in no way mean to diminish the significance for journalism of recent trends in the wider social structure of the news industry. Indeed, any assessment of journalists as an occupational group or of the forces which shape mass news in our society would be incomplete if it failed to take these developments into account.

Many of these changes are familiar, and have been discussed in the literature—the growth of local media monopolies (Nixon, 1968); the emergence of national and regional media chains or "baronies" (Atlantic Editors, 1969); the demise of mass magazines (Welles, 1971); and the impact of offset printing on the community press (Bowers, 1969). These centralizing trends have brought about greater homogenization in the news, have increased the control of national and regional news organizations over local outlets, and have integrated the news media even more firmly within the corporate nexus of American industry.

Journalists today cannot be viewed simply as individual communicators, nor for that matter even as representatives of independent news organizations. A majority of practicing newsmen today—we would estimate about two-thirds—work for organizations which are tied to larger chains, groups, or networks, many of which are controlled ultimately by industrial conglomerates whose principal interests and functions lie outside the field of communications altogether.

Other changes in our society in recent decades have also had their effects on newswork, the most significant of which would have to be the expanding complexity of government and of society more generally. As many have observed, the task of covering the federal government is much more difficult today than it was a half-century ago, and the same could probably be said for science, urban affairs, international relations, and a great many other fields. These developments tax the physical and intellectual resources of the news media. Partly in response to the growing complexity, both the public and private sectors of the economy have institutionalized their own public information machinery, and personnel in these agencies generate an enormous flow of communications to the news media. This has further complicated the social processes by which information enters the news system, and constitutes a new pressure point on the independence of the news media.

Finally, the more recent introduction of computer technology into the news industry (Bagdikian, 1971) heralds a whole new dimension of change, and will further broaden the repertoire of technical skills necessary to do newswork.

Perhaps the most general conclusion to be drawn from the study is how very much modern newswork is a collective enterprise, and how very intricate is the process by which occurrences in the real world come to be translated into news stories. As participants in modern life, we are able to apprehend directly just a tiny fraction of the events which shape our lives: yet to realize that only some proportion of those whose full-time occupation it is to report these events to us are involved first-hand in their observation and evaluation is an even more startling revelation. It is important, then, to know that so many journalists devote the major share of their time and energy to processing and transmitting information structured by others: awareness of this fact should better enable us to evaluate the information the media provide. Mass news is very much an organizational phenomenon, and with increasing centralization in the industry and increasing complexity in newsroom technology, it is likely to become even more so.

Newswork in contemporary America takes place in a variety of organizational environments, and in the course of our analysis we have demonstrated that these settings differ markedly in the types of editorial personnel they recruit and in the kinds of influences they exert on those who work for them. The most visible difference here is between the broadcast and print media. Compared with their counterparts in print journalism, newsmen in broadcasting are younger, are more likely to be men, and are less likely to be college graduates. When these factors are controlled, they also turn out to be better paid. The most striking difference between the sectors, however, is in the comparative stability of their manpower: journalists on the whole are a fairly transient occupation group, but the extent to which this is true is much greater in radio and television than it is in the print media. As a result, news people in broadcasting are less likely to establish roots and ties in local communities, and are more clannish in their patterns of social relations. These differences can probably be attributed in large part to the relative ages of the two segments of the industry and to the lack of tradition in broadcast journalism, but they may also reflect in part the influence in broadcast journalism of show business values such as the "star" system, where journalists are transformed into media personalities whose fortunes wax and wane with changing audience tastes. Whatever the explanation, rates of job mobility among personnel in the two sectors differ sharply.

Knowing the characteristics of broadcast journalists is especially important in view of the changing influence of print and broadcast journalism on American public opinion. During the past decade, television has become the principal source of information and opinion for American adults, and it is significant, therefore, to know that journalists in this sector represent such a small proportion (about a tenth) of the total editorial manpower in the country. The growing influence of television journalism has hardly gone unnoticed, of course, and in its recent struggles with the press the administration mounted the main thrust of its offensive against the broadcast media.

Many other factors contribute to differences between the nature and quality of newswork in the two major sectors, of course, and many of these have more to do with economic, technical, legal, and historical differences between the media than with the nature of the news personnel they employ. As Philpot (1973) observes, the lack of First Amendment protections, the absence of advocacy or editorial traditions, the scrutiny of the FCC, the weaker position of television vis-à-vis advertisers, the lack of effective information archives in radio and television, and natural differences between print and the spoken word in the amount of information which can be communicated in a given time period all make broadcast newswork very different from journalism in the print sector.

A second prominent contextual factor which affects news-work is organization size, and herein lies a paradox for the contemporary journalist. Newsmen much prefer to work in small news organizations than in large ones, primarily, it turns out, because they have more editorial autonomy in smaller organizations—more freedom to select the stories they work on, more freedom in deciding how to play a story, and less day-to-day interference from editors and news processors. These aspects of newswork are of considerable importance to journalists, and just as Pelz and Andrews (1966), Miller (1967), and others have found for scientists, there are certain kinds of organizational settings in which they are better able to realize them.

At the same time, however, newsmen like to be identified with news organizations which command respect and prestige in the professional community, and despite their verbalizations to the contrary, they are happier with their jobs when they are paid better. The dilemma here, of course, is that there are very few small news organizations which enjoy much national visibility or prestige (though there are plenty of large ones which do not either), and that earnings in journalism are in large part a function of organization size. Many journalists, in other words, must trade off certain of their professional ideals for higher earnings and better opportunities for professional recognition.

What many young journalists seem to be saying today is that they find contemporary newswork alienating because their work is too fragmented, they are too dependent on others, they too often are assigned passive editorial functions, or because of ubiquitous deadlines they have insufficient opportunity to utilize their most important skills. Mass production in newswork is an aspect of the contemporary news-media experience which few journalists regard with warmth, and we would conclude that it is one of the principal reasons that many highly trained young news people find it difficult to commit themselves to long-term careers in the media.

This situation is not unique to journalism, of course, and grievances of this sort can be heard among workers throughout the industrial order. The situation is not unlike the familiar industrial dilemma of how to maximize productivity and efficiency without alienating the worker from his tasks. The classical sociological answer to this dilemma has been to decentralize authority and to create smaller and more autonomous work units.

We feel that the strain between the needs of formal organizations to regulate and control their functions and the needs of individual workers for autonomy is especially critical for journalism because of current trends in the organization of the news industry. Increasing centralization leads inevitably to greater bureaucratization, and this together with the introduction of computerized routines in the newsroom will further increase the necessity for coordination and control over newswork. It is not unlikely, therefore, that this source of strain will be exacerbated in news-media journalism in the near future.

Our results suggest that it is fundamentally this issue which underlies the so-called "reporter power" movement which has surfaced in a number of American news organizations recently, and for which full-blown models already exist in Europe as well as in the alternative sector of the American news media. We expect that these themes will be heard more and more regularly on the American scene in the near future, and that eventually the news media will have to face the issue head-on if they hope to retain their more lively and potentially most promising young talent.

Despite their importance, we have also attempted to show in the analysis that structural factors do not entirely wash out or explain away the effects that individual journalists have on the news. In the current argot, where a newsman is "coming from" is at least as important as "where he is," and we would argue that to truly picture the complexity of mass-media phenomena it is necessary to have accurate information not only about organizational and environmental contexts but about the personal traits of journalists as well. We feel it is significant, for example, that journalists are predominantly male, emanate from the middle-classes of American society, and are disproportionately concentrated within large urban places and in the Northeast. If it is true, as critics have argued, that our media give disproportionate attention to the affairs of established groups in the society, to events, such as sports, which are of interest primarily to men, and to experiences in the urban environment, then these propensities are entirely consistent with the social and geographic makeup of news-media personnel. *Who* and *where* the people are who gather and assemble the news, in other words, can significantly influence what is portrayed as newsworthy by the media. As has been observed before, the media may not be able to tell us what to think, but by the emphasis they give to or withhold from events, they very effectively tell us what to think about.

Perhaps the most compelling evidence as to the importance of individual backgrounds is that which shows that the type of training journalists get has a lasting impact on the perspectives they bring to their work. Currently, American newsmen are split sharply between those oriented to what we term "neutral" and "participant" brands of professionalism, and from our analysis we conclude that this differentiation is basically a consequence of how newsmen are trained. Educational backgrounds, significantly, have stronger effects on professional values than do subsequent career experiences such as the sector of the media journalists work in, the level of their organizational responsibilities, the size of the community they work in, and the nature of their social and professional integration. Moreover, these outcomes are more a function of the *amount* of schooling one has had than of the *field* of specialization one has studied. In view of this, value segmentation among journalists is probably more pronounced today than it ever has been in the past or may ever be in the future: since just over half of all practicing journalists in the United States today are college graduates, current variability in educational backgrounds is close to the maximum possible. This situation is changing rapidly, however, and a college degree is already virtually a universal prerequisite for recruitment into the media. This source of differentiation will therefore all but disappear within two or three decades.

Fields of specialization are also extremely diverse among contemporary newsmen, and it is not unlikely that this variation will become a more important basis of value segmentation in the future. In other occupations and professions marked by diversity in how their practitioners are trained, ideological cleavages are often evident among the subgroups with different backgrounds. The most prominent example of this is in psychiatry. As university training becomes more universal within journalism, we would anticipate that the main source of value conflict and ideological debate within the field will be between graduates of professional programs and those who enter the media from the humanities or the social sciences.

Because value positions among journalists were better predicted by education than by age, we concluded that differences on these dimensions should not be interpreted primarily as a manifestation of generational conflict. Yet it would be inaccurate to say that generational strains are entirely absent within the field today: on a variety of issues of current relevance to journalism there was much greater consensus of opinion *within* age groups than *between* them. At the same time, however, we would guess that there is a greater homogeneity of professional perspective among young journalists today than will be the case for entering cohorts in a decade or so. Most young newsmen today are products of the era of campus unrest and student dissent, and if not active participants in the student movement of the sixties are likely at least to have been deeply influenced by its values. The decline in sociopolitical involvement which has been evident among American college students since about 1971, however, is likely to weaken the solidarity of ideological perspective so evident among college students of the late sixties. Declining "age-grade consciousness" (Johnstone, 1970) among college students, in other words, will probably result in a broadened range of viewpoints regarding press functions among newly forming cohorts of journalists, and, we would predict, a decline in commitment to advocacy journalism and related themes of the so-called "new journalism."

American journalism today is an extremely diverse occupational field, and there is little agreement as to what constitutes the most appropriate training for entering the field. This lack of agreement stems in large part from the diversity of background found among current practitioners, but not entirely so, since not insubstantial numbers of newsmen felt that their own field of preparation in college may not have been the most appropriate. Different sectors of the news media also demand different mixes of talents and skills, but it is not clear that in recent decades the media have always taken sufficient care to match the backgrounds of their recruits to the work demands of their particular branch of journalism. We are particularly struck by the degree to which imbalances were evident in the wire services, where a sizable number of those with journalism degrees seemed to be saying that a broad liberal arts background would be more useful to them, and in the broadcast media, where many felt they would be better off if they had been professionally trained. While the field may well require diversity in the types of personnel it recruits, it is also a field in which there is some lack of fit between recruitment practices and the particular demands of the work.

In overview, one cannot but be impressed by the quality of talent entering news-media journalism today. Veteran newsmen are also favorably impressed by the credentials of young persons entering the media, and will readily comment on their knowledgeability and sophistication. Veterans do have negative things to say about the new recruits, of course, most notably that they lack professional dedication, are opinionated, lack objectivity, and are too self-interested. Yet few score them on the basis of their formal credentials for doing newswork. To conclude, we would assess the question of the quality of manpower in American journalism with both optimism and concern. There is little doubt but that the qualifications of persons entering the field today are higher than they have been in the past, and it is likely that they will continue to rise. We would be concerned, however, with whether the news media as presently constituted will be able to hold their most promising recruits. To do so, many American news organizations may soon find it necessary to reassess how they control newswork, and eventually to vest greater editorial autonomy with those who do news gathering, news writing, and news reporting.

Appendix: Tables and Charts

TABLE 2.1
*Estimated Full-Time Editorial Manpower
in American News Media, April, 1971*

Media Sector	Number	Percent
Daily newspapers	38,800	55.8
Weekly newspapers	11,500	16.5
News magazines	1,900	2.7
Total print media	52,200	75.1
Television (and combined TV and radio stations)	7,000	10.1
Radio only	7,000	10.1
Total broadcast media	14,000	20.2
News services	3,300	4.7
Total manpower	69,500	100.0

TABLE 2.2
*Regional Distribution of Journalists Compared
with Labor Force and Total U.S. Population*
(Percent in Each Region)[a]

Region	Journalists (1971)	U.S. Civilian Labor Force[b] (1970)	Total Population[c] (1970)
New England	7.5	6.2	5.8
Middle Atlantic	28.8	18.1	18.3
East North Central	15.3	20.7	19.8
West North Central	7.4	8.0	8.0
South Atlantic	11.0	15.1	15.1
East South Central	4.6	6.0	6.3
West South Central	9.1	9.0	9.5
Mountain	6.4	3.7	4.1
Pacific	9.9	13.2	13.1
Total	100.0	100.0	100.0
Total Northeast	36.3	24.3	24.1
Total North Central	22.7	28.7	27.8
Total South	24.7	30.1	30.9
Total West	16.3	16.9	17.2

[a]In this and subsequent tables in this volume, the "elite" and "rank-and-file" strata are combined into a single sample weighted by their probabilities of selection. All calculations reported are computed from the weighted case bases.

[b]Source: U.S. Bureau of the Census, 1971, Table 336, p. 215.

[c]*Ibid.*, Table 11, p. 12.

TABLE 2.3
Distribution of Journalistic Manpower and of
Total Population, 1970, by Size of Community
(Percent in Each Type of Community)

Size of Community	Journalists (1971)	Total Population[a] (1970)	Ratio of Journalists to Population
1,000,000 or more	41.0	34.9	1.17
500,000 - 1,000,000	13.8	7.1	1.94
250,000 - 500,000	15.1	6.1	2.48
50,000 - 250,000	18.4	10.2	1.80
10,000 - 50,000	7.6	8.2	.93
Under 10,000	4.0	33.5[b]	.12
Total	99.9	100.0	

[a]Source: U.S. Bureau of the Census, Census of Population 1970. Vol. I, Characteristics of the Population, Part A, *Number of Inhabitants*. U.S. Government Printing Office, Washington, D.C., 1972, Table 4, pp. 1-43. (Cited elsewhere as U.S. Bureau of the Census, 1972b.)

[b]Consists of 26.5 percent from rural places, and 7.0 percent from places under 10,000 outside of urbanized areas.

TABLE 2.4
Size of Editorial Staff per 1,000 Circulation in Daily and
Weekly Newspapers, by Size of Circulation

Size of Circulation	Median Number of Editorial Employees per 1,000 Circulation	Number of Papers
Under 10,000	1.33	46
10,000 - 50,000	.87	41
50,000 - 250,000	.48	32
250,000 - 500,000	.44	24
More than 500,000	.34	18

TABLE 2.5
Age Composition of Manpower in Journalism
(Percent in Each Age Group)

Age Group	Journalists	U.S. Civilian Labor Force 18 and Older[a] (Nov., 1971)
Under 20	.7	5.1
20 - 24	11.3	13.9
25 - 29	21.1	12.2
30 - 34	12.2	10.0
35 - 39	11.7	9.5
40 - 44	10.5	10.5
45 - 49	10.6	11.0
50 - 54	8.2	10.0
55 - 59	7.0	8.4
60 - 64	4.3	5.7
65 - 69	2.0	2.3
70 and older	.3	1.6
Total	99.9	100.2[b]
Median age	36.5	39.2

[a]Source: U.S. Department of Labor, 1971, Table A-3, p. 29.
[b]Does not total to 100 percent because of rounding.

TABLE 2.6
Sex Composition of Journalistic Manpower
(Percent)

Sex	Journalists	Total Full-Time U.S. Labor Force 20 and Older[a] (November 1971)
Male	79.7	66.4
Female	20.3	33.6
Total	100.0	100.0

[a]Source: U.S. Department of Labor, 1971, Table A-2, p. 28.

TABLE 2.7
Representation of Women in News Media, by Media Sector

Media Sector	Percent Women	Case Base	
		Weighted	Unweighted
Radio	4.8	418	89
Television (and combined TV and radio)	10.7	519	162
Wire services	13.0	232	46
Daily newspapers	22.4	3,194	920
Weekly newspapers	27.1	825	78
News magazines	30.4	102	33

TABLE 2.8
Representation of Women in Journalism and in U.S. Labor Force, 1970, by Age
(Percent Women)

Age Group	Journalism	Total Labor Force[a] (1970)
Under 25	25.5	40.9
25 - 34	17.9	32.3
35 - 44	15.5	35.6
45 - 54	22.5	38.4
55 - 64	25.5	36.8
65 and older	9.1	32.8

[a]Source: U.S. Bureau of the Census, 1971, Table 328, p. 211.

TABLE 2.9
Ethnic Origins of Journalists Compared with Total Population
(Percent in Each Group)

Ethnicity	Journalists	Adult Population[a] (1967)
Anglo-Saxon	39.0	23.8
German	17.5	16.8
Irish	13.6	10.4
Scandinavian	5.0	4.4
French	4.0	1.5
Black	3.9	14.9
Jewish	3.3	2.6
Italian	3.2	4.1
Polish	1.4	2.1
All other groups	9.1	19.3
Total	100.0	99.9
Weighted case base	(4,934)	—
Unweighted sample size	(1,225)	(2,482)

[a]Source: Gabriel A. Almond and Sidney Verba's 1968 national survey of political participation of adults.

TABLE 2.10
*Fathers' Occupations of Journalists Compared with Those
of Self-Employed and Salaried Professionals*
(Percent of Fathers in Each Occupational Group)

Father's Occupation	Professional Males, 1962[a]			1971 Journalists
	Self-Employed	Salaried	Total	
Professional, technical, and kindred	21.5	13.4	14.4	23.7
Managers, proprietors, and officials	27.2	17.5	18.7	25.1
Clerical	4.9	7.3	7.0	4.1
Sales	6.5	5.7	5.7	9.0
Total white-collar	60.1	43.9	45.8	61.9
Craftsmen and foremen	10.8	18.5	17.6	16.6
Operatives	8.0	13.9	13.2	6.6
Service workers	2.3	3.7	3.5	4.1
Farmers	11.2	10.8	10.8	4.5
Laborers, including farm	1.3	3.5	3.3	3.4
Total blue-collar	33.6	50.4	48.4	35.1
No answer	6.3	5.7	5.8	3.0
Total	100.0	100.0	100.0	100.0

[a]Source: Peter M. Blau and O. D. Duncan, *The American Occupational Structure* (New York: Wiley, 1967), Table 2.8, p. 39.

TABLE 3.1
Amount of Formal Schooling, by Age
(Percent with Different Amounts of Schooling)

Highest Educa-tional Attainment	Under 25	25-34	35-44	45-54	55 and Older	Total
Some high school	1.7	.8	1.8	1.8	3.9	1.8
Graduated from high school	3.8	8.6	11.4	12.3	28.8	12.2
Some college	44.4	26.6	22.7	29.9	21.8	27.9
Graduated from college	41.4	41.4	42.7	37.8	31.5	39.6
Some graduate training	6.0	13.9	9.9	10.6	7.4	10.5
Graduate degree(s)	2.7	8.7	11.4	7.6	6.6	8.1
Total	100.0	100.0	99.9	100.0	100.0	100.1
Weighted case base	(631)	(1,748)	(1,171)	(990)	(715)	(5,255)
Unweighted sample size	(130)	(409)	(310)	(274)	(180)	(1,303)

TABLE 3.2
Number of College Graduates, by Media Type
(Percent Who Graduated from College)

Media Type	Percent	Case Base (Weighted)
News magazines	88.2	102
Wire services	80.4	232
Daily newspapers	62.6	3,189
TV (and combined TV-radio)	58.7	519
Weekly newspapers	43.6	825
Radio	36.6	418
Total print sector	59.4	4,116
Network broadcasting	65.5	116
Non-network broadcasting	45.2	821
Total broadcast sector	47.7	937
Total sample	58.2	5,285

TABLE 3.3
Number of College Graduates in News Media,
by City Size and by News Organization Size
(Percent Who Graduated from College)

Size of City and Staff	Percent	Case Base (Weighted)
A. Size of city:		
Under 10,000	40.8	493
10,000 - 50,000	44.7	1,101
50,000 - 250,000	54.1	1,503
250,000 - 500,000	61.3	810
500,000 - 1,000,000	78.5	540
Over 1,000,000	76.6	850
B. Size of editorial staff:		
1 - 10	44.0	1,603
11 - 25	48.1	668
26 - 50	58.1	621
51 - 100	59.4	839
Over 100	76.2	1,565

TABLE 3.4
Number of College Graduates in News Media, by Media Type and City Size
(Percent Who Are College Graduates)

Media Type	Size of City		
	Under 50,000	50,000 to 500,000	Over 500,000
Daily newspapers	47.1 (768)[a]	61.9 (1,611)	78.5 (811)
Television (and combined TV and radio)	47.2 (53)	50.3 (342)	78.9 (123)
Total print media	44.5 (1,404)	61.4 (1,758)	77.7 (957)
Total broadcast media	39.3 (178)	41.8 (557)	71.5 (200)

[a]Case bases are weighted.

TABLE 3.5
Percent Who Graduated from College, and Percent of Graduates Who Attended
Schools Rated as Very Selective, by Region of Current Employment

Region	Percent Who Graduated from College	Base (Weighted)	Percent of Graduates from Schools Rated Very Selective	Base (Weighted)
New England	52.2	397	52.4	207
Middle Atlantic	61.0	1,524	61.3	933
East North Central	58.5	799	41.6	468
West North Central	52.4	391	38.2	205
South Atlantic	58.1	579	56.5	334
East South Central	59.1	248	15.9	146
West South Central	52.9	480	17.8	253
Mountain	58.2	354	5.3	206
Pacific	61.8	523	33.5	324
Total sample	58.2	5,295	42.9	3.076

TABLE 3.6
Fields of Study in College and Graduate School

Subject	Major Field in College		Major Field in Graduate School	
	Percent of Sample	Percent of All Subjects	Percent of Sample	Percent of All Subjects
Journalism	22.6	34.2	6.9	34.9
Radio-TV	1.8	2.8	.3	1.6
Other communication specialties	3.1	4.7	1.6	8.0
Total communication field	27.5	41.7	8.8	44.5
English, creative writing	15.1	22.9	2.0	10.3
History	6.4	9.7	1.6	8.2
Other humanities	2.9	4.4	.9	4.7
Political science, government	5.0	7.5	2.2	10.9
Other social sciences	3.6	5.5	1.3	6.4
Liberal arts, unspecified	1.1	1.6	.1	.5
Mathematics	.4	.6	.1	.5
Physical or biological sciences	.8	1.2	.1	.5
Total liberal arts-science	35.3	53.4	8.3	42.0
Agriculture	.2	.3	.1	.7
Business	1.0	1.5	.1	.7
Education	.5	.8	1.0	5.2
Law	a	.1	.6	2.9
All other fields	1.5	2.3	.8	4.1
Total other fields	3.2	5.0	2.7	13.6
Total	66.0[b]	100.1	19.8[c]	100.1

[a]Less than one-tenth of 1 percent.

[b]Does not total to 100 percent because some journalists are not college graduates, and does not total to percent of college graduates because some majored in more than one subject.

[c]Does not total to 100 percent because many journalists did not attend graduate school, and does not total to percent attending graduate school because some studied more than one field.

TABLE 3.7
Content of College and Graduate Degrees, by Period of Graduation
(Percent of All Fields Reported as Majors)

Major Field	College Degrees			Graduate Degrees		
	Date of Graduation			Date of Graduation		
	1944 or earlier	1945-59	1960 or later	1944 or earlier	1945-59	1960 or later
Journalism	23.6	42.5	32.0	45.8	54.9	41.4
Other communica-tion fields	.8	6.8	10.4	–	7.5	16.7
Total communi-cation fields	24.4	49.3	42.4	45.8	62.0	58.1
English, creative writing	35.4	20.9	19.7	14.6	2.1	12.1
History	11.1	7.3	11.0	–	4.8	11.1
Other humanities	8.6	3.1	3.9	12.5	10.2	–
Political science, gov-ernment	3.2	6.2	10.2	–	5.9	8.1
Other social sciences	4.7	5.8	4.8	4.2	–	2.5
Other liberal arts and science	6.0	2.1	4.1	–	2.7	2.5
Total liberal arts and science	69.0	45.4	53.7	31.3	25.7	36.4
Total other fields	6.6	5.4	3.9	22.9	12.3	5.6
Total	100.0	100.1	100.0	100.0	100.0	100.1
Base (weighted)	(619)	(1,227)	(1,653)	(48)	(187)	(198)

TABLE 3.8
Fields of Study Recommended for Persons Entering News Media Today,
by Respondent's Education Level and Major Field of Study in College
(Percent Who Mentioned Each Field of Preparation)

Fields Recommended	Major Field in College		Did Not Graduate from College	Total Sample
	Jour-nalism	All Other Subjects		
General liberal arts	43.4	46.6	34.9	40.8
Social sciences	47.7	38.4	29.5	37.1
English, literature, creative writing	30.2	32.6	41.5	35.7
Journalism	35.1	26.5	32.0	31.1
Other communication specialties	2.6	4.1	4.1	3.7
All other fields	4.6	3.8	6.5	5.2
Anything, does not matter	1.8	6.2	4.7	4.4
Total	165.4 [a]	157.6 [a]	153.2 [a]	158.0 [a]
Base (weighted)	(1,403)	(1,649)	(2,217)	(5,269)

[a]Totals exceed 100 percent because some persons recommended more than one field.

TABLE 3.9
Recommended Fields of Study, by Sector of News Media in Which Employed
(Percent Who Mentioned Each Field of Preparation)

Fields Recommended	Daily News-papers	Weekly News-papers	News Maga-zines	Wire Services	Radio	Televi-sion
General liberal arts	41.4	36.0	66.7	56.5	33.3	37.2
Social sciences	37.3	36.0	47.1	34.5	33.7	36.0
English, literature, creative writing	35.4	50.2	39.2	36.6	28.5	21.6
Journalism	28.4	33.7	9.8	21.6	44.7	39.7
Other communication specialties	2.3	1.3	–	4.3	12.9	9.2
All other fields	4.3	5.3	6.9	6.5	8.9	4.0
Anything, does not matter	4.8	1.3	2.0	2.2	6.5	3.7
Total	153.9[a]	163.8[a]	171.7[a]	162.2[a]	168.5[a]	151.4[a]
Base (weighted)	(3,194)	(825)	(102)	(232)	(418)	(519)

[a]Totals exceed 100 percent because some persons recommended more than one field.

TABLE 3.10

Numbers Trained in Journalism and Numbers Who Recommend Training in Journalism, by Media Sector

Media Sector	Percent Who Hold Degrees in Journalism	Percent Who Recommend Training in Journalism	Difference
Wire services	39.1	21.6	−17.5
Daily newspapers	32.6	28.4	− 4.2
Weekly newspapers	19.9	33.7	+13.8
Television	14.7	39.7	+25.0
News magazines	12.7	9.8	− 2.9
Radio	8.9	44.7	+35.8

TABLE 3.11

Educational Pursuits Subsequent to Entering News Media
(Percent Involved in Educational Pursuits of Each Type)[a]

Total active in structured educative pursuits since entering news media			35.7
Total who studied professional topics		17.7	
Journalism skills and specialties	12.7		
Management training courses	1.9		
Other vocationally relevant topics	5.1		
Total who studied academic subjects		20.5	
English, literature, creative writing	7.0		
Politics, government, public affairs	4.4		
All other academic subjects	9.4		
Total who studied other subject matter		2.5	
Total not active in educative pursuits since entering news media			64.3
Total			100.0

Base	5,272	
No information	29	
Total (weighted)	5,301	

[a]Subcategory totals do not add to category totals because some persons studied more than one subject.

TABLE 3.12
Topics Journalists Would Like to Know More About
(Percent Who Mentioned Each Topic)

Total who said some type of additional training, study, or refresher course would be helpful		57.7
Journalism	10.1	
Political science, government	8.9	
English, literature, writing	7.2	
History	3.9	
Economics	3.6	
Law	2.7	
Business	2.6	
Photography	2.2	
News analysis, clinics, seminars, etc.	1.7	
Shorthand	1.5	
Modern languages	1.5	
Total who did not feel additional training or study would be helpful		42.3
Total		100.0

Base	5,287
No answer	14
Total (weighted)	5,301

TABLE 4.1

Age of Decision to Enter Communications Field, by Father's Socioeconomic Status
(Percent Who Decided to Enter Field at Each Age)

| | Socioeconomic Background | | | |
Age	Lower Quartile	Middle Half	Upper Quartile	Total
12 or younger	8.7	10.9	10.0	10.0
13 - 16	23.5	18.9	19.3	20.3
17 - 20	31.2	33.8	28.9	31.7
21 - 24	14.5	20.8	26.2	20.4
25 or older	22.1	15.6	15.6	17.5
Total	100.0	100.0	100.0	99.9
Base	(1,470)	(2,233)	(1,373)	(5,076)
Median age	18.8	18.9	19.4	19.0

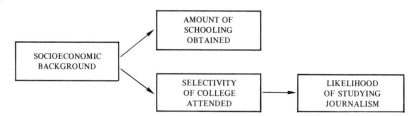

FIGURE 4.1
Influence of Socioeconomic Origins on Early Stages of Journalism Careers

TABLE 4.2

Amount of Formal Schooling, by Socioeconomic Background

A. Percent with Different Amounts of Schooling			
	Socioeconomic Background		
Amount of Schooling	Lower Quartile	Middle Half	Upper Quartile
Some high school or less	1.9	1.6	1.7
Completed high school	17.0	11.3	7.7
1-3 years of college	31.0	28.4	23.8
Graduated from college	35.6	40.7	43.3
Some graduate study	8.3	10.1	13.0
Graduate degree	6.2	7.9	10.5
Total	100.0	100.0	100.0
Base	(1,482)	(2,270)	(1,384)

B. Proportion Continuing Their Education from One Level to the Next				
	Socioeconomic Background			
Level of Schooling	Lower Quartile	Middle Half	Upper Quartile	Difference
Completing high school	.981	.984	.983	.002
Entering college if a high school graduate	.827	.885	.922	.095
Graduating from college if entered college	.618	.674	.737	.119
Entering graduate school if a college graduate	.289	.307	.352	.063
Completing a graduate degree if entered graduate school	.428	.439	.447	.019

TABLE 4.3
*Location of Entry into Labor Force, by Level of Education
and Type of College Major*
(Percent of All First Job Locations)[a]

Labor Force Sector	College Graduates		Non-College Graduates	Total
	Journalism Majors	All Other Majors		
News media	80.7	69.8	62.5	70.0
Total non-news media	19.3	30.2	37.5	30.0
Business and industry	9.4	15.6	30.8	20.1
Educational institutions	2.4	10.2	.6	4.1
Government	3.4	2.2	3.4	3.0
All other sectors	4.1	2.2	2.7	2.8
Total	100.0	100.0	100.0	100.0
Base (weighted)	(1,356)	(1,516)	(1,999)	(4,874)

[a]Excludes those whose first employment was in the armed forces.

TABLE 4.4
*Locations of First Jobs of Those Entering News Media Directly out of School,
and Net Manpower Shifts between Entry Points and Current Locations*

Media Sector	Percent of All First Jobs in News Media	Ratio of Current Share of Manpower to Share of Entry Locations[a]
Television	5.2	1.88
Weekly newspapers	14.1	1.11
Daily newspapers	58.2	1.04
Wire services	4.6	.95
News magazines	2.3	.84
Radio	15.5	.51

[a]Proportion currently in media sector divided by proportion whose first media job was in that sector.

TABLE 4.5
Previous Occupations of Journalists Entering News Media
from Other Fields of Employment
(Percent of Previous Occupations Held)

Type of Occupation	Most Recent Employment	All Employment Prior to Most Recent
Professional and technical	31.4	24.4
Managerial and administrative	24.4	17.3
Clerical	18.1	22.4
Sales	8.3	11.2
Total white collar	82.2	75.3
Craftsmen and foremen	3.1	6.6
Operatives	2.3	4.6
Service workers	7.8	8.9
Laborers	4.5	4.5
Total blue collar	17.7	24.6
Total	99.9	99.9
Base (weighted)	(977)	(1,592)
Mean occupational prestige score	43.9	35.8

TABLE 4.6
Average Tenure on Jobs, Working Backward through Career Stages

Job Order	Mean Number of Years	Case Base (Weighted)
Current employer	9.35	5,269
Most recent employer	3.99	4,174
Second most recent employer	2.97	2,896
Third most recent employer	2.95	1,835
Fourth most recent employer	2.44	1,011

TABLE 4.7

Job Mobility among Journalists, by Years of Experience in News Media

	Mobility Measures		
Years of Experience	Percent Who Have Changed Media Jobs	Mean Number of Previous Jobs Held	Estimated Annual Job Mobility at Specific Career Stages[a]
1 or less	11.3	.113	.113
2	28.4	.315	.202
3	47.0	.769	.454
4	54.4	.847	.078
5	57.5	.961	.114
6 - 10	68.5	1.419	.092
11 - 15	74.9	1.821	.080
16 - 20	81.6	1.989	.034
21 - 25	74.6	1.787	b
More than 25	62.5	1.660	b

[a]Mean number of previous jobs held minus mean number of jobs held by succeeding cohort, divided by number of years represented within cohort.

[b]No estimate possible because of inversion of trend line.

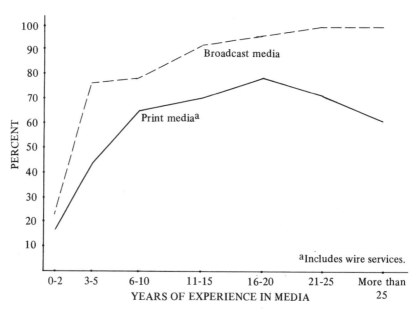

FIGURE 4.2

Number Who Have Held Previous Media Jobs, by Media Sector and Number of Years in News Media

(Percent who have changed media jobs one or more times)

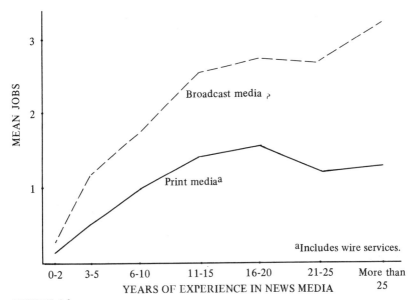

FIGURE 4.3
Mean Number of Previous Jobs Held, by Media Sector
and Number of Years in News Media
(Mean number of previous jobs per person)

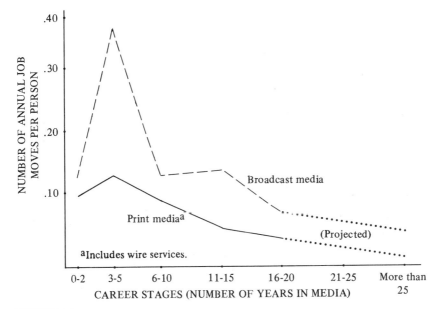

FIGURE 4.4
Estimated Annual Rates of Job Mobility at Selected Career Stages, by Media Sector
(Mean number of previous jobs held minus mean number of jobs held by succeeding
cohort, divided by number of years represented within cohort)

TABLE 4.8

Intermedia Job Moves

(Proportion of All Job Changes among News Organizations)

| Type of Organization Person Left | Recruiting Organization | | | | | | Total (Departures) |
	Daily Newspaper	Weekly Newspaper	News Magazine	Wire Service	Radio	Television	
Daily newspaper	.3879	.0571	.0116	.0303	.0065	.0092	.5026
Weekly newspaper	.0789	.0619	.0007	.0042	.0018	.0000	.1475
News magazine	.0085	.0050	.0028	.0009	.0000	.0009	.0181
Wire service	.0264	.0059	.0017	.0063	.0026	.0004	.0433
Radio	.0122	.0042	.0000	.0028	.1371	.0534	.2097
Television	.0042	.0000	.0004	.0028	.0194	.0521	.0789
Total (recruits)	.5181	.1341	.0172	.0473	.1674	.1160	1.0001[a]

[a]Base equals 5,414 intermedia job moves (weighted).

TABLE 4.9

Patterns of Imbalance in Intermedia Job Moves

(Ratio of Actual to Expected Job Moves)

| Type of Organization Person Left | Recruiting Organization | | | | | |
	Daily Newspaper	Weekly Newspaper	News Magazine	Wire Service	Radio	Television
Daily newspaper	1.49	.85	1.35	1.27	.08	.16
Weekly newspaper	1.03	3.13	.29	.61	.07	.00
News magazine	.91	2.06	8.82	1.09	.00	.44
Wire service	1.18	1.02	2.25	3.06	.36	.07
Radio	.11	.15	.00	.28	3.91	2.19
Television	.10	.00	.27	.74	1.47	5.70

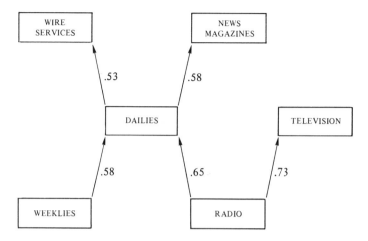

FIGURE 4.5
*Most Frequent Paths of Interorganizational Job
Mobility, and Main Directions of Exchange*
(Numbers Represent the Proportion of Moves in the Direction of the Arrows)

TABLE 4.10
Where News Organizations Recruit Their Editorial Manpower
(Percent of All Recruits)

	Recruiting Organization						
Source of Recruitment	Daily News-paper	Weekly News-paper	News Maga-zine	Wire Service	Radio	Tele-vision	All News Media
Directly from school or from no pre-vious employ-ment	32.3	28.6	37.1	31.1	31.0	18.6	30.4
From other news organi-zations	44.5	42.3	42.1	49.4	51.8	63.8	47.1
From other types of employment	23.2	29.1	20.8	19.5	17.2	17.6	22.5
Total	100.0	100.0	100.0	100.0	100.0	100.0	100.0
Base (weighted)	(6,303)	(1,718)	(221)	(518)	(1,750)	(984)	(11,494)

TABLE 4.11
*Region of Current Employment by Region of Birth among
Journalists (1971) and Heads of U.S. Households (1962)*[a]
(Proportion in Each Combination of Locations)

| Birthplace | Current Employment | | | | Total (Birthplaces) |
	Northeast	North Central	South	West	
	A. Journalists (1971)				
Northeast	.283	.018	.035	.014	.350
North Central	.030	.180	.039	.045	.294
South	.024	.019	.160	.014	.217
West	.013	.005	.009	.083	.110
Non-U.S.	.013	.005	.004	.007	.029
Total (current location)	.363	.227	.247	.163	.1.000
	B. Heads of U.S. Households (1962)				
Northeast	.165	.010	.016	.008	.199
North Central	.008	.215	.029	.044	.296
South	.012	.038	.274	.026	.350
West	.001	.002	.003	.068	.075
Non-U.S.	.033	.023	.006	.019	.080
Total (current location)	.219	.288	.328	.165	1.000

[a]Source: John B. Lansing and Eva Mueller, *The Geographic Mobility of Labor* (Ann Arbor: Institute for Social Research, University of Michigan, 1967), p. 35, Table 10.

TABLE 4.12
*Regions from which Journalists Earned College Degrees, by Major Field of Study,
and Regional Distribution of Journalism Degrees Awarded in 1970-71*
(Percent of Total Degrees Awarded by U.S. Colleges and Universities)

| Region | Major Field of Study | | | All U.S. Jour-nalism Degrees Awarded in 1970-71[a] |
	Journalism	All Other Subjects	Total	
Northeast	16.5	31.3	26.1	10.2
North Central	37.1	25.6	29.7	33.0
South	29.8	28.8	29.2	35.4
West	16.6	14.2	15.0	21.3
Total	100.0	99.9	100.0	100.0
Base	(1,546)[b]	(2,298)[b]	(3,844)[b]	(8,304)

[a]Source: *Editor and Publisher Yearbook, 1971.*
[b]Bases are weighted.

TABLE 4.13
Flow Patterns of Journalistic Manpower for Subregions of the United States

Subregion	Migration Ratio
Middle Atlantic	1.52
Pacific	1.41
Mountain	1.16
South Atlantic	1.03
East North Central	.97
East South Central	.92
West South Central	.74
New England	.61
West North Central	.49

[a]Calculated from all previous job changes reported by journalists. For each subregion the values indicate the ratio of in-migrants to out-migrants.

TABLE 5.1
Types of Job Functions Journalists Perform, by Media Sector
(Percent Engaged in Each Type of Activity)

Functions	Print Sector[a] (N = 4,353)[b]	Broadcast Sector (N = 937)	Total Sample (N = 5,290)
A. Reporting, news gathering, and news writing functions			
Total who do reporting	78.3	80.5	78.8
Cover a specialized newsbeat	37.1	23.5	34.7
Write editorials	28.1	20.7	26.8
Write a column	29.4	1.3	24.4
Write features	11.9	3.8	10.4
Do news commentaries	6.3	13.3	7.5
Write reviews	4.7	0.0	3.9
Produce documentaries or news specials	.5	11.7	2.5
Produce or host a discussion program	.4	8.2	1.7
B. Editing and news processing functions			
Total who edit or process other people's work	71.9	70.3	71.6
Edit for content	65.9	59.8	64.8
Edit for grammar or spelling	65.6	52.2	63.2
Edit for factual accuracy	63.3	56.2	62.1
Edit for length	62.2	55.0	60.9
Edit for technical quality	58.0	53.9	57.2
Do rewrites	57.1	51.8	56.1
C. Managerial and supervisory functions			
Total with managerial or supervisory duties	41.6	42.7	41.9
Influence hiring and firing	27.5	31.3	28.1
Supervise one or more reporters	27.0	31.7	27.9
In charge of a department	16.3	17.6	16.5
Manage a budget	12.2	16.8	12.9
Manage an entire news operation	11.4	9.8	11.1
In charge of a news desk	9.8	5.8	9.1

[a]Includes the wire services.

[b]Bases are weighted.

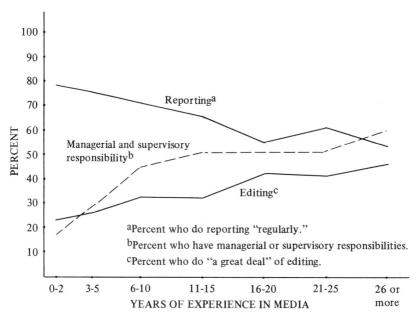

FIGURE 5.1
Types of Journalistic Functions Performed, by Years of Experience in News Media

TABLE 5.2
Median Ages of Print and Broadcast Journalists
Who Perform Various Journalistic Functions

Type of Function	Median Age	Base (Weighted)
A. Print journalists		
Covers a specific news beat	35.2	1,602
Does reporting regularly	35.6	2,941
Covers "hard news" a majority of the time	36.9	2,495
Writes features	37.0	508
All print journalists	38.1	4,316
Does news analysis, or interpretive or in-depth reporting a majority of the time	38.4	624
Writes a column	40.6	1,303
Manages a news desk	41.5	424
Does reviews	41.5	174
Does a great deal of editing	41.7	1,596
Manages a department	42.1	689
Writes editorials	44.8	1,212
Has an influence on hiring and firing	45.2	1,187
Manages a weekly newspaper	46.9	309
Manages a daily newspaper	48.5	137
B. Broadcast journalists		
Does news commentaires	29.3	123
Does news analysis, or interpretive or in-depth reporting a majority of the time	29.7	116
Does a great deal of editing	29.7	192
Produces or hosts a discussion program	29.9	76
Covers a specific news beat	30.6	219
All broadcast journalists	30.8	934
Does reporting regularly	31.0	613
Covers "hard news" a majority of the time	31.0	574
Has an influence on hiring and firing	32.8	303
Produces documentaries or news specials	33.1	109
Writes editorials	34.4	193
Manages a news department	36.2	164

TABLE 5.3

Correlations among Job Activities Performed by Print and Broadcast Journalists
(Pearson Correlations)

					PRINT MEDIA JOURNALISTS						
Variables	(1)	(2)	(3)	(4)	(5)	(6)	(7)	(8)	(9)	(10)	(11)
(1)		.728	.450	-.241	.368	.073	.009	-.045	–	–	–
(2)	.731		.339	-.407	.233	-.004	.011	-.056	–	–	–
(3)	.240	.204		-.317	.188	.028	.001	.001	–	–	–
(4)	-.119	-.237	-.133		.016	.105	.000	.104	–	–	–
(5)	.332	.188	.112	.048		.165	.042	.020	–	–	–
(6)	–	–	–	–	–		-.072	-.084	–	–	–
(7)	–	–	–	–	–	–		.057	–	–	–
(8)	–	–	–	–	–	–	–		–	–	–
(9)	.040	.125	.121	.067	-.040	–	–	–		–	–
(10)	.138	.032	.033	.154	.162	–	–	–	.020		–
(11)	-.044	.015	-.124	.113	-.017	–	–	–	-.084	-.117	

BROADCAST MEDIA JOURNALISTS

Legend

(1) *Managerial responsibilities.* (Q4) Do you have any managerial responsibilities, or do you supervise any editorial employees? Yes (1), No (0). Print newsmen Mean = .412, SD = .493; broadcast newsmen Mean = .432, SD = .496.

(2) *Number of employees responsible for.* (Q6) Altogether, how many editorial employees report to you either directly or indirectly? More than 25 (5), 11-25 (4), 6-10 (3), 3-5 (2), 1-2 (1), none (0). Print newsmen Mean = .887, SD = 1.45; broadcast newsmen Mean = .858, SD = 1.35.

(3) *Editing.* (Q17) How much editing or processing of other people's work do you do? A great deal (2), some (1), none at all (0). Print newsmen Mean = 1.088, SD = .801; broadcast newsmen Mean = .914, SD = .704.

(4) *Reporting.* (Q25) How often do you do reporting? Regularly (3), occasionally (2), seldom (1), never (0). Print newsmen Mean = 2.372, SD = 1.019; broadcast newsmen Mean = 2.382, SD = .973.

(5) *Editorial writing.* (Q41) Do you ever write editorials? Yes (1), no (0). Print newsmen Mean = .281, SD = .450; broadcast newsmen Mean = .209, SD = .407.

(6) *Writing a column.* (Q48) Are there any other types of writing or production that you do that we haven't covered? Mentioned writing a column (1), didn't mention writing a column (0). Print newsmen Mean = .295, SD = .456.

(7) *Writing reviews.* (Q48) Mentioned writing reviews (1), didn't mention writing reviews (0). Print newsmen Mean = .047, SD = .212.

(8) *Writing features.* (Q48) Mentioned writing features (1), didn't mention writing features (0), Print newsmen Mean = .119, SD = .324.

(9) *Produces documentaries or news specials.* (Q48) Mentioned documentaries or news specials (1), didn't mention documentaries or news specials (0). Broadcast newsmen Mean = .118, SD = .323.

(10) *Does news commentaries.* (Q48) Mentioned news commentaries (1), didn't mention news commentaries (0). Broadcast newsmen Mean = .128, SD = .334.

(11) *Produces or hosts a discussion program.* (Q48) Mentioned a discussion program (1), didn't mention a discussion program (0). Broadcast newsmen Mean = .082, SD = .286.

TABLE 5.4
Organization Size and Specialization of Function
(Correlation between Number of Editorial Employees in an Organization and
Whether or Not a Journalist Performs Specific Functions)

Functions	Correlations (Pearson)
Among executives, number who have an influence on hiring and firing	−.350
Number who write editorials	−.311
Among executives, number who make final gate-keeping decisions	−.262
Among staffers, number who cover a specific news beat	.216
Number who do editing or news processing	−.184
Number who have managerial or supervisory responsibilities of any type	−.163
Among executives, number who make final gate-keeping decisions on news stories	−.115
Number who do reporting	−.076

TABLE 5.5
*Indicators of Professional Autonomy among Those Who
Do Reporting, by Size of News Organization*

Indicators of Autonomy	Number of Editorial Employees			
	Less than 25 (N = 1,855)	26 – 100 (N = 1,045)	More than 100 (N = 1,184)	Total Who Do Reporting (N = 4,084)[a]
Percent who say				
A. They have almost complete freedom in deciding which aspects of a news story should be emphasized	84.3	65.0	72.0	75.9
B. They have almost complete freedom in selecting the stories they work on	73.1	50.2	48.3	60.1
C. They make their own story assignments	57.7	37.1	36.2	46.2
D. Their stories are not edited by other people	46.3	25.5	16.1	32.3

[a]Bases are weighted.

TABLE 5.6
Newsmen's Ratings of Media Performance
(Percent)

Ratings	News Media in General[a]	Respondent's Own Organization[b]
Outstanding	17.8	14.9
Very good	36.3	38.1
Good	30.6	31.2
Fair	11.2	13.1
Poor	3.7	2.0
No opinion or no answer	.3	.7
Total	99.9	100.0
Base (weighted)	(5,301)	(5,301)

[a]Question 64. On the whole, how good a job of informing the public do you think the news media are doing today?

[b]Question 65. How good a job of informing the public do you think your own news organization is doing?

TABLE 5.7
Newsmen's Ratings of Top Twenty-Five American News Organizations

Fairest and Most Reliable News Organization		Votes[a]	News Organization Relied on Most Often in Respondent's Work		Votes[a]	Overall Prominence		Combined Votes
	Organization			Organization			Organization	
1.	New York Times	600	1.	New York Times	408	1.	New York Times	1008
2.	Associated Press	310	2.	Associated Press	388	2.	Associated Press	698
3.	Washington Post	214	3.	United Press International	274	3.	United Press International	456
4.	Wall Street Journal	204	4.	Washington Post	158	4.	Washington Post	372
5.	United Press International	182	5.	Wall Street Journal	129	5.	Wall Street Journal	333
6.	Christian Science Monitor	129	6.	Time	72	6.	Los Angeles Times	190
7.	Los Angeles Times	127	7.	Los Angeles Times	63	7.	Newsweek	165
8.	Newsweek	111	8.	Newsweek	54	8.	Christian Science Monitor	148
9.	CBS News	90	9.	CBS News	31	9.	Time	145
10.	Time	73	10.	San Francisco Chronicle	27	10.	CBS News	121
11.	St. Louis Post-Dispatch	43	11.	Washington Star	25	11.	Chicago Tribune	61
12.	NBC News	42	12.	New York Daily News	24	12.	NBC News	56
13.	U.S. News & World Report	40	13.	Chicago Daily News	23	13.	U.S. News & World Report	56
14.	Chicago Tribune	38	14.	ABC News	23	14.	ABC News	54
15.	ABC News	31	15.	Chicago Tribune	23	15.	St. Louis Post-Dispatch	53
16.	National Observer	29	16.	Minneapolis Tribune	21	16.	Washington Star	52
17.	Washington Star	27	17.	Christian Science Monitor	19	17.	Chicago Daily News	45
18.	Milwaukee Journal	25	18.	Charlotte Observer	18	18.	National Observer	44
19.	Miami Herald	23	19.	Salt Lake City Tribune	18	19.	New York Daily News	41
20.	Chicago Daily News	21	20.	U.S. News & World Report	16	20.	Minneapolis Tribune	38
21.	Louisville Courier	21	21.	Chicago Sun-Times	16	21.	Milwaukee Journal	37
22.	Boston Globe	21	22.	National Observer	15	22.	San Francisco Chronicle	35
23.	Minneapolis Tribune	17	23.	Houston Post	15	23.	Boston Globe	34
24.	Baltimore Sun	17	24.	NBC News	14	24.	Chicago Sun-Times	32
25.	New York Daily News	17	25.	Boston Globe	13	25.	Philadelphia Inquirer	29
			26.	Philadelphia Inquirer	13	26.	Houston Post	29

[a]Vote counts are unweighted, and indicate the number of newsmen out of 1,349 (1,313 from the national sample plus thirty-six listed in the Congressional Directory 1971) who named each news organization.

TABLE 5.8
Distribution of Sample in Terms of Prestige, Influence, and
Overall Prominence of Organizations Newsmen Work For
(Percent Employed in Organizations of Each Type)

Number of Times Named	Dimension of Prestige or Influence		
	Fairness and Reliability	Organizations Newsmen Rely On	Overall Prominence
More than 100	7.1	6.5	7.9
26 - 100	2.1	1.3	5.9
11 - 25	3.6	7.6	9.5
6 - 10	9.9	15.6	13.1
3 - 5	12.6	7.8	15.0
1 - 2	23.7	20.4	15.8
None	41.0	40.9	32.8
Total	100.0	100.0	100.0
Base (weighted)	(5,301)	(5,601)	(5,301)

TABLE 5.9
Selected Characteristics of Journalists in Prominent and Nonprominent
News Organizations, by Status Level in Organization

Characteristics	Prominent Organizations		Nonprominent Organizations	
	Executives (N = 404)[a]	Staffers (N = 828)	Executives (N = 1,816)	Staffers (N = 2,247)
A. *Social origins and personal characteristics*				
(1) Father's education—percent who were college graduates	25.0	31.6	17.9	19.7
(2) Father's occupation—percent who were employed in professional or managerial occupations	66.0	59.2	46.0	47.7
(3) Religious background—				
Protestant	59.7	55.7	63.8	62.1
Catholic	22.4	22.5	26.0	24.4
Jewish	11.9	10.4	5.9	4.3
Other or none	6.0	11.4	4.4	9.3
Total	100.0	100.0	100.1	100.1

(Cont.)

TABLE 5.9 (Cont.)

(4) Racial background–percent who are black	0.0	3.6	6.3	2.8
(5) Sex–percent who are women	9.0	21.8	14.0	26.9
(6) Birthplace (U.S. born only)–				
Northeast	37.5	34.4	33.8	38.4
North Central	31.5	27.8	36.2	25.9
South	26.7	25.6	20.8	21.6
West	4.3	12.2	9.2	14.0
Total	100.0	100.0	100.0	99.9
B. *Education and Training*				
(7) College region (U.S. college graduates only)–				
Northeast	36.8	25.6	27.6	26.4
North Central	30.1	29.2	31.1	28.4
South	28.7	31.9	26.8	24.5
West	4.4	13.3	14.5	20.6
Total	100.0	100.0	100.0	99.9
(8) College graduates–percent who graduated from college	75.1	79.7	54.8	49.9
(9) Advanced degrees–percent with graduate degrees	10.9	16.7	7.4	4.9
(10) Selectivity of college–percent who graduated from colleges rated among most selective in country	19.9	16.3	10.0	5.3
C. *Political dispositions*				
(11) Party affiliation–				
Democrats	44.0	43.2	31.1	35.3
Republicans	8.5	15.6	31.8	27.8
Independents	44.7	33.7	30.6	31.8
Other	2.7	7.4	6.5	5.2
Total	99.9	99.9	100.0	100.1
(12) General political leanings–				
Pretty far to the left	6.8	12.4	4.1	9.5
A little to the left	56.1	40.4	24.4	31.0
Middle of the road	27.1	29.9	46.7	41.0
A little to the right	8.7	15.1	19.7	15.3
Pretty far to the right	1.4	2.2	5.1	3.2
Total	100.1	100.0	100.0	100.0

[a]Bases are weighted.

TABLE 6.1

Membership of Newsmen in Journalism Associations
(Percent Who Are Members of Each Type of Organization)

Type of Organization			Percent
Total who belong to one or more journalism associations			45.3
A. Professional associations		33.4[a]	
National professional associations	12.8[a]		
Radio and Television News Directors Association	1.5		
National Newspaper Association	1.2		
Baseball Writers Association of America	.8		
Football Writers Association of America	.8		
National Photographers Association	.7		
White House Correspondents Association	.7		
American Society of Newspaper Editors	.7		
Associated Press Managing Editors Association	.6		
All other national professional organizations	5.8		
Local and regional professional associations	24.9		
B. Greek-letter societies		15.7	
Sigma Delta Chi	15.1		
Theta Sigma Phi	1.3		
All other Greek-letter societies	.9		
C. Social organizations		8.2	
Total who do not belong to any journalism associations			54.7
Total			100.0
Base (weighted)			(5,296)

[a]Subtotals exceed category totals because of multiple memberships.

TABLE 6.2

Number of Professional Associations Belonged To, by Media Sector
(Percent)

Number of Associations or Societies	Media Sector				
	Daily News-papers	Tele-vision	Total Print[a]	Total Broad-cast	Total Sample
More than one	10.9	9.2	10.8	8.9	10.4
One	20.8	26.9	22.6	24.7	23.0
None	68.3	63.8	66.6	66.5	66.6
Total	100.0	99.9	100.0	100.1	100.0
Base (weighted)	(3,194)	(519)	(4,351)	(937)	(5,288)
Mean	.477	.503	.484	.467	.481

[a]Includes wire services.

TABLE 6.3
Extent of Informal Social Contacts among Journalists, by Media Sector
(Percent of People Seen Socially Who Are Connected
with Journalism or the Communications Field)

Percent of Social Contacts Which Are with Journalists	Daily Newspapers	Television	Total[a] Print	Total Broadcast	Total Sample
50 or more	34.5	41.8	31.4	44.5	33.7
11 - 49	24.1	27.4	24.7	22.6	24.3
1 - 10	31.2	23.5	33.0	26.5	31.8
Zero	10.2	7.2	10.9	6.4	10.1
Total	100.0	99.9	100.0	100.0	99.9
Base (weighted)	(3,159)	(517)	(4,308)	(930)	(5,238)
Mean	30.00	35.79	28.42	36.27	29.81

[a]Includes wire services.

TABLE 6.4
Factors Influencing Formal and Informal Identification with Journalism

Predictors	Standardized Regression Coefficients	Simple r
A. Formal Identification (Number of Professional Organizations Belonged To)		
1. Professional age (number of years in the news media)	.226	.211
2. Scope of managerial responsibilities	.198	.216
3. Organization size	.063	.009
4. Years of schooling	.062	.031
5. Chronological age	−.061	.145
6. Number of employees who report to respondent	−.033	.151
7. Media sector (being in the broadcast sector)	.028	−.013
8. Size of city	−.027	.007
9. Organization prominence	−.023	−.007

(Cont.)

TABLE 6.4 (Cont.)

B. Informal Identification
(Percentage of People Seen Socially Who Are Connected with
Journalism or the Communications Field)

1. Chronological age	-.191	-.179
2. Media sector (being in the broadcast sector)	.175	.113
3. Organization size	.137	.216
4. Organization prominence	.101	.225
5. Size of city	.100	.259
6. Professional age (number of years in the news media)	.052	-.102
7. Years of schooling	.025	.116
8. Number of employees who report to respondent	.013	-.008
9. Scope of managerial responsibilities	-.001	-.077

TABLE 6.5
Importance Journalists Assign to Different Job Aspects, by Media Sector
(Mean Scores)[a]

Job Aspects	Daily News-papers (N = 3,194)[b]	Tele-vision (N = 519)	Total Print (N = 4,353)	Total Broad-cast (N = 937)	Total Sample (N = 5,301)
A. Public service— the chance to help people	1.54	1.64	1.57	1.66	1.59
B. Autonomy	1.45	1.52	1.48	1.48	1.48
C. Freedom from supervision	1.38	1.36	1.40	1.35	1.39
D. Job security	1.34	1.25	1.34	1.34	1.34
E. Pay	1.08	1.16	1.04	1.18	1.06
F. Fringe benefits	1.02	.93	.98	.92	.97

[a]Where 2 = very important; 1 = fairly important; and 0 = not too important.
[b]Bases are weighted.

TABLE 7.1

Importance Journalists Assign to Various Mass Media Functions
(Percent)

Media Functions	Level of Importance						
	Extreme-ly Impor-tant	Quite Impor-tant	Some-what Impor-tant	Not Really Impor-tant at All	No Opinion	Total	Mean[a]
(1) Investigate claims and statements made by the government	75.8	19.1	3.5	.9	.6	99.9	2.71
(2) Provide anal-ysis and inter-pretation of complex problems	61.0	25.2	10.9	2.5	.4	100.0	2.45
(3) Get informa-tion to the public as quickly as possible	56.0	29.7	11.2	2.3	.8	100.0	2.40
(4) Discuss na-tional policy while it is still being developed	55.2	26.8	12.1	4.6	1.4	100.1	2.34
(5) Stay away from stories where factual content can-not be verified	50.9	19.0	16.8	9.7	3.6	100.0	2.15
(6) Concentrate on news which is of interest to the widest possible public	38.7	31.5	20.8	7.9	1.1	100.0	2.02
(7) Develop intel-lectual and cultural interests of the public	30.3	35.1	25.7	8.1	.9	100.1	1.88
(8) Provide enter-tainment and relaxation	16.6	28.1	41.5	13.3	.5	100.0	1.48

[a]Where "extremely important" = 3, "quite important" = 2, "somewhat important" = 1, and "not really important at all" = 0.

TABLE 7.2
*Other Issues which Differentiate Participant and Neutral
Conceptions of Press Functions*

Issues	Percent
A. Number of crusaders and social reformers in the news media[a]	
Too many	22.3
Too few	34.9
About the right number	39.1
No opinion	3.6
Total	99.9
Base (weighted)	(5,301)
B. Perceived utility of the underground press[b]	
Very useful	11.3
Somewhat useful	47.5
Not useful at all	36.6
No opinion	4.5
Total	99.9
Base (weighted)	(5,301)

[a]Do you feel there are too many, too few, or about the right number of crusaders and social reformers in the news media today?

[b]How useful a role do you think the underground media are playing on the American scene today?

TABLE 7.3
Joint Distribution of the Sample on Participant and Neutral Professional Values

Neutral Values	Participant Values			Total
	Upper Fourth	Middle Half	Lower Fourth	
Upper fourth	4.1	14.1	9.7	27.9
Middle half	9.1	27.0	11.0	47.1
Lower fourth	8.5	12.3	4.3	25.1
Total	21.7	53.4	25.0	100.1

TABLE 7.4
Main Criticisms of News Media, by Type of Professional Orientation
(Percent of Total Criticisms Cited)

Type of Criticism	Professional Orientation					
	Predomi-nantly Partici-pant	Moder-ately Partici-pant	Balanced	Moder-ately Neutral	Predomi-nantly Neutral	Total Sample
A. *What* the media cover						
Content covered too much	4.0	8.4	12.7	13.8	15.3	11.4
Content not covered enough	24.3	19.4	16.5	13.8	14.8	17.0
Total	28.3	27.8	29.2	27.6	30.1	28.4
B. *How* the media handle information						
Bias, lack of objec-tivity	11.4	21.3	25.3	30.3	38.8	25.7
Superficiality, lack of depth	29.8	31.4	22.3	17.5	15.9	23.3
Other performance faults	10.4	6.9	8.1	9.8	7.9	8.4
Total	51.6	59.6	55.7	57.6	62.6	57.4
C. All other criticisms	20.0	12.7	15.2	14.8	7.2	14.2
Total	99.9	100.1	100.1	100.0	99.9	100.0
Base—total re-sponses (weighted)	(604)	(1,515)	(2,325)	(1,599)	(647)	(6,690)
Base—total persons (weighted)	(444)	(1,125)	(1,857)	(1,313)	(510)	(5,249)

TABLE 7.5
Predictors of Professional Values among Journalists

Variables	Participant Values (R = .347)		Neutral Values (R = .340)	
	Standardized Regression Coefficients (Beta)	Correlation Coefficients	Standardized Regression Coefficients (Beta)	Correlation Coefficients
A. Age, sex, and education:				
Years of schooling	.180	.230	-.170	-.218
Chronological age	-.067	-.106	.194	.159
Professional age	-.019	-.089	-.070	.098
Sex (being a man)	-.092	-.039	-.081	-.120
B. Organizational status:				
Income	.128	.080	-.063	-.090
Number of employees responsible for	-.109	-.071	.085	.030
Scope of managerial responsibility	.029	-.086	-.024	.021
C. Community and organizational setting:				
Size of city	.085	.212	-.176	-.218
Size of news organization	.091	.175	.136	-.087
Prominence of news organization	-.083	.143	-.054	-.121
D. Professional and community integration:				
Number of professional associations belonged to	-.052	-.031	.004	-.007

(Cont.)

TABLE 7.5 (Cont.)

Extent of informal social contacts in the professional community	.072	.155	−.009	−.100
Number of community organizations belonged to	−.099	−.157	.033	.104

TABLE 8.1
Incomes in 1970 among American Journalists

Income Bracket	Percent
Under $4,000	7.0
$4,000 - 5,999	7.0
$6,000 - 7,999	10.9
$8,000 - 9,999	15.5
$10,000 - 11,999	16.9
$12,000 - 13,999	13.5
$14,000 - 15,999	10.7
$16,000 - 17,999	5.0
$18,000 - 19,999	2.8
$20,000 - 21,999	3.1
$22,000 and higher	7.5
Total	99.9
Base (weighted)	(4,577)
Median income	$11,133

TABLE 8.2
Median Income in 1970, by Media Sector, Region,
Size of City, and Size of News Organization

Factors	Median Income 1970
A. Media sector	
News magazines	$15,571
Television	11,875
Wire services	11,833
Daily newspapers	11,420
Radio	9,583
Weekly newspapers	8,786
B. Region	
New England	11,274
Middle Atlantic	11,622
Total Northeast	11,532
East North Central	11,702
West North Central	9,600
Total North Central	11,187
South Atlantic	11,484
East South Central	7,846
West South Central	8,920
Total South	10,005
Mountain	9,118
Pacific	13,573
Total West	11,661
C. Size of city	
Under 10,000	8,314
10,000 - 49,999	8,945
50,000 - 249,999	10,742
250,000 - 499,999	10,895
500,000 - 999,999	13,806
1,000,000 and over	14,787
D. Size of news organization	
1 - 10 editorial employees	8,632
11 - 25 editorial employees	9,866
26 - 50 editorial employees	11,657
51 - 100 editorial employees	10,892
Over 100 editorial employees	13,550

TABLE 8.3

Median Income in 1970, by Sex, Age, Years of Schooling, Selectivity of College Attended, and Scope of Managerial and Administrative Responsibilities

Factors	Median Income 1970
E. Sex	
Male	$11,955
Female	7,702
F. Age	
Under 25	6,492
25 - 34	10,031
35 - 44	13,322
45 - 54	12,847
55 and older	12,000
G. Years of schooling	
High school graduate or less	10,992
Some college	10,164
Graduated from college	11,617
Some graduate training	11,424
Graduate degree	12,823
H. Selectivity of college attended	
High	13,440
Average	11,671
Low	10,521
I. Scope of managerial responsibility	
Organization as a whole	12,958
Department	13,148
News desk or news program	11,710
None at all	10,034
J. Number of editorial employees responsible for	
More than 25	17,793
11 - 25	14,822
6 - 10	12,612
3 - 5	12,868
1 - 2	11,500
None	10,073

TABLE 8.4
Median Income of Journalists in 1970, by Sex and Age

Age	Median Income		Difference
	Men	Women	
Under 25	$ 6,934	$ 5,111	$1,823
25 - 34	10,243	8,744	1,499
35 - 44	14,041	8,579	5,462
45 - 54	14,042	8,000	6,042
55 and older	14,321	7,710	6,611
Total	11,955	7,702	4,253

TABLE 8.5
Predictors of Income Level in the Sample as a Whole and among College Graduates

	Predictors	Standardized Regression Coefficients	Simple r
	A. Total Sample ($N = 4,531$; $R = .683$; $R^2 = .467$)		
1.	Professional age (number of years in news media)	.278	.439
2.	Size of city	.259	.362
3.	Sex (being a man)	.237	.349
4.	Scope of managerial responsibilities	.182	.281
5.	Region	.123	.194
6.	Number of editorial employees supervised	.096	.343
7.	Size of organization	.077	.299
8.	Chronological age	.064	.324
9.	Media sector	.060	.133
10.	Prominence of news organization	.025	.260
11.	Years of schooling	.019	.115
	B. College Graduates ($N = 2,439$; $R = .672$; $R^2 = .452$)		
1.	Professional age	.309	.432
2.	Sex (being a man)	.240	.332
3.	Size of city	.211	.299
4.	Number of editorial employees supervised	.154	.351
5.	Region	.131	.221
6.	Scope of managerial responsibilities	.117	.272
7.	Selectivity of college attended	.106	.204
8.	Media sector	.074	.146
9.	Prominence of news organization	.044	.212
10.	Size of organization	.042	.240
11.	Chronological age	.028	.341

TABLE 8.6
*Job Satisfaction among Journalists (1971) Compared
with Labor Force as a Whole (1962)[a]*
(Percent)

Level of Satisfaction[b]	Journalists (1971)	Labor Force (1962)
Very satisfied	48.5	45.2
Fairly (moderately) satisfied	38.6	37.8
Somewhat (a little) dissatisfied	11.7	13.1
Very dissatisfied	1.2	3.9
Total	100.0	100.0
Base	(5,301)[c]	(1,808)

[a]Source: National Survey of the Educational Pursuits of American Adults, National Opinion Research Center, 1962.

[b]Brackets indicate phrasing in 1962 survey.

[c]Base is weighted.

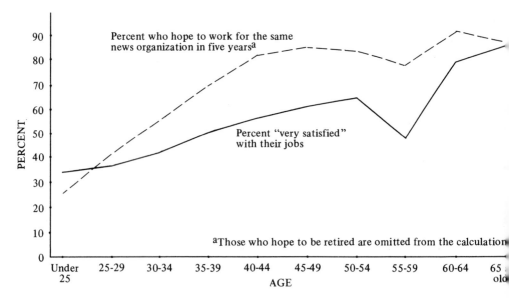

FIGURE 8.1
Organizational Commitment and Job Satisfaction, by Age

TABLE 8.7
Employment Aspirations in Five Years, by Age
(Percent in Each Grouping)

Age	Employment Aspirations						Weighted Base
	Work for Same News Organization	Work Elsewhere in News Media	Work Outside News Media	Retire	Undecided	Total	
Under 25	26.3	58.0	8.9	—	6.8	100.0	631
25 - 29	42.4	33.8	12.9	—	10.9	100.0	1,108
30 - 34	56.0	22.8	5.8	—	15.4	100.0	641
35 - 39	69.4	16.5	2.6	—	11.5	100.0	618
40 - 44	81.8	9.9	3.2	—	5.0	99.9	555
45 - 49	85.2	7.2	7.0	—	.7	100.1	559
50 - 54	83.8	6.0	4.2	1.2	4.8	100.0	433
55 - 59	74.9	8.4	4.3	4.6	7.8	100.0	370
60 - 64	75.0	2.2	1.8	18.9	2.2	100.1	228
65 and older	81.8	—	1.7	7.4	9.1	100.0	121
Total	62.0	21.8	6.6	1.4	8.2	100.0	5,264

TABLE 8.8
*Selected Characteristics of Newsmen 25 to 34
with Different Employment Commitments*

Characteristics	Types of Newsmen				Total in Age Group (N = 1,749)
	Stayers (N = 830)[a]	Shifters (N = 519)	Defectors (N = 180)	Undecideds (N = 220)	
(1) Percent male	78.7	84.5	85.5	86.4	82.1
(2) Percent who are college graduates	56.3	67.4	58.1	88.7	63.9
(3) Percent who hold advanced degrees	6.5	7.1	8.9	20.7	8.7
(4) Percent of college graduates who were journalism majors	44.1	47.1	34.6	27.9	41.3
(5) Percent of college graduates who attended more selective schools[b]	31.0	40.9	51.1	46.0	38.6

(Cont.)

TABLE 8.8 (Cont.)

(6) Percent employed in broadcast sector	23.6	32.3	26.7	12.2	25.2
(7) Median income in 1970	$10,193	$9,411	$8,967	$11,962	$9,970
(8) Percent employed by highly prominent news organizations[c]	11.7	7.7	7.8	27.5	12.1
(9) Percent who hold participant values[d]	24.4	46.0	52.0	64.8	38.4
(10) Percent high on perceived autonomy[e]	40.7	37.4	28.7	27.4	36.9

[a]Bases are weighted.

[b]Colleges and universities rated in the top four of six categories on selectivity by Cass and Birnbaum (1970).

[c]News organizations cited for fairness and reliability or for their usefulness by more than 100 newsmen in the sample.

[d]Newsmen classified as "predominantly participant" or "moderately participant" in their professional values in Table 7.4.

[e]Scores of 3 or 4 on Index of Perceived Autonomy described on pages 86-87.

TABLE 8.9
Commitment to News-Media Careers among Journalists 25 to 34,
by Level of Formal Schooling

Amount of Schooling	Percent Who Are Stayers or Shifters	Base (Weighted)
High school graduate or less	89.2	166
1 to 3 years of college	82.4	465
College graduates	76.1	723
Some graduate training	72.7	242
Advanced degrees	59.5	153

TABLE 8.10

Selected Correlates of Job Satisfaction among Journalists, by Age
(Pearson Correlations)

Characteristics	Under 40 (N = 2,998)	40 and Older (N = 2,266)
A. Background characteristics		
1. Sex (being a man)	–.028	–.094
2. Years of formal schooling	–.095	–.066
3. Selectivity of college attended	–.020	–.077
B. Community and organizational characteristics		
4. City size	–.001	–.070
5. Organization size	–.067	–.034
6. Prominence of news organization	.014	.026
7. Media sector (working in the broadcast sector)	.054	–.152
C. Job functions and rewards		
8. Amount of reporting done	.001	.007
9. Amount of editing and news processing done	.029	–.055
10. Scope of managerial responsibilities	.126	.097
11. Number of editorial employees responsible for	.066	.067
12. Income	.171	.041
D. Job milieu		
13. Percentage of time under deadline pressure (reporters only)	–.163	–.077
14. Amount of freedom in selecting stories to work on (reporters only)	.162	.256
15. Amount of freedom in deciding how stories should be played (reporters only)	.150	.108
16. Amount of editing stories get (reporters only)	–.066	–.053
17. Percentage of stories considered to be improperly edited (reporters only)	–.305	–.085
18. Amount of freedom in deciding what to say in editorials (editorial writers only)	.190	.212
19. Amount of freedom in deciding topics for editorials (editorial writers only)	.102	.141
20. Amount of professional respect for editor or superior	.298	.356
21. Rating of performance of one's own news organization in informing the public	.357	.290
E. Professional values		
22. Strength of neutral values	.120	.060
23. Strength of participant values	–.137	–.068

TABLE 8.11

Relative Strength of Seventeen Predictors of Job Satisfaction among Journalists in Two Age Groups

Predictors	Standardized Regression Coefficients (Beta)
A. *Journalists under 40* $(R = .514, R^2 = .264)$	
1. Rating of performance of one's own news organization	.256
2. Professional respect for editor or superior	.234
3. Income	.175
4. Level of perceived autonomy	.144
5. Frequency of deadline pressures	-.128
6. Strength of neutral professional values	.080
7. Sex (being a man)	-.066
8. Prominence of news organization	.062
9. Organization size	-.058
10. Scope of managerial responsibilities	.057
11. Level of formal schooling	-.048
12. Chronological age	-.045
13. Professional age	-.031
14. Number of editorial employees supervised	-.027
15. City size	.020
16. Media sector (working in the broadcast sector)	-.014
17. Strength of participant professional values	.008
B. *Journalists 40 and older* $(R = .582, R^2 = .339)$	
1. Professional respect for editor or superior	.328
2. Prominence of news organization	.227
3. Sex (being a man)	-.215
4. Rating of performance of one's own news organization	.179
5. Level of perceived autonomy	.155
6. Organization size	-.154
7. Number of editorial employees supervised	.133
8. Scope of managerial responsibilities	.125
9. Media sector (working in the broadcast sector)	-.109
10. Professional age	.103
11. Income	.088
12. Frequency of deadline pressures	-.086
13. City size	-.076
14. Strength of neutral professional values	-.074
15. Chronological age	-.020
16. Level of formal schooling	.011
17. Strength of participant professional values	-.002

TABLE 9.1
Estimated Manpower in the Alternative Media

Media Type	Number of Organizations	Average Size	Number of Personnel
Newspapers	800	6	4,800
Broadcast media	200	1.5	300
Other	200	4	800
Total	1,200		5,900

References

Almond, Gabriel A., and Sidney Verba. 1968. *The Five Nation Study*. Ann Arbor: Inter-University Consortium for Political Research.

Alsop, Joseph, and Stewart Alsop. 1958. *The Reporter's Trade*. New York: Reynal and Company.

Atlantic Editors. 1969. "The American Media Baronies, and a Modest Atlantic Atlas." *The Atlantic* 224, No. 1 (July), 82-84, 90-94.

Ayer, N. W., and Son. 1970. *Directory: Newspapers and Periodicals*. Philadelphia: N. W. Ayer & Son.

Bagdikian, Ben H. 1971. *The Information Machines: Their Impact on Men and the Media*. New York: Harper and Row.

Becker, Howard S. 1962. "The Nature of a Profession." In *Education for the Professions: Sixty-first Yearbook of the National Society for the Study of Education, Part II*. Chicago: National Society for the Study of Education, 27-46.

Berelson, Bernard. 1959. "The State of Communication Research." *Public Opinion Quarterly* 23, No. 1 (Spring), 1-15.

Birmingham, John. 1970. *Our Time Is Now: Notes from the High School Underground*. New York: Praeger.

Blau, Peter M., and O. D. Duncan. 1967. *The American Occupational Structure*. New York: Wiley.

Bleyer, Willard G., ed. 1918. *The Profession of Journalism*. Boston: Atlantic Monthly Press.

Blumler, J. G., and John Madge. Undated. *Citizenship and Television*. London: Political and Economic Planning.

Bogue, Donald J. 1969. *Principles of Demography*. New York: Wiley.

Boorstin, Daniel J. 1962. *The Image*. New York: Atheneum.

Bowers, David R. 1969. "The Impact of Centralized Printing on the Community Press." *Journalism Quarterly* 45, No. 1 (Spring), 43-46.

Bowman, William W. 1974. "Distaff Journalists: Women as a Minority Group in the News Media." Ph.D. dissertation, Department of Sociology, University of Illinois at Chicago Circle.

Boyd-Barrett, Oliver. 1970. "Journalism Recruitment and Training: Problems in Professionalization." In J. Tunstall, ed., *Media Sociology*. Urbana: University of Illinois Press, 181-201.

Breed, Warren. 1950. "The Newspaperman, News and Society." Ph.D. dissertation, Department of Sociology, Columbia University.

———. 1955. "Social Control in the Newsroom." *Social Forces* 33 (May), 326-335.

———. 1958. "Mass Communication and Sociocultural Integration." *Social Forces* 37 (December), 109-116.

Broadcasting. Yearbook Issue. 1971. Washington: Broadcasting Publications.

Bucher, M. Rue, and Anselm Strauss. 1961. "Professions in Process." *American Journal of Sociology* 66 (January), 325-335.

Carey, James W. 1969. "The Communications Revolution and the Professional Communicator." *The Sociological Review Monograph* 13 (January), 23-37.

Cass, James, and Max Birnbaum. 1970. *Comparative Guide to American Colleges*. (1970-71 ed.). New York: Harper and Row.

Cater, Douglass, 1959. *The Fourth Branch of Government*. Boston: Houghton Mifflin.

Chittick, William O. 1970. *State Department, Press, and Pressure Groups: A Role Analysis*. New York: Wiley-Interscience.

Cohen, Bernard C. 1963. *The Press and Foreign Policy*. Princeton: Princeton University Press.

DeFleur, Melvin L. 1964. "Occupational Roles as Portrayed on Television." *Public Opinion Quarterly* 28, No. 1 (Spring), 57-74.

Desmond, Robert W. 1949. *Professional Training of Journalists*. Paris: UNESCO.

Dunn, Delmer D. 1969. *Public Officials and the Press*. Reading: Addison-Wesley.

Editor and Publisher International Year Book. 1970. New York: Editor & Publisher.

Emery, Edwin, Phillip H. Ault, and Warren K. Agee. 1970. *Introduction to Mass Communications*. New York: Dodd, Mead and Company.

Ennis, Philip H. 1961. "The Social Structure of Communication Systems: A Theoretical Proposal." *Studies in Public Communication*, No. 3 (Summer), 120-144.

Epstein, Edward Jay. 1973. *News from Nowhere*. New York: Random House.

Erskine, Hazel. 1971. "The Polls: The Politics of Age." *Public Opinion Quarterly* 35, No. 2 (Fall), 482-495.

Flacks, Richard. 1967. "The Liberated Generation: An Exploration of the Roots of Student Protest." *Journal of Social Issues* 23 (July), 52-75.

———. 1971. *Youth and Social Change*. Chicago: Markham.

Form, William H., and Delbert C. Miller. 1949. "Occupational Career Pattern as a Sociological Instrument." *American Journal of Sociology* 54 (January), 317-329.

Freidson, Eliot. 1970. *Profession of Medicine: A Study of the Sociology of Applied Knowledge*. New York: Dodd, Mead and Company.

Gans, Herbert J. 1972. "The Famine in American Mass-Communications Research." *American Journal of Sociology* 77, No. 4 (January), 697-705.

Gerbner, George. 1967. "Newsmen and Schoolmen: The State and Problems of Education Reporting." *Journalism Quarterly* 44, No. 2 (Summer), 211-224.

Gieber, Walter. 1956. "Across the Desk: A Study of 16 Telegraph Editors." *Journalism Quarterly* 33, No. 4 (Fall), 423-432.

Gieber, Walter, and Walter Johnson. 1961. "The City Hall 'Beat': A Study of Reporter and Source Roles." *Journalism Quarterly* 38, No. 3 (Summer), 289-297.

Glaser, Barney G. 1968. *Organizational Careers: A Sourcebook for Theory*. Chicago: Aldine.

Glessing, Robert J. 1970. *The Underground Press in America*. Bloomington: Indiana University Press.

Greenwood, Ernest. 1957. "Attributes of a Profession." *Social Work* 2, No. 3 (July), 44-55.

Gross, Neal. 1956. *The Schools and the Press: A Study of the Relationships between Newspapermen and School Administrators in New England*. Cambridge: New England School Development Council.

Hall, Richard H. 1968. "Professionalization and Bureaucratization." *American Sociological Review* 33, No. 1 (February), 92-104.

Hohenberg, John. 1968. *The News Media: A Journalist Looks at His Profession*. New York: Holt, Rinehart and Winston.

Hughes, Everett C. 1959. "The Study of Occupations." In Robert K. Merton, ed., *et al., Sociology Today*. New York: Basic Books, 442-458.

———. 1970. *The Sociological Eye: Selected Papers*. Chicago: Aldine.

Janowitz, Morris. 1952. *The Community Press in an Urban Setting*. Glencoe: Free Press.

Johnstone, John W. C., and Ramon Rivera. 1965. *Volunteers for Learning*. Chicago: Aldine.

Johnstone, John W. C. 1970. "Age-Grade Consciousness." *Sociology of Education* 43, No. 1 (Winter), 56-68.

Johnstone, John W. C., Edward Slawski, and William Bowman. 1973. "The Professional Values of American Newsmen." *Public Opinion Quarterly* 36 (Winter), 522-540.

Kimball, Penn. 1965. "Journalism: Art, Craft, or Profession?" In Kenneth Lynn, ed., *The Professions in America*. Boston: Beacon Press, 242-260.

Kornhauser, William. 1962. *Scientists in Industry: Conflict and Accommodation*. Berkeley: University of California Press.

Krieghbaum, Hillier. 1957. *When Doctors Meet Reporters*. New York: New York University Press.

———. 1967. *Science and the Mass Media*. New York: New York University Press.

Kruglak, Theodore E. 1955. *The Foreign Correspondents*. Geneva: Droz.

Lambert, Donald A. 1956. "Foreign Correspondents Covering the United States." *Journalism Quarterly* 33, No. 3 (Summer), 349-356.

Lansing, John B., and Eva Mueller. 1967. *The Geographic Mobility of Labor.* Ann Arbor: Institute for Social Research, University of Michigan.

Leamer, Lawrence. 1972. *The Paper Revolutionaries: The Rise of the Underground Press.* New York: Simon and Schuster.

Lerner, Daniel. 1963. "Toward a Communication Theory of Modernization." In Lucian Pye, ed., *Communication and Political Development.* Princeton: Princeton University Press, 327-350.

Liebling, A. J. 1961. *The Press.* New York: Ballatine Books.

Lyons, Louis M. 1965. *Reporting the News.* Cambridge: Harvard University Press.

MacDougall, Curtis D. 1963. *Newsroom Problems and Policies.* New York: Dover.

Matejko, Aleksander. 1970. "Newspaper Staff as a Social System." In J. Tunstall, ed., *Media Sociology.* Urbana: University of Illinois Press, 168-180.

Maxwell, J. William. 1956. "U.S. Correspondents Abroad: A Study of Backgrounds." *Journalism Quarterly* 33, No. 3 (Summer), 346-348.

McQuitty, L. L. 1964. "Capabilities and Improvements of Linkage Analysis as a Clustering Method." *Educational and Psychological Measurement* 24 (Fall), 441-456.

Miller, George. 1967. "Professionals in Bureaucracy: Alienation among Industrial Scientists and Engineers." *American Sociological Review* 32, No. 5 (October), 755-768.

Molotch, Harvey, and Marilyn Lester. 1974. "News as Purposive Behavior: On the Strategic Use of Routine Events, Accidents, and Scandals." *American Sociological Review* 39 (February), 101-112.

Moore, Wilbert E. 1969. "Occupational Socialization." In D. A. Goslin, ed., *Handbook of Socialization Theory and Research.* Chicago: Rand McNally.

Newspaper Fund. 1969. "Where They Went to Work 1964-68." Princeton.

———. 1971. "1971 Supplement: Where They Went to Work." Princeton.

Nimmo. Dan D. 1964. *Newsgathering in Washington.* New York: Atherton.

Nixon, Raymond. 1968. "Trends in U.S. Newspaper Ownership: Concentration with Competition." *Gazette* 14, No. 3, 181-193.

Pelz, Donald C., and Frank M. Andrews. 1966. *Scientists in Organizations.* New York: Wiley.

Philpot, Frank A. 1973. "A Note on Television News and Newspaper News." In Ithiel de Sola Pool, Wilbur Schramm, *et al.*, eds., *Handbook of Communication.* Chicago: Rand McNally, 551-558.

Porter, John. 1965. *The Vertical Mosaic.* Toronto: University of Toronto Press.

Rein, Martin. 1970. "Social Work in Search of a Radical Profession." *Social Work* 15 (January), 15-28.

Reiss, Albert J., *et al.* 1961. *Occupations and Social Status.* New York: Free Press of Glencoe.

Reston, James B. 1945. "The Job of the Reporter." In New York *Times* Staff, *The Newspaper: Its Making and Its Meaning.* New York: Scribner.

Rivers, William L. 1960. "The Washington Correspondents and Government Information." Ph.D. dissertation, Department of Government, American University.

———. 1962. "The Correspondents after 25 Years." *Columbia Journalism Review* 1, No. 1 (Spring), 4-10.

———. 1965. *The Opinionmakers.* Boston: Beacon Press.

———. 1971. *The Adversaries: Politics and the Press.* Boston: Beacon Press.

———. 1973. "The Press as a Communication System." In Ithiel de Sola Pool, Wilbur Schramm, *et al.*, eds., *Handbook of Communication.* Chicago: Rand McNally, 521-550.

Roper, Elmo, and associates. 1965. *The Public's View of Television and Other Media, 1960-64.* New York: Television Information Office.

Rosten, Leo. 1937. *The Washington Correspondents.* New York: Harcourt, Brace and Company.

Samuelson, Merrill. 1962. "A Standardized Test to Measure Job Satisfaction in the Newsroom." *Journalism Quarterly* 39, No. 3 (Summer), 285-291.

Sherlock, Basil J., and Richard T. Morris. 1967. "The Evolution of the Professional: A Paradigm." *Sociological Inquiry* 37 (Winter), 27-46.

Siebert, Fred. 1956. "The Libertarian Theory." In Fred Siebert *et al.*, *Four Theories of the Press.* Urbana: University of Illinois Press.

Sigelman, Lee. 1973. "Reporting the News: An Organizational Analysis." *American Journal of Sociology* 79 (July), 132-151.

Skornia, Harry J. 1968. *Television and the News.* Palo Alto: Pacific Books.

Slater, Philip. 1970. *The Pursuit of Loneliness: American Culture at the Breaking Point.* Boston: Beacon Press.

Stone, Vernon A. 1970. "Broadcast News Educators and the Profession." *Journalism Quarterly* 47, No. 2 (Spring), 162-165.

Sutton, Albert A. 1945. *Education for Journalism in the United States from Its Beginnings until 1940.* Evanston: Northwestern University Press.

Tuchman, Gaye. 1969. "News, the Newsman's Reality." Ph.D. dissertation, Department of Sociology, Brandeis University.

———. 1972. "Objectivity as Strategic Ritual: An Examination of Newspapermen's Notion of Objectivity." *American Journal of Sociology* 77, No. 4 (January), 660-679.

———. 1973. "Making News by Doing Work: Routinizing the Unexpected." *American Journal of Sociology* 73, No. 1 (July), 110-131.

Tunstall, Jeremy. 1970. *The Westminster Lobby Correspondents.* London: Routledge and Kegan Paul.

———. 1971. *Journalists at Work.* London: Constable.

The News People

U.S. Bureau of the Census, 1963a. Census of Population, 1960. Subject Reports, Final Report PC(2)-7A, *Occupational Characteristics*. Washington, D.C.: U.S. Government Printing Office.

U.S. Bureau of the Census, 1963b. *Statistical Abstract of the United States*. Eighty-fourth edition. Washington, D.C.: U.S. Government Printing Office.

U.S. Bureau of the Census, 1971. *Statistical Abstract of the United States*. Ninety-second edition. Washington, D.C.: U.S. Government Printing Office.

U.S. Bureau of the Census, 1972a. *Statistical Abstract of the United States*. Ninety-third edition. Washington, D.C.: U.S. Government Printing Office.

U.S. Bureau of the Census, 1972b. Census of Population, 1970. Vol. I, Characteristics of the Population, Part A, *Number of Inhabitants*. Washington, D.C., U.S. Government Printing Office.

U.S. Bureau of the Census, 1973a. Census of Population, 1970. Subject Reports, Final Report PC(2)-7A, *Occupational Characteristics*. Washington, D.C.: U.S. Government Printing Office.

U.S. Bureau of the Census, 1973b. Census of Population, 1970. Subject Reports, Final Report PC(2)-8B, *Earnings by Occupation and Education*. Washington, D.C.: U.S. Government Printing Office.

U.S. Department of Labor, 1971. *Employment and Earnings*, 18, No. 6 (December). Washington, D.C.: U.S. Government Printing Office.

UNESCO. 1958. *The Training of Journalists: A Worldwide Survey of the Training of Personnel for the Mass Media*. New York: UNESCO Publications Center.

Valleau, John F. 1952. "Oregon Legislative Reporting: The Newsmen and Their Methods." *Journalism Quarterly* 29, No. 2 (Spring), 158-170.

Weisberger, Bernard. 1961. *The American Newspaperman*. Chicago: University of Chicago Press.

Welles, Chris. 1971. "Can Mass Magazines Survive?" *Columbia Journalism Review* 10 (July-August), 7-14.

Wilensky, Harold. 1964. "The Professionalization of Everyone?" *American Journal of Sociology* 70, No. 2 (September), 137-158.

Index

Editorial writing: number who do, 75; related to career path, 82

Editors and reporters: in 1960 census, 8; in 1970 census, 17n; number who are women, 23

Educational aspirations: of alternative journalists, 177

Educational levels: in alternative media, 170; in broadcast networks, 33; changes over time in, 32; and city size, 33, 47n; and commitment to journalism, 148-149; and income, 138, 141; and job mobility, 58; and job satisfaction, 152; of journalists, 31; and media sector, 33; of men and women, 156n; in nationally prominent media, 91-92; and organization size, 33, 47n; and professional values, 124-125, 186; and region, 34-35. *See also* Fields of study; Training in journalism

Epstein, Edward Jay: on control over newswork, 4

Ethnic origins: of journalists, 25-26

FCC Broadcasting Directory, 161

Features: number who write, 75

Fields of study: changes over time in, 37-40; effects of diversity of, 186; in graduate school and college, 35-37. *See also* Training in journalism

Fifth Estate, 165

Flacks, Richard: on college radicals, 171-172; on effects of the student movement, 113

Foreign policy: coverage of, 3

Freelance writing; number who do, 19

Generational conflict: in contemporary journalism, 187

Geographic mobility: interregional, 67-69, 71; of journalists compared with labor force, 66-68; related to economic opportunities, 69, 136

Gieber, Walter: on city hall reporters, 4; on wire editors, 164

Glaser, Barney: on occupational careers, 48

The Great Speckled Bird, 157, 165, 169

Greenwood, Ernest: on professions, 102

High School Independent Press Service, 162

Hughes, Everett: on development of professions, 98; on historic occupations, 26

Ideology: in alternative journalism, 178; of objectivity, 114

Income levels: in alternative media, 172-173; and career aspirations, 145-147; importance of to journalists, 110; and job satisfaction, 150, 153; in journalism compared to other occupations, 134; of journalists in 1970, 133-134; and migration, 136; predictors of, 139-142; and professional values, 127-128; refusal of journalists to divulge, 155n

Informal colleague networks: factors related to, 107-108; functions of, 108; and membership in voluntary associations, 130; among print and broadcast journalists, 106, 107; and professional values, 129-130

International Editorial Association, 100

Interviews: how conducted, 10-11

Investigative reporting: endorsement of by journalists, 117; and "participant" journalism, 116-117

Job functions: in alternative media, 168; in broadcast media, 78, 79-80, 81, 82, 83; and career stage, 77-78; and income level, 140-141; in journalism, 73; and organizational size, 84; in print media, 78, 81, 82-83; relationships among, 76-77, 81-83; specialization of, 83-85

Job histories: of alternative journalists, 173; of journalists, 53-55, 56-57

Job mobility: and career stage, 56-60; changes over time in, 58, 70; common and rare paths of, 62-64; and education, 58; of print and broadcast journalists, 59-60, 71; related to migration, 68; within and across media sectors, 60-64, 71. *See also* Career aspirations; Geographic mobility

Professional standards: and job satisfaction, 149, 153
Professional values: factors related to, 123-130; history of debate over, 113-116; and job satisfaction, 151, 153; of journalists, 120
Professionals: work attitudes of, 108-109
Pulitzer prizes, 128

Racial origins: of journalists, 26, 90-91
Radio: attrition of manpower from, 54, 63; number of women in, 23; premium of youthfulness in, 80; as recruitment sources, 65. *See also* Broadcast journalists; Broadcast networks
Radio and Television News Directors Association, 101, 103
Region: and average earnings, 135-136; and educational levels of journalists, 34-35; and migration, 66-69; and training in journalism, 67-68; where alternative journalists born, 169; where journalists born, 66, 91; where journalists employed, 20, 28
Reiss, Albert: on occupational prestige, 71-72n
Religious backgrounds: of alternative journalists, 170; of journalists, 90
Reporting: and career stage, 77; numbers who do, 74; types of, 74
Rivers, William: on press-government conflict, 3; on Washington correspondents, 3, 56
Rolling Stone, 157, 158, 168-169
Rosten, Leo: on Washington correspondents, 2, 56

Sample: of alternative media, 160; design of, 8-10; execution of, 9-11; universe defined, 6-8
Samuelson, Merrill: on job satisfaction, 154, 156n
San Francisco *Chronicle*, 89
Screw magazine, 162
The Seed, 158
Sensationalism: avoidance of in "neutral" journalism, 114; journalists criticize media for, 121

Sex: and average earnings in professional occupations, 155n; and criticisms of the news media, 126-127; distribution of journalists by, 22-23, 28; and income level, 137, 140, 141; and job satisfaction, 151, 153-154; of journalism students, 23; and professional values, 126-127. *See also* Women in journalism
Sex ratios: in print and broadcast journalism, 24
Sigelman, Lee: on control over newswork, 4
Sigma Delta Chi: number of members, 103; mentioned, 100, 101, 104
Skornia, Harry: on television codes, 102
Slater, Philip: on avoidance of responsibility by media, 175
Social class background: of alternative journalists, 169-170; and career beginnings, 70; and decisions to enter journalism, 49-50; and education, 50-51, 52, 70; of journalists, 27-28, 71-72n; related to colleges attended, 51, 52, 70; related to major in college, 72n
Society of Professional Journalists. See Sigma Delta Chi
Specialization of function: absence of in alternative media, 167-168; in mainstream news media, 76-77; and organization size, 79, 83-85
Staff size: in broadcast media, 78; related to circulation, 21
St. Louis *Globe-Democrat*, 100
St. Louis *Post-Dispatch*, 89
Strauss, Anselm: on occupational segments, 123
Superficiality: journalists criticize media for, 121

Television: credibility of as news source, 19, 29n; flow of manpower to, 61, 62, 64; income levels in, 135; recruitment sources for, 65. *See also* Broadcast journalists; Broadcast networks
Theta Sigma Phi, 101
Time, 165
Top Value TV, 162